The European Union

A Political Sociology

Chris Rumford

Blackwell
Publishing

350 Main Street, Malden, MA 02148–5018, USA
108 Cowley Road, Oxford OX4 1JF, UK

First published 2002 by Blackwell Publishers Ltd, a Blackwell Publishing company

Library of Congress Cataloging-in-Publication Data

Rumford, Chris, 1958–
    The European Union : a political sociology / Chris Rumford.
        p.   cm.
Includes bibliographical references and index.
    ISBN 0–631–22617–6 (alk. paper) – ISBN 0–631–22618–4 (alk. paper)
    1. European Union. 2. Globalization. 3. Civil society—European Union countries. 4. European Union countries—Social conditions.
I. Title
    JN30 .R87   2002
    306.2'094—dc21   2001007095

A catalogue record for this title is available from the British Library.

Set in 10.5/12.5 Palatino
by SetSystems Ltd, Saffron Walden, Essex
Printed and bound in the United Kingdom
by TJ International Ltd, Padstow, Cornwall

For further information on
Blackwell Publishing, visit our website:
http://www.blackwellpublishing.com

Contents

Acknowledgments

For their advice and encouragement I should like to thank Martin Albrow, Barrie Axford, Andrew Barry, Roland Robertson, and Kathleen White. I am also grateful to Daniel Fascione and Danny Cleary for their unfailing willingness to obtain articles and other material. Ken Provencher at Blackwell Publishing has provided excellent editorial assistance. My colleagues at Istanbul Kultur University have been most helpful, and I thank Tamer Koçel, Ülkü Demirdöğen, Mensur Akgün, Mesut Eren, Bianca Kaiser, and Melike Akkaraca for their support. Special thanks to Füsun and Lara for helping in so many ways.

1 Introduction: A New Approach to Studying European Integration

Studying European Integration

Many books on European Union (EU) integration or contemporary European issues have been published in the past few years. The vast majority of these books have been generated by the academic disciplines of politics, international relations (IR), geography, economics, and history. The number of books on the EU from the field of political sociology is much smaller. Indeed, very few exist. This itself is an interesting issue. Why should political sociology, and sociology more generally, fail to generate an impressive literature on what most people would agree is an important aspect of our contemporary world? In part the answer lies in the nature of political sociology as a sub-discipline of sociology. So what has prevented political sociology from taking its place in the study of European integration?

Bottomore (1993: 1) claims that it is impossible "to establish any significant theoretical distinction between political sociology and political science," as both are concerned with relations between social and political life. On the face of it this makes political sociology's non-contribution to EU studies more puzzling. But there is one crucial difference between political science and political sociology that Bottomore does not take into consideration. As Nash (2000: 1) points out, political sociology has tended to focus on politics at the level of the nation-state. "It has shared what may be seen as the prejudice of modern sociology for taking 'society' as the unit of analysis and treating it as a distinct, internally coherent and self-regulating entity, organized around the nation-state." On this reading, political sociology is unprepared for a study of social and political life in contexts other than that of the nation-state – the European Union, for example.

Political sociology cannot ignore the European Union. Whatever aspect of contemporary Europe we wish to investigate – ranging from international relations and domestic politics to welfare policy, the politics of community and identity, unemployment and individual rights – the EU looms large. What exactly do we mean when we talk of the European Union? Strictly speaking, the EU was established by the Treaty on European Union, agreed between 12 member states, and came into existence in 1993.[1] As commonly understood, the European Union denotes several things. Most obviously, an economic and political bloc consisting of 15 member states.[2] It is also synonymous with the project of European integration: the objective of "ever closer union" was enshrined in the founding Treaty of Rome, and the Single European Act of 1986 established that European union was the ultimate aim of integration. Since the mid-1980s the EU has grown much more influential – its role strengthened by the collapse of communism – and has become synonymous with Europe itself, for example when the question of European identity is raised.

The EU has both positive and negative connotations. On the one hand, its origins are associated with the worthy aim of preventing future wars in Europe. Similarly, it is referred to in terms which express the loftiest motives associated with a rejection of a narrow nationalist outlook. The EU is often linked with growth and development and constitutes an economic bloc which can counter the might of the US and Japan. Equally, the EU is deemed to endow European nation-states (particularly the smaller ones) with a political voice in world affairs which they could never achieve on their own. The EU is also strongly associated with the idea of human rights, setting standards which it insists that others follow. On the other hand, the EU is also associated with a "democratic deficit," an idea which draws attention to the lack of accountability of its institutions to its citizens. Similarly, the EU is viewed as distant and remote by its citizens for whom the benefits of EU citizenship remain rather abstract. The EU is often seen as a defensive structure, a "fortress Europe" keeping out immigrants and refugees. To many people the EU remains first and foremost a giant market place, valuing trade and economic growth above all else. The EU is a "capitalists' charter," enabling the owners of enterprises to increase their wealth at the expense of the workers, thereby increasing the gap between rich and poor. To non-members the EU is a hegemon, controlling and regulating trade and aid throughout Europe, increasingly interfering in domestic political and economic affairs, and setting stringent standards for aspirant countries.

This book aims to substantiate the claim that political sociology – defined here as the study of relationships between state, society, and the individual – can make an extremely valuable contribution to thinking about the nature of, and problems besetting, the European Union. One way in which political sociology can do this is by confronting EU studies with a set of concerns and preoccupations not foregrounded in political science or international relations approaches. Existing studies of the EU tend to centre on integration and its implications for European governance, particularly the changing role of member states *vis-à-vis* the institutions of the EU. Within this broad field EU scholars investigate the likelihood of the EU developing a form of political integration to match that already achieved in the economic sphere, the decision-making powers of various EU institutions, the development of European-level democracy, policy developments and conflicts, and a host of technical and constitutional issues such as the balance of power within and between institutions, and the implementation of legislation.

The extent to which the EU is developing supranational powers at the expense of, or in addition to, those of its member states places integration as the central issue in EU studies. We can see the extent to which an integrative logic is dominant if we consider the following terms associated with EU policy: cohesion, community, competition, enlargement, harmonization, regional autonomy. All of them obtain their current meanings from, and in turn contribute to, the idea of an integrated European Union. Upon examination each reveals a series of issues which are resolved within the dominant discourse on the EU in terms which contribute to the idea that the EU is becoming more coordinated, unified, harmonious, integrated. Even the extent to which the EU is internally divided is frequently interpreted as evidence that the EU has the ability to overcome such problems in such a way as to bring about a greater degree of unification. Thus, harmonization, which acknowledges that a diversity of standards and practices exists, suggests that a system of EU norms is being instituted; the notion of cohesion, which signifies that within the EU there exist great variations in the levels of economic development, is held to represent the means of overcoming such divisions; the idea of regional autonomy, challenging member states "from below," provides the foundation for an integrated "Europe of the regions."

The point is not that a political sociology of the European Union should seek to deny that European integration is taking place or that it is a process with important ramifications for a multiplicity of interested parties: sectors, interest groups, enterprises, citizens, regions, member states, candidate countries and non-members. Rather, the point is to begin from a different starting point and view the process of integration not as natural or inevitable but to view it as one process, albeit a very important one, occurring within the EU alongside other processes which may run counter to it or exist largely beyond the control of the EU. Murray (2000) points out that "the term integration is used in almost every article written about the EU, yet it is rarely defined." We might want to add that it is even rarer to find a challenge to the idea that integration is the dominant process. Integration needs to be problematized, in the course of which the dynamics of the EU may well start to look rather different and rather more complex. A key element of a political sociology of the European Union then, is that it questions the dominant nature of integration, as currently understood, and questions the extent to which the EU controls and shapes all of the processes taking place within its sphere of influence.

Sociological Studies of European Integration

Is the European Union a strange topic for sociological study? There is no reason why it should be, but at the same time we have already established that there are few existing studies in this field. There are of course many sociological contributions to a broad range of issues pertaining to the EU: unemployment, the welfare state, democracy, social exclusion, networks, citizenship. However, there is no recognizable sociological approach to studying the EU, and other disciplines have tended to ignore sociology when they are looking to borrow concepts and theories in order to explicate processes such as supranationalism, integration, and regionalism.

One noteworthy sociological study of European integration is that of Etzioni (1965), a comparative study of several attempts to create political unification: the United Arab Republic, the Federation of the West Indies, the Nordic Associational Web, and the EEC. His sociological approach to international relations concentrates on the forces leading towards integration, or unification as he terms it, and the role of leaders and elites in this process. The study has two main features which are of particular interest. First, he concludes that in its initial phases EU integration depended very heavily upon US support mobilized through the Marshall plan on the back of a perception of the Soviet threat. Etzioni establishes that the unifying ambition of the EEC in the early days was not matched by the level of integrating power, and the success of the European Coal and Steel Community was only possible because of its limited practical ambitions: the multinational harmonization of only two industries, steel and coal, rather than whole economies (Etzioni 1965: 264–6).[3] Etzioni sees meaningful integration as something for the future, not something that has been achieved already. For him, unification is conceived in federalist terms and will only be realized when a political community has been instituted.

Second, Etzioni makes a strong case for the European project being bolstered by a series of myths. For example, that the EEC could overcome the political divisions inherited from the past, when it was "hardly more than an evolving customs union" (Etzioni 1965: 253). Also, the relative prosperity, high levels of growth and increasing trade in the period up until the mid-1960s (and which were to continue until the early '70s) gave rise to "a myth of success that was supportive of the Community's institutions and gratifying to its adherents" (Eztioni 1965: 272). Although the real benefits of the EEC do not easily yield to measurement, "prosperity became more closely associated with the formation of the EEC than economic analysis would demonstrate" (Etzioni 1965: 251).

Etzioni's work can be properly placed within a tradition of sociological work on international relations rather than a milestone on the road to establishing a sociological tradition of EU studies, which has remained underdeveloped. Sociology has not taken part in the grand theorizing on European integration that has dominated, some would say disfigured, the study of the EU over the past 40 years. Nevertheless, at the present time the distance between sociological interests and EU studies is much smaller than at any time since Etzioni examined the nascent integration of the EEC. This is not, however, because sociology has oriented itself towards a study of regional integration. It is the result of the fact that EU studies have increasingly coalesced around issues such as citizenship, democratization, social movements, social exclusion, globalization, media and communication, nationalism, and the environment, on which there is an extensive sociological literature. Another contributing factor is the rise of "constructivism," a new IR paradigm that draws upon social theory in an attempt to understand the historical contexts and power relations which inform the structures of world politics (Rosamond

2000: 171–4). Rather than sociology embracing EU studies, the study of the EU has come to sociology.

There is also another key trend. Sociology has become interested in transnational flows, global networks, and society beyond the (nation-) state. A sea-change has resulted from significant efforts within sociology to refocus its concerns, its theoretical underpinnings and the scope of its investigation. Rex (1999) makes the point that events in the world have impacted upon political sociology in such a way as to transform its core concerns. Political sociology no longer focuses on the structure of national societies and class distinctions, and in the contemporary setting "these foci seem inadequate or misleading as we seek to come to terms with a post-national globalised world, as some nation states and empires break up giving rise to sub-national ethnic conflict, and as some of the existing nation states seek to regroup themselves in supra-national but not world wide organisations" (Rex 1999: vii).

The work of the globalization theorists has been especially important in this regard, and we should single out Albrow (1996), Beck (1992), Robertson (1992) and Urry (1999) for their contribution to a redefinition of the range of issues, processes, and relations central to sociological investigation. Beck (2000: 25) points out that one feature of the globalization debate is a "dispute about which basic assumptions and images of society, which *units for analysis,* can *replace* the axiomatics of the national state." In other words, the study of globalization works to undermine the traditional (national) base of sociology, which in turn causes it to seek more appropriate fields of enquiry, one candidate for which is the European Union. In addition, the "cultural turn" in sociology has also contributed to the recasting of the traditional concerns of the discipline (Nash 2001). What this means is that political sociology now has an interest in a much wider range of social and political issues and possesses a much greater range of tools with which to study non-national, transnational and global phenomenon.

Issues for a Political Sociology of European Integration

It would be a mistake to assume that the EU is a "European polity," simply an enlarged version of the nation-state. Nevertheless, the idea of political sociology as a study of the structures which shape the relationship between an individual and the formal institutions of the society he or she lives in, whether that society be local, national or transnational remains a valid one. In this section we will look at the shifting focus of sociology and how a political sociology adequately equipped to deal with contemporary issues can offer unique insights into the processes comprising and compromising European integration.

Many important issues in relation to the contemporary EU centre on the type of state that the EU represents, the nature of European society, and the role of the individual in European public spaces. In the case of the state, one version of the debate centres not only on whether the EU is a nation-state writ large or an internationalization of the national state, but also the extent to which the EU represents a form of multi-level governance, with sub-national regional government and the supranational EU increasingly carrying out what were previously the tasks of the nation-state. The development of the EU and the advent of pan-European structures of governance cause us to reconsider the whole idea of society, and invite us to consider the structure and organization of social and political life in a globalized world where transnational flows and linkages are becoming ever more important. The corollary of this is that it is increasingly difficult to talk of integrated national societies and we need to recognize the plurality of social groups existing within (and across) nation-states, as well as the formation of transnational communities. As for the individual, there are many considerations invited by the ongoing processes of European integration. Some of the most prominent of these are the changing nature of citizenship, involvement in or exclusion from democratic processes, and the politics of identity. In sum, a sociological inquiry of European integration recasts the relationship between the individual, society, and state to take into account new levels of state power, the existence of societies beyond states, and a reordering of the role and responsibilities of the individual.

A political sociology of contemporary Europe must investigate other, more fundamental, changes. The changing relationship between state and society outlined above assumes that to a significant extent each remains largely unaltered by the processes that have contributed to European integration. They are merely extended and aggregated to a new level, or fractured and divided into new components. Such an analysis also assumes that sociology can continue to employ traditional concepts and theories with which to understand these changes. We must recognize that state, society and the individual have been fundamentally transformed, and that it is the proper task of political sociology to identify and deploy the most appropriate tools with which to investigate such a transformation.

It is no longer possible to talk of the state – either the nation-state or its sub- or supranational variants – as the primary locus of political power and the exercise of government. A criticism often levelled at traditional political sociology is that its focus was the central state, its powers, and the party politics associated with state rule. Contemporary sociology must examine the state within the wider field of forms of government. In the case of the EU the state is better thought of as but one element in a decentered array of government and authority. To study the EU we must examine the type of government consistent with the ways in which the EU seeks to regulate a harmonized European economic space. In this context the work of the governmentality theorists, sometimes referred to as the Anglo-Foucauldians, is of great relevance. They hold that government is accomplished not simply through the apparatuses of state but via a multiplicity of actors and agencies (Dean 1999 and Rose 1999). When applied to the EU this insight enables us to see how EU policies encourage responsibility and self-regulation in a whole range of actors: regions, enterprises, citizens.

A sociological study of the EU offers an opportunity to examine the nature of European societies under conditions of globalization. A study of contemporary European societies must begin with the recognition that in the same way that the state has undergone many changes, society too has been transformed. If the EU is not a nation-state writ large then neither can European society be simply an enlarged and expanded version of that found within nation-states. We must accept the need for a new conceptual approach to the study of societies. One of the key elements of such an approach is to problematize the notion of civil society. Civil society is a frequently used concept in sociology, political science and other discourses and is taken to represent a sphere of democracy, autonomy and freedom, distinct from (and in some versions protected by) the state. The idea has also been taken up by some globalization theorists who argue for an emerging global civil society. This book argues against the usefulness of the idea of civil society, finding it too liberal and optimistic, and too heavily associated with the sociology and imagery of the nation-state. The idea of society developed in this book is one which emphasizes the existence of a multiplicity of social spheres and public spaces not patterned according to the logic of an overarching principle. This frees us from the necessity to study the EU in terms of either an integrated supranational entity or the aggregate of its member states. This idea of a constellation of European public spaces also allows us to move away from a rigid cartographical notion of the EU. We can begin to think of the EU not as a totality or an integrated whole, but as a series of overlapping networks and diffuse power centres.

Thus far we have addressed some key features of, and new relationships between, society and the state occasioned by the European Union. The need to go beyond an approach that merely refocuses sociological inquiry to accommodate the existence of new levels of state power and the existence of societies beyond states has been emphasized. To this end a political sociology which acknowledges changing forms of political governance and the concomitant reordering of society is a prerequisite. However, there is still another dimension of political sociology that we have not yet discussed: the role of the individual. We can say that one of the most important aspects of a whole range of theorizing in the field of political sociology (especially work associated with postmodernism and post-Marxism) has been to challenge established notions of the individual (the subject). The notion of the subject associated with modernity, the purposive, self-conscious, reflexive, rational human agent has given way under the influence of postmodern thought (broadly construed) to a notion of the decentered, fragmented and partial subject whose identity is neither given a priori nor fixed, but open, contingent and malleable. This has implications for the individual both as a political actor and as a member of a collectivity. In the same way as societies are no longer thought to be unitary with respect to ethnic and national identity, our collectives selves are increasingly seen as fractured, fragmented and multiple. These shifts have several consequences. First, the object of politics is no longer what it was under conditions of modernity. Collective political action is no longer centered on the politics of state power: it is increasingly an ethical politics centered on the expression and furtherance of self-identity. Second, political and social transformation does not necessarily proceed according to previously accepted models. The politics of emancipation have given way to a politics of identity recognition in the passage from modernity to postmodernity and post-materialism. These changes have a particularly important bearing on the way we study social exclusion, citizenship, and the nature of European democracy.

Organization of the Book

This book aims to establish a framework within which a sociological study of European integration can be conducted. To this end the book advances three central propositions. The first is that European integration confronts political sociology with two major problems. These are that it poses questions which fall beyond sociology's traditional field of competence – state-centric political rule and nationally bounded cleavages – and that there exists a weak sociological tradition in the field upon which to build. In order to study European integration from a political sociology perspective we need to construct political sociology afresh and demonstrate its relevance and applicability.

The second proposition is that a political sociology informed by recent contributions to social theory can be made adequate to the task.[4] Political sociology may not feature large within the field of EU studies but this should not be taken to mean that it is not capable of making a significant contribution. Borrowing from social theory, or more accurately drawing upon the productive debates between sociology and social theory that have taken place over the past 20 years or so on issues such as modernity, postmodernity, globalization, subjectivity, and identity is a good way of enhancing the contribution that sociology can make.

The third proposition is that the resulting political sociological framework is potentially a very productive one with which we can begin to understand the EU. To this end a political sociology of the EU must engage with the existing literature on the EU, stemming mainly from political studies and international relations, and demonstrate that it has something new and relevant to say. More than this it has to establish that the dynamics of European integration, its problems and prospects, can be better apprehended and revealed through a sociological analysis.

The book is organized in the following way. Chapter 2 looks at the EU from the perspective of globalization. Globalization is central to this study not only because it is possibly the most important process acting upon and shaping the EU, but also because it is a crucial issue from the perspective of how to study the EU. A number of different sociological approaches to globalization are examined (Castells, Albrow, Robertson) and compared with the chief alternative represented by the work of Held. It is shown that sociological studies of globalization can yield important insights into the dynamics of integration and it is argued that it is essential to place globalization centrally within a political sociology of the EU. The usefulness of the model of globalization advanced in the chapter, and which serves as a framework of interpretation throughout the rest of the book, is demonstrated in an exploration of the oft-quoted idea that "capital is global, workers local," which is shown to be weak, sociologically speaking. This is linked to a discussion of the recent revision of the German nationality law and the closely related issue of European and German immigration policy and the need to recruit skilled workers from abroad. This section links arguments about globalization and the Europeanization of immigration policy to the discussions about unemployment and labor developed in chapter 5.

The idea that the EU represents a "super-state" is a common one, at least in popular and journalistic discourse. It rarely features in academic studies, although attempts to classify the EU as some kind of a state are a noticeable feature of the literature. However, the EU is not a monolithic entity and comprises several institutions: the European Commission, the Council and the Council of Ministers, the European Parliament, and the European Court of Justice. Chapter 3 deals with the thorny problem of what kind of state the EU represents (although it should be stated at the outset that it does not concern itself with the detailed workings of the above mentioned institutions). Various non-sociological approaches to the question of the European state are considered (Stone-Sweet and Sandholtz, Majone, Anderson, Dehousse), all of whom are orientated toward the debate on the extent to which the EU is an intergovernmental or supranational organization, and these are then compared to sociological approaches which deal with the EU as an "internationalization of the state." It is argued that sociological approaches to globalization (especially Albrow) offer a particularly useful way of looking at the EU, not as a state but in terms of forms of rule. Additionally, the governmentality theorists (Dean, Rose) demonstrate that the EU is best conceived of not as a state, or a multi-level polity, but as a multiplicity of agencies involved in the business of governing. The advantages of the preferred sociological approach are demonstrated in an analysis of the EU's Common Agricultural Policy (CAP), until recently dominated by statist forms of intervention and supranational protectionism but increasingly aligned with new forms of European governance.

Many sociologists profess to study society – information society, civil society or network society, for example – or features, characteristics or elements imputed to society. This book actually does study society: its very form and existence in contemporary Europe in its specificity and diversity. The question of whether a European society exists is a pertinent one for political sociology, particularly as it is commonly asserted that European integration has proceeded in the economic and, to a certain extent, political direction, but that there is no evidence of a European society in the making. Moreover, the very status of the sociological meaning of society is in some disarray as a result of the impact of globalization on sociological thought. As Nash (2000: 47) points out, globalization has problematized "the founding sociological image of society as a bounded and coherent set of structures and practices governed by the sovereign nation-state." Chapter 4 reviews recent sociological literature on the possibility of a European society (Delanty, Mann). It also advances a critique of the notion of civil society, for so many the cornerstone of political sociology, and looks at the ways in which the idea of civil society has been used to characterize democratic developments in national, supranational, and global contexts. The contributions of globalization and governmentality theory are utilized in order to advance the idea that European society should not be seen as a unified and coherent whole but as a series of non-integrated, fragmented, and autonomous public spheres. The chapter also explores how the issue of society is a growing preoccupation of the EU, particularly in relation to the problem of the "democratic deficit." The shifting constructions of society within EU discourse are examined to reveal a perceived need to develop new forms of governance.

Chapter 5 examines the interrelated issues of unemployment, social exclusion, and citizenship. The phenomenon of "jobless growth," often associated with the EU, is investigated to highlight the importance of a political sociology informed by globalization theory. The work of Esping-Anderson on welfare regimes is considered and its contribution to understanding the dynamics of unemployment in Europe assessed. The issues of social exclusion and citizenship are then considered within a framework which builds upon the work on globalization and the nature of society undertaken in earlier chapters. The connections between work, citizenship and participation in society assumed by "traditional" sociology, are shown to be in need of substantial revision in the light of developments in contemporary Europe.

The image of a "Europe of the regions" has become an important metaphor of integration. The idea that the EU has worked to empower and bring autonomy to sub-national regions which are increasingly "being disembedded from their national states" (Smith 1999: 247) is a pervasive one. Regional autonomy and cohesion (EU attempts to reduce regional disparities) are considered in chapter 6. Both are subjected to a critique from a globalization and governmentality perspective and the idea that Europe's regions contribute to integration is called into question. It is suggested that the sociological notions of "subpolitics" (associated with the work of Beck) and autonomization (driving from the work of the governmentality theorists and designating that neo-liberal economic policies tend to fragment and divide in their pursuit of growth) are particularly useful in understanding the way in which regions are animated in contemporary Europe. It is argued that an investigation of the role of regions in the EU and the workings of the EU's cohesion policy reveal a dynamic of growth and development which is concealed by more orthodox accounts.

Europe's core/periphery relations come under consideration in chapter 7, in the context of the model of growth that the EU assumes derives from this relationship. Stated simply, the orthodox view is that the peripheries are dependent upon the core for growth, and EU policies are devised accordingly. The globalization-inspired critique of the EU's regions developed in the previous chapter is employed to demonstrate that core/periphery hierarchies have become destabilized and that territorialist assumptions about integration need to be revised. It is argued that the idea of peripherality deployed by the dominant discourse on the EU serves to legitimize EU policies on regional development, competitiveness, and growth. An approach to peripheries based on a theory of networks rather than territory is proposed. To this end a number of sociological and political science theories of networks and flows (Appadurai, Axford and Huggins, Barry, Castells, Urry) are introduced in order to develop a different model of the dynamics of EU growth. The idea of a "Europe of the network" is rejected in favour of an understanding of networks which emphasizes their openness and fluidity and the ways in which global flows impact on EU structures.

The idea of a "democratic deficit" in the EU is considered by many commentators to constitute a major barrier to greater integration and is frequently linked to the lack of a true European identity. Chapter 8 deals with the question of democracy, and more particularly Europe's democratic identity. The issue of what European identity comprises or should comprise is a fraught one, and it is often conceived in terms of exclusivity borrowed from the language of nationalism. Key approaches to this issue in the literature are reviewed, particularly the work of Laffan, Giorgi, Siedentop, and Moravcsik. Two alternative approaches to the issue of democracy and democratic identity in the EU are considered. Cosmopolitan democracy (Held and Archibugi) argues for new international institutions of democracy to sit alongside existing nation-states with a view to ensuring that the democratic nation-state is the global norm. These theorists argue that the EU is an example of cosmopolitan democracy and by further extending postnational democratic practices the EU's "democratic deficit" can be eradicated. Another model, agonistic democracy (Mouffe), emphasizes the need for Others in the democratic process (struggle between contending forces is central to democracy), and demonstrates the impossibility of maintaining a strict "us and them" approach to outsiders. Both approaches enable us to think about democracy beyond the nation-state.

Will the EU double its membership over the new few years? EU enlargement is the theme of chapter 9, in which one key element of the enlargement process, the Copenhagen criteria in respect of democracy and human rights, is considered in relation to one country, Turkey. The EU believes that its human rights values are universal values and that it has a moral duty to impose these on candidate and non-member countries. There are several important sociological approaches to the question of universalism, most (but not all) deriving from a globalization perspective. The work of Beck, Laclau and Robertson on universalism is applied to an understanding of human rights and democracy in Turkey in particular, and the enlargement process in general, and the contested and contingent nature of human rights norms are asserted. The chapter investigates the reasons why the norms and principles of the EU, as codified in the Copenhagen criteria, and the way in which the EU projects these values and expectations as universal, remain largely unchallenged within the accession processes. Chapter 10 concludes the book and aims to draw together some of the main themes developed in the preceding chapters. In particular, it addresses the key issues of how best to study European integration, and the contribution that political sociology can make to the future of a subject for so long dominated by political science and international relations.

2 The European Union and Globalization

An "Inclusive Globalization Paradigm"

Globalization is currently the biggest and most complex issue in relation to European integration. More than this, it is the most important issue in terms of *how* to study the European Union. In order to understand why it is so important in both of these contexts we must establish exactly what we mean by globalization, and the ways in which it is transforming the EU. This is a far from straightforward task as there are numerous meanings attached to globalization and a whole range of interpretations as to its importance for studying the EU. It is hardly an exaggeration to say that every academic discipline works with its own version of globalization, and even within a discipline such as sociology there are several contending interpretations. This makes coming to terms with globalization as an intellectual idea "whose time has come" (Held et al. 1999: 1) much more complicated than it would otherwise be. In EU studies no consensus exists on the extent to which globalization (even when conceived narrowly as an economic phenomenon) is a factor in shaping the role and direction of the EU, or the ways in which globalization acts upon and is in turn furthered by the European Union. Indeed, it is quite common to encounter accounts of European integration that accord no role to globalization in shaping contemporary events.

The position adopted here is that a political sociology of the European Union cannot hope to be successful unless it comes to terms with globalization. At the same time, political sociology can contribute something very useful to the study of the EU's involvement with the processes comprising globalization. The incorporation of a sociological perspective on globalization makes the study of the EU a more exciting and yet more exacting proposition. To appreciate why this is so we must first recognize the way in which globalization has come to be understood in both popular and academic discourse. Globalization is most commonly thought of as a series of transnational economic processes making the world into one large market place, and in doing so undermining the authority of, and need for, the nation-state. On the basis of this interpretation the relationship between globalization and the EU is one in which the former dictates that integration is necessary in order that the latter can ensure competitiveness in the global economy, the sovereign nation-state no longer being able to fulfil this function. Globalization constitutes the environment in which the EU operates, and the threat that it represents provides the stimulation for greater cooperative economic action. The EU, and more particularly the single market and monetary union, are rational and calculated responses to economic problems which are too large to be controlled by any one nation-state. This is not an understanding of the relationship between globalization and the EU that finds favour in this book.

The idea that globalization is primarily an economic phenomenon and that it has impacted on the EU by acting as a catalyst of greater integration has become something of a commonplace. The rise of this economistic model poses some problems for sociology however, and, as it will become clear, for a study of the EU. Robertson (2001) makes the point that:

> The current tendency to regard globalization in more or less exclusively economic terms is a particularly disturbing form of reductionism, indeed of fundamentalism. Nowadays invocation of the word 'globalization' almost automatically seems to raise issues concerning so-called economic liberalism, deregulation, privatisation, marketization and the crystallization of what many call a global economy (or global capitalism).

That an economistic interpretation has become fashionable in recent times should not blind us to the fact that the study of globalization has a long tradition in sociology, stretching back to the late 1960s and developing strongly through the 1980s and 90s. Furthermore, this sociology of globalization (at least in the hands of its more able practitioners) is also reflexive sociology. That is to say it has made a considerable contribution to thinking about sociology itself and reordering the discipline in the light of changing circumstances. This is most evident in the way sociology has been forced to acknowledge that it has hitherto tended to study societies contained within nation-states in a way that contributed to the "naturalness" of these entities. Sociology has, since its inception as a discipline in the nineteenth century, been an accomplice in the project of legitimizing and institutionalizing the nation-state as the universal form of social and political organization.

The sociology of globalization (and the work on globalization imported from the broader field of social theory) has encouraged the study of a whole range of transnational and global processes which render such assumptions untenable, and caused sociology to challenge some very basis assumptions. For instance, if we ask the question "what is sociology the study of?" and give as an answer "society," we are forced to ask a further question: "what sort of society?" The answer given to this second question will nearly always be couched in terms of a particular national society; French, German, American, and so on. It is commonly assumed, both within sociology and in more popular contexts, that when we talk of society we implicitly refer to national forms of society. We need to consider whether society has to be contained within a national form, or whether it can have an existence beyond national borders; a European society, for example.

The transnational and global interactions characteristic of our contemporary world make the study of a "nationally sequestered society" (Robertson 1992) something of an anachronism. It is more interesting and pertinent to examine how these "societies" are subjected to forces which originate from a distant source, the networks and flows which traverse their space, and the ways in which the groups and individuals which comprise them are organized and mobilized according to non-national criteria. But this is not to say that the nation-state is irrelevant under conditions of globalization. As we shall see, the nation-state is simultaneously weakened and strengthened by globalization, and it is frequently the impact of global processes on the nation-state which produce the most interesting phenomena of contemporary times.

Our sociological interpretation of globalization refers to a wide-ranging and complex series of processes occurring over a long period of time, and through which the world has become increasingly interconnected and the consciousness of the world as a single place has increased (Beck 2000, Robertson 1992). The globalization paradigm facilitates a new approach to a whole array of issues ranging from the nature of society and mechanisms of social cohesion, to the construction of identities and the nature of social movements and conflicts. At the same time as globalization is moving sociology beyond a parochial set of concerns, sociology strives to provide an efficacious antidote to the tendency to reduce globalization to economic processes. The chapter advances the case that a sociological approach to globalization provides us with a more productive way of thinking about the dynamics of European integration. Not only is it able to throw fresh light on perennial questions such as how globalization is shaping the EU and the extent to which the state is being rendered obsolete (or not), but it also reveals new questions and new areas to explore. For example, it causes us to reconsider the relationship between Europe's core and periphery, the autonomy of its regions, and the meaning of citizenship in the contemporary EU.

This chapter is organized in the following way. First, we will examine the dominant interpretation of the relationship between globalization and the European Union (having first inserted the caveat that not all accounts of EU integration allow for any relationship at all). There is much support for the view that globalization constitutes an external threat which closer integration can combat. Second, we will look at the way that globalization has been conceived within sociology, concentrating our attention on the work of Albrow and Robertson, via consideration of the sociology of Castells. The work of Albrow and Roberston has important differences but has sufficient commonality to be said to represent an "inclusive globalization paradigm."[1] The benefits of this model *vis-à-vis* its main rivals will then be considered and its usefulness for a study of the EU outlined.

Globalization and EU Integration

It is common to read that no consensus exists on the meaning and impact of globalization on the EU (Hudson and Williams 1999: 5). It would be more accurate to say that there is no consensus that globalization has any significant impact on the EU. Many books explore European integration, European identity and Europe's relationship to the rest of the world, in terms which do not acknowledge the existence of globalization (however conceived) as a factor contributing to, shaping or determining the EU's policy choices, economic development, or internal problems.[2]

However, where a relationship is acknowledged, a broad consensus does exist. Globalization is conceived in economic terms – international trade and global flows of capital – and is responsible for creating the environment in which a much greater degree of European integration is deemed necessary (the EU being just one of a number of regional trading blocs brought into being by the same set of processes) (Starie 1999). There is also broad agreement that globalization implies a diminution in the powers of the nation-state and the concomitant empowerment of the sub-national region. This consensus is reinforced by a growing volume of literature which seeks to refute these claims and argue that nothing much has changed and that the nation-state is still a major player in world affairs (Hirst and Thompson 1996).

One area of debate within this wider consensus is the extent to which the EU is the product of globalization, or whether it is active in shaping it. There are those who hold that increased European integration is the logical response to a world dominated by global financial flows and transnational corporations. On this understanding globalization has acted upon the EU by encouraging the replacement of an economic space of independent trading regions and nations by a single Europe-wide corporate economy (Amin and Tomaney 1995: 33). One consequence of the "greater transnational uniformity in culture, communication, information, financial regulation and national economic policies" (Rhodes, Heywood and Wright 1997: 5) engendered by globalization is that the nation-state needs the security offered by membership in an economic bloc such as the EU. The existence of globalization legitimizes European integration in the name of the need for greater EU competitiveness. This is in fact the dominant theme in the EU's own appreciation of the impact of globalization. For example a Commission White Paper (European Commission 1993) states that:

> The globalization of economies and markets, which involves the intensification of international competition through the emergence of a potentially unique worldwide market for an expanding range of goods, services and factors, brings out the full importance of that responsibility on the part of national and Community authorities as regards competitiveness.

Globalization is presented as a challenge to be met and an incentive to pursue ever-greater steps towards economic integration, trade liberalization and competitiveness. In other words, globalization presents the EU and its member states with both the motive and the opportunity to enhance competitiveness. Delanty (1998) argues that the perspective on European integration that has emerged since the 1980s and encapsulated by the Maastricht Treaty is the product of an increasingly global world order. On this model of integration nation-states surrender a degree of their sovereignty in order to survive under conditions of globalization. "In short, globalization is the condition which has replaced the need for peace in the justification of European integration today."[3] For some writers EU integration and globalization are interrelated to the point where the two sets of processes are difficult to distinguish. They are mutually implicated: one calling forth the other: one finding expression in the other. This is a more sophisticated version of the "justification for integration" argument. For example, Castells (1998: 338) sees integration as being both a reaction to globalization and its most advanced expression, and Ross (1998) is of the opinion that European integration has had the effect of promoting globalization, rather than being conditioned by it. Held et al. (1999) whose work we will consider in detail later in the chapter, subscribe to the view that the EU has strengthened European nation-states in the face of US and Japanese economic dominance, and in doing so has given them the means to shape and direct globalization.

We should dispel the idea that thinking about the EU in terms of a project to empower European countries is the preserve of a political science discourse ignorant of the sociological dimensions of the globalization debate. Beck (2000) also sees in EU integration evidence of a desire to be an active participant in the face of globalization rather than a passive recipient. Europe should be the active political tamer and moulder of economic globalization. Only by creating a transnational political space can the EU become, at some future point, a "shape-giving subject of globalization" (Beck 2000: 158). What this example demonstrates is that the idea of the EU as a defensive reaction to globalization is a pervasive one, as is the economistic logic that drives it.

A Sociological Understanding of Globalization

It would be misleading to suggest that sociologists and social theorists have uniformly managed to extract themselves from the gravitational pull of this economistic "black hole." In fact, they have bought into this model in a big way, or at least some of them have. Probably the most widely read, and possibly the most influential sociological account of globalization is that offered by Castells in his trilogy entitled *The Information Age*.[4] In this work Castells charts "the rise of the network society," the outcome of wide-ranging and epochal transformations in the fields of technology, economy, culture, the state (Castells 2000c).[5] Before turning to his conceptualization of globalization we should first appreciate the broad contours of *The Information Age* and understand some of its most fundamental claims.

Its range of concerns and the questions which it poses makes *The Information Age* a work of great relevance. According to Castells, the coming of the network society marks a fundamental change from the industrial age, and by implication we need a sociology capable of grasping emerging forms of social organization and conflict. The purpose of *The Information Age* is "to propose some elements of an exploratory, cross-cultural theory of economy and society in the information age, as it specifically refers to the emergence of a new social structure" (Castells 2000a: 26). Like Urry (1999), Castells is searching for a "sociology beyond societies." The network society, which is taking shape and already "permeates most societies in the world," cannot be easily controlled and regulated. Social order is at the same time social disorder: "the new social order, the network society, increasingly appears to most people as a meta-social disorder. Namely, as an automated, random sequence of events, derived from the uncontrollable logic of markets, technology, geo-political order, or biological determination" (Castells 1996: 6–7).

From the industrial age where power was located in political institutions such as the state, we are moving to the network society in which, "political institutions are not the site of power any longer. The real power is the power of instrumental flows, and cultural codes, embedded in networks" (Castells 2000c). A corollary of this shift of power away from the state is that forms of political opposition are less readily apparent. In industrial societies conflict centered on production and the antagonism between capital and labor. This is no longer a characteristic of the network society in which capital is global, labor local and therefore no longer pitted in struggle. Castells seeks a candidate to replace the industrial working class, an agent who could take on global capital and transform the world for the better. However, he finds only "communes of resistance" (communities of faith, minorities, environmental protest groups, for example) whose local struggles do not promise generic social change. As one commentator states, Castells is hoping for "salvation through total societal transformation but finds no evidence for it." Local struggles are "insufficiently transformative (havens not heavens)" (Friedman 2000: 119). So on the one hand Castells recognizes that the old categories of sociology are insufficient to apprehend the extent to which globalization continues to transform our lives, on the other he still expects social movements to have universal pretensions.

We have already come across two indications of what Castells has in mind when he talks about globalization, although at the time that we encountered them we did not draw out their significance. First, there was the suggestion that the new social order represented by the network society is a "meta-social disorder." I take this to be a reference to the idea that the networks and flows to which Castells refers are global in scope and work to destabilize the structures of nation-state societies. Meta-social (beyond or above the social) being a metaphor for global. The global is the disordered state of affairs incurred by the supercession of industrial (nation-state) society. This is an interesting conceptualization in as much as it draws attention to the contingent and unpredictable nature of contemporary events, and fits well with the idea of the network society "careening out of control" (Friedman 2000: 112). The second indication as to the model of globalization with which Castells is working is the reference to a global/local dichotomy. Socially defining cleavages are not possible where capital is global and labor local: they reside at different ends of the continuum therefore and can never engage in meaningful conflict in the way that was definitive of industrial society.[6] The assumption of global/local dichotomy is common to many branches of the study of globalization, but as we shall see is far from the most productive way to view the relationship of the local to the global.

When Castells talks about globalization it is invariably in terms of a global economy. Globalization is driven by "strategic economic activities" integrated "through electronically enacted networks of exchange of capital, commodities, and information" (2000b: 348). Contemporary capitalism differs from its historical predecessors in that it is global and "structured to a large extent around a network of financial flows" (2000a: 502). The global economy (working as a unit in real time) is a new phenomenon and should be distinguished from a world economy (in which capitalist accumulation proceeds throughout the world). For Castells, globalization has transformed European integration from a series of "defensive projects" into a network state (Castells 2000b: 339). These "defensive projects" were political reactions to serious economic problems: the threat of another war and the concomitant need to bring under a European authority those industries central to any future war effort (coal and steel); the perception of a "technology gap" between Europe, the US, and Japan resulting in the Single European Act of 1987; the collapse of communism and the unification of Germany. Castells' interpretation of globalization is a sophisticated version of the model alluded to at the opening of this chapter in which globalization provides the incentive needed for the EU to become competitive in the global economy, the sovereign nation-state acting alone no longer being able to do this.

What are we to make of Castells' claim (2000b: 348) that the EU has not only been constructed as a response to globalization, but is in fact its most advanced expression? One interpretation would be that the EU is integrated most fully into the flows and networks of "the information age." The making of the global economy, led by financial and currency markets, "induces and shapes the current process of European integration" (Castells 2000b: 348). Another interpretation would be that he is not simply pointing to the presence of global economic networks propelling Europe towards integration and thereby rendering the nation-state obsolete. The EU is also the most advanced expression of the tensions and conflicts thrown up by global networks acting on the European nation-state. The global works to shape EU integration but it does so "on the basis of European institutions constituted around predominantly political goals" (Castells 2000b: 348). Elsewhere, he adds that globalization does not act alone in shaping European integration: "the trends which I have identified as critical in configuring the Information Age – globalization, identity and the crisis of the nation-state – are shaping European unification" (Castells 2000b: 340). As an example of the tensions revealed by the impact of globalization on EU integration Castells points to the rise of nationalism. While the EU has been gaining power in its search for competitiveness in the global economy, rising social problems – unemployment, inequality, job insecurity – coupled with the perception of a "democratic deficit" have led citizens to believe that their nation-states are becoming "captives of European supernationality" (Castells 2000b: 357). One reaction to this has been an affirmation of nation against state. European integration has spawned (divisive) nationalism, not federalism. "Thus, confronted with a decline in democracy and citizen participation, at a time of globalization of the economy and Europeanization of politics, citizens retrench in their countries, and increasingly affirm their nations" (Castells 2000b: 359).

The Global Age

Castells' *The Information Age* advances a sophisticated version of the thesis that globalization is an economic process to which European integration is a reaction. The creation of a single world market which is at the heart of this interpretation is an example of what Albrow (1996) would term a modernist vision of a globalized world: an attempt to apprehend a new set of circumstances through familiar concepts and categories. Albrow is another theorist who sees globalization instituting a new epoch in human existence. When referring to globalization he believes that it is a mistake to talk about "global modernity."[7] Equally it is not possible to adequately explain the profound transformations that herald the Global Age through the conceptual imagery of modernity. The project of modernity was "to extend human control over space, time, nature and society. The main agent of this project was the nation-state working with and through capitalist and military organization" (Albrow 1996: 7). Modernity has come to an end, replaced by the Global Age, a transformation which requires a new conceptual framework. In the Modern Age the nation-state was the basic unit of social organization and experience: in the Global Age the globe becomes the frame within which human activity is conceived and takes place. "Fundamentally the Global Age involves the supplanting of modernity with globality and this means an overall change in the basis of action and social organization for individuals and groups" (Albrow 1996: 4).

Albrow is keen to distinguish claims that we are experiencing an epochal transformation from the teleological idea that there is anything inevitable about these processes, and that they are in any sense a culmination of human history. Rather than being the latest stage in a long process of development, globalization is "the arrest of what was taken for granted" (Albrow 1996: 101).[8] In other words, there is nothing "natural" about the social, institutional, and economic arrangements characteristic of modernity. We take it for granted that modernity embodies progress but it is not necessary or inevitable. Globalization challenges many of the assumptions upon which modernity was founded: that the nation-state constitutes the dominant frame for social organization or that nature can be controlled and tamed. For instance, the project of modernity has set ideas about the relationship between state and society: the former acts to control the latter. Society must be managed and conflict contained in order that the continued unity of the nation-state can be assured. The Modern Age has run its course when "the social takes on a meaning outside the frame of reference set by the nation-state. This happens when the state is no longer able to control new forms of social organization" (Albrow 1996: 58). We shall explore Albrow's ideas on society in the Global Age in greater detail in chapter 4.

Albrow's definition of globalization coalesces around the general process of becoming global (whether considered as incremental change or epochal transformation) and comprises "the active dissemination of practices, values, technology and other human products throughout the globe" (Albrow 1996: 88). Globalization can be said to be occurring when our consciousness of the globe shapes our activities, and when global practices impact on our lives. It should be noted that there is no special role reserved for the economy in causing these things to occur.

This way of thinking ushers in a new and very important way of interpreting the relationship between the global and the local. Again a comparison with Castells is useful. As we have already seen, Castells views the global and the local as being polar opposites. By contrast, Albrow sees them as interrelated and mutually implicated, the local being produced by the global. It is readily understood that globalization brings greater interconnectedness across large distances.

> At the same time, what used to be connected is often disconnected. People are separated by highways where once there were fields and village streets. Neighbours no longer come from the same class or even country. One generation fails to understand another's music. Night is divided from day by danger on the street. This is daily experience of living in a locality. (Albrow 1996: 110)

Globalization does not lead inevitability to a decline in locality but it does change its meaning. There are two main senses in which this is true. First, activities which occur side-by-side in geographical space may be disconnected from each other in a profound sense (as with the examples contained in the above quote). There is no necessary integration of activities which occur in a given locality (what Albrow terms "disconnected contiguity"), nor can these localities be automatically grouped together or aggregated to form larger entities as was the case with the nation-state. Secondly, with the deterritorialization of social life locality is less about where an activity takes place, and increasingly a "site for multiple coexisting worlds" (Albrow 1996: 156). People can participate in any number of groups and communities, of varying size and extension, in a way which bears little relation to the physical spaces they occupy in their daily lives. Locality no longer acts as a necessary focal point for community. Communities of kin and interests groups can be created and sustained at a distance via modern communications. Economic and political interests are pursued by many groups – women, the elderly, ethnic minorities, homosexuals to name but a few – whose members are dispersed and whose organization does not rely on territorial proximity as the basis for commonality.

Albrow's understanding of globalization also introduces a new perspective on the issue of the global economy. He talks of the "denationalization of the economy," by which he means the break with the idea so characteristic of modernity that the national economy (in a world of national economies) was the focus of analysis (Albrow 1996: 128). Free trade and global markets are not the keys to understanding the global economy: globalization is not driven by free trade. It is economic organization rather than the market which underscores the globalization of the economy. The transnational corporation and the globalization of production and consumption are more important than global markets in the creation of globalization, as are mobility of capital, and international financial institutions. These processes also have an impact on local activity: as the nation-state is forced to adapt to a diminished role in the regulation of economic activity there arises "the possibility of subnational forms of activity which owe something to the boundary-dismantling effects of globalization but little to organization at the global level" (Albrow 1996: 133). The local emerges in the spaces opened up by the play of the global on the nation-state. In other words, the local is both freed from national restrictions and at the same time enjoys a freedom from similar constraints at the global level. This gives a whole new meaning and status to the local.

Albrow also talks about the "relativization of identity" and the way globalization has the potential to detach identity from group membership. This is another example of the way in which globalization causes us to re-assess our sociological concepts and categories. The political society of modernity would address the individual within a framework based upon the assumption that identity was derived from a structural location within a (more or less) integrated whole, and that the individual's position would be the outcome of the interplay of state and societal forces. These assumptions are challenged by Albrow's assertion that "The problem of the individual and society has moved away from what used to be the central issue, agency and structure, to the problem of identity" (Albrow 1996: 150). In other words, the structure/agency debate – the extent to which we act freely (have agency) or our actions are determined by external structures (such as the economy) – is itself founded upon the type of social science characteristic of modernity. Such modes of sociological analysis are found wanting in the quest to understand identities relativized by global social change, and which subvert traditional hierarchies and detach themselves from recognizable structural settings.

He illustrates the point through the use of two examples: nationalism and fundamentalism. Modern social theory wants to interpret contemporary nationalism as a primordialist response to the disruption of the modern state caused by the collapse of communism and/ or the advent of globalization. In a similar way, fundamentalism is seen as a desire for certainty and fixity in an uncertain and fluid world. Both explanations are couched in "old modern social scientific discourse." They "explain contemporary movements in terms of the human attempt to re-establish a firm structure after an earlier one had been lost" (Albrow 1996: 150–1). In both cases globalization is seen as negative force. As we have already seen, one consequence of the liberation of locality, community and society from the territorially constructed hierarchies of the nation-state is that the individual can inhabit "multiple worlds." Under conditions of globality identity is acquired by membership in a multiplicity of groups all of which have different dimensions and different intensities. There is no longer the same pressure for individuals to assimilate to proximate or traditional groups, or to subscribe to a hierarchy of identities headed by nation and class. Identity is a property of self rather than an attribute of group membership. People increasingly have recourse to universal personhood rights, as enshrined in various UN Charters which institutionalise the right of the individual to assert their chosen identity (Soysal 1997). "Identity is a unique particularity recognized in the universality of the right to be a distinct human being" (Albrow 1996: 151).

Attachments to religion, territory or ethnicity are frequently portrayed as a rejection of globalization, or a regression to ancient collectivities or tribal loyalties. As Robins (1997: 41) points out, the (western-generated) image of Islamic fundamentalism is notable for the way it positions fundamentalism in opposition to globalization.[9] For example, "attempts by some Islamic countries to ban satellite television have seemed to symbolize resistance to global information and communication flows," and appear to represent a defensive response to the disruptions of global modernity. Another way of interpreting these phenomena is to view them as assertions of identity within an emerging global field and "the aspiration to create a space within global culture." As another commentator points out, "the central thrust is to make Islam and Muslims more determinative in the world system, not to reverse globalization. The intent is to shape global reality, not to negate it" (Beyer quoted in Robins 1997: 42). A Global Age understanding of nationalism and fundamentalism emphasizes the extent to which both are no longer necessarily tied to the project of the nation-state, and appeal precisely to those people who were previously excluded. Indeed, it the extent to which these movements evade the control and restrictions of domestic and international agencies which gives them their political potency, a feature which is enhanced by the fact that they can be animated from afar and sustained by transnational networks.

Albrow's globalization thesis performs two important functions. First, it outlines ways in which we can begin to think about social relations, networks, and institutions beyond the nation-state. Globalization reorders the borders and parameters within which social relations take place. Secondly, it emphasizes that in order to do this we must move beyond the conceptual confines dictated by the sociology of modernity. Globalization calls upon sociology to question its own methodological assumptions. From such a platform it is possible to develop a sophisticated analysis of European integration in the Global Age.[10]

Albrow identifies three features of the Global Age which are relevant to a study of European integration: the internationalization of technical systems; the floating of nationality; the liberation of territorial locality. The first of these refers to the way in which the EU has worked to govern European space through the harmonization of technical practices and standards (see also Barry 2001). For Albrow this is the real meaning of integration, but it is not something which divides Europe from the rest of the world or forges a distinctive European identity. His ideas are in marked contrast to the majority of accounts of European integration which see it as the construction of an economic bloc designed to compete against other such entities in an increasingly competitive global environment.

The harmonization which is constitutive of the EU as a single economic and social space also frequently leads to greater harmonization with the rest of the world. He cites the Euro, a new "worldwide medium of exchange" as one example, and standards of air safety as another. Human rights would constitute yet another, EU practices being conditioned by, and in turn promoting, universal values. "The search for rational standards, which are technically robust brings with it the requirement that they should fit international standards. There is no point in having standards of air safety simply over Europe" (Albrow 1998a).

The second feature of the Global Age which has a particular bearing on the EU is the floating of nationality, related of course to the changing role of the nation-state under globalization. In short, nation and state have become detached and citizenship is less and less dependent upon the nation-state. Belonging to a nation means something different from what it did in the Modern Age when the nation-state was the standard reference point for political allegiance. In a similar way, society is freed from the constraints of the state. Society is expanding and overflows the borders of the nation-states which formerly contained it.

The final feature of the Global Age to which Albrow draws our attention is the "liberation of territorial locality." We have already seen how the local takes on a different set of meanings in the Global Age. From the point of view of the EU the autonomy of locality consequent upon globalization is a significant factor in explaining sub-national regional dynamism in the contemporary EU, but not necessarily in predictable ways (see chapter 5). One way in which globalization impacts on the EU is to free locality from traditional national and supranational bindings. This means not only that Euro-regions can gain independence from their national capitals but can also enjoy an existence separate from EU control. Cities and regions are capable of taking advantage of the global networks and flows which act upon the EU but originate in distant places. In the Global Age, local autonomy is global autonomy.

Albrow's thesis revolves around the notion that the Global Age supplants the Modern Age, and he advances a compelling case for why we should embrace the logic of globality. In order to understand the Global Age we must dispense with the familiar intellectual tools of modernity, and recognise "our own time and its unique configuration" (Albrow 1998a).[11] One of the limitations of modernity is that "it cannot imagine the future except as its own continuation, or chaos"(Albrow 1996: 9). Modernity is in a state of flux in which the only constant is that "all that is solid melts into air" (Berman 1983). As such, modernity claims a monopoly on the terms with which we describe change and understand history. In order to break with this logic we must accept the arrival of a new epoch beyond modernity. According to Albrow (1998b) the idea of epochal change is "a necessary intellectual resource for understanding the present and as a counterweight to the inevitabilism which disfigures much of globalization theory." Nevertheless, the epochal schema is an element of his work which we might want to criticize, and we might want to question why a series of changes which have been a long time in the making have to be narrated as a sharp break between two distinct periods. The emphasis on epochal change or far reaching transformation may work to suppress continuities which are equally important. One way of exploring these issues is to look at the question of postmodernity, and how Albrow conceptualises the relationship between modernity, postmodernity, and the Global Age.

The first point to note is that just as the nation-state is not completely obliterated by globalization – it continues to exert a powerful influence and interacts in important ways with global networks – modernity is not totally wiped out by the onset of the Global Age. Modernity is accorded "a subordinate place within the configuration of the new epoch, which derives its defining features from the global" (Albrow 1996: 78). People will continue to think and make judgment according to modernist categories and according to established norms. The institutions of the Modern Age do not "melt into air" overnight. The difference is that new forms of thought and new institutional arrangements become dominant under conditions of globalization. We can draw an analogy with the way in which Marx conceptualized modes of production. The advent of capitalism does not mean that previous modes of production cease to exist. Feudalism and slavery continue in our own times, but they are no longer dominant, merely residual elements of previous modes of production.

Albrow interprets postmodernity as a continuation of modernity, not a break with it. Postmodern thinking is rooted in the modern, as evidenced by its emphasis on the importance of technology, for example. The postmodern imagination is also unable to envisage an alternative to itself, short of complete chaos. For these reasons post-modern thought never manages to convince in its accounts of the onset of a new era. The main weakness of postmodern thought is that it remains trapped in a critique of (western) modernity. For Albrow, a more productive way forward is to acknowledge the contribution of the pre-modern and the non-western in order to both construct a better model of what comes after and to build in a greater sense of continuity over a much longer historical period (Albrow 1996: 210). In short, Albrow feels the need to establish a break between the Modern and Global Ages in order to prevent the distinctive and innovative characteristics of the latter being subordi-nated to the logic of the former. Postmodernity is no substitute as it serves only to maintain modernity as the entire horizon for thinking about the consequences of globalization.

The debate on the relationship of modernity and postmodernity to globalization runs deep within the sociological literature. There are two main issues, the first concerns causality, the second periodiza-tion. In the case of causality the biggest issue is whether or not globalization has been produced by modernity. In Albrow's thesis the Global Age follows the Modern Age, but is not simply the consequence of it. In the work of other theorists, Giddens (1990) being the most famous example, globalization is produced by modernity. Robertson (1992) challenges this view and puts the case for modernity being a consequence of globalization.

Giddens holds that modernity has entered a new and radical phase, termed postmodernity by some, reflexive modernization by Beck, Giddens, and Lash (1994). In the terms mapped out by Albrow above, Giddens can be categorized as a theorist who sees a good deal of continuity (alongside the discontinuity) between the modern and the postmodern and who continues to analyse the transition "via a consideration of the institutions of modernity" (Robertson 1992: 140). For Giddens, this radical or reflexive modernity possesses inherent globalizing tendencies. Globalization amounts to "an intensification of worldwide social relations which can link distant localities in such a way that local happenings are shaped by events occurring many miles away and vice versa" (Giddens 1990: 64). Globalization becomes a metaphor for the expansion of modernity and bringing the entire globe within its remit.

We have seen how Albrow establishes his case for the Global Age by emphasising that new social arrangements and institutions can only be properly comprehended by going beyond a modernist logic, and at the same time by insisting that we establish cultural and temporal continuities with much earlier epochs. For Giddens, globalizing tendencies inhere within modernity, indeed globalization is a consequence of modernity (Giddens 1990: 175). Giddens' view only holds if we subscribe to the idea that globalization is a recent phenomenon and not part of a much longer period of development. We can contrast this with Robertson's argument that globalization constitutes "the vital setting" for the emergence of modernity and for modernization. He argues that aspects of the globalization process such as "the growth of the 'world religions', voyages of discovery, early map-making, the spread of the Gregorian calendar, and so on were both pivotal attributes of globalization and preconditions of *different types* of modernity" (Robertson 2001). In other words, globalization ushered in modernity. In terms of epochal designations Robertson also eschews postmodernity, arguing that much of what has been discussed in the debate about postmodernity and postmodernism, the relativization of perspectives and emphasis on difference and heterogeneity for example, "has been incorporated into and recast in the contemporary debate about globality, globalization and globalism" (Robertson 2001).[12] Let us now look at some of the key elements of Robertson's work on globalization.

Global Culture

The development of globalization as a focus of sociological study is closely associated with Robertson's work. In Robertson's hands the sociology of globalization becomes a vehicle for exploring and pointing up the limitations of traditional sociological frameworks. In other words, Robertson's sociology of globalization is a very good example of what I referred to earlier as reflexive sociology. His book *Globalization: Social Theory and Global Culture* (Robertson 1992) is as much about sociology as it is about globalization. Of his own work he says that it constitutes "an extension and refocusing of sociological work, work which enables sociology and more generally social theory to transcend the limitation of the conditions of its own maturation in the so-called classical period of the discipline" (Robertson 1992: 9). Of especial interest is the problem alluded to earlier, the tendency of sociology to assume a congruity between society and nation-state. In other words, that the class structure, social mobility, culture and traditions, socio-economic inequalities or whatever are being studied are "naturally" contained within the framework of a given nation-state. Sociology has been responsible for the "institutionalisation of the idea of the culturally cohesive and sequestered national society" (Robertson 1992: 50).

For Robertson the concept of globalization "refers both to the compression of the world and the intensification of the consciousness of the world as a whole" (Robertson 1992: 8). The world has become more interconnected, a development which is closely tied up with an increased awareness that this is so. It should be noted that the interconnectedness and the compression of the world do not simply equate to the unification or integration of the world. Robertson prefers to talk of the "unicity" of the globe in preference to its unity, and in doing so emphasizes that it is possible to think of the globe as a single place and its uniqueness (its "oneness"), but in ways which do not imply that it is constituted as such by global institutions.

The economistic globalization discourse prevalent at the present time prefers to see globalization as a recent phenomenon, a product of the post-Cold War world order dominated by the global spread of capital. In contrast, Robertson emphasizes that globalization has been a very long historical process, over a thousand years in the making (Robertson 1990). As we have already discussed, this historical line-age means that for Robertson it is not possible to view globalization as an outcome of modernity. During the past five hundred or so years "the world has increasingly taken a particular overall shape consisting of nation-states; individual selves; the system of inter-national relations; and humankind" (Robertson 2001). What this means is that globalization has, over a protracted time period, worked to shape the world in to the form that we recognize it today, and, at the same time, has sharpened our sense of what the world is and of what it consists. It is Robertson's contention that the "global field" thus constituted is the lens through which we conceive the unicity of the world. If modernity is not responsible for globalization, the question of what drives it becomes more intriguing. Robertson wishes to avoid economic determinism and argues that different forces (religious, cultural, economic) have been at the forefront at different periods in history.

From the point of view of constructing a political sociology of European integration, one of the most important of Robertson's contributions is his work on the global–local relationship. Rather than being at opposite ends of a continuum, or placed in an antagonistic relationship (the global denies the local, or the local resists the global)

Robertson is emphatic that the two exist in a complex and productive relationship: the local is globally produced.[13] He states: "much of what is called local is in large degree constructed on a trans- or super-local basis. In other words, much of the promotion of locality is in fact done from above or outside" (Robertson 1995). The important point is that the global and the local are not separate or unconnected. The local is not that which is excluded or residual when we are looking at globalization, neither is it the "victim," disempowered or destroyed by global processes. One outcome of the globalization process has been an increased emphasis on the local: the local has become globalized. The ways in which European localities have been energized by extra-EU sources, which was one of the points made by Albrow, can only be understood from a perspective which holds that the global acts upon the local, produces the local, and offers mobility for the local through transnational networks. The local is not incidental to globalization nor is it by-passed by global flows: the local is integral to these processes. If we want to turn these abstractions into more concrete examples we might point to the ways that the rights to difference, identity, self-determination and human rights for example, or national self-determination (which has taken a fresh turn in the post-communist period) have been globally institutionalized in the twentieth century. All of these things have in their own way led to an increase in the incidence of the local. But the local is a relative term and in the more contemporary period it has become more associated with both sub-national regions and ethnic nationalism and trans-national communities of interest. In all cases we are witnessing the assertion of local identity within a globally determined frame.

McDonald's is frequently evoked as an example of a multinational corporation whose sales and marketing strategies obliterate local difference in the pursuit of product homogenization. The argument runs that all over the world people eat the same fast food and drink the same soft drinks, and that this is an example of how global cultural homogenization eradicates local differences. In fact, McDonald's frequently uses local ingredients and develops products which are unique to local markets: in Brazil passion fruit juice, and guava sauce for ice cream. In India, McDonald's took the decision not to serve beef and pork (respecting religious sensitivities), resulting in the chicken and lamb "Maharaja Mac." Similarly, in countries such as Greece and Turkey meals appropriate to religious holidays have been introduced.[14] Robertson (2001) points out that "relatively few global or near-globally marketed goods or services are in fact sold in a standardized form," and draws attention to the way that successful global marketing requires sensitivity to local circumstances, identities and practices.[15] The packaging and product will and does vary in ways which demonstrate that globalization is a complex mixture of homogenization and heterogenization: the local is visible in global processes, and vice versa. Robertson (2001) also cites the case of jeans, worn worldwide by young people. Their ubiquity does not equate to homogenization as the type of jeans worn and how they are combined with other clothing varies enormously. Dutch students wear torn jeans while Spanish students prefer designer labels and wear them with fashionable jackets, for example.

Global Transformations

In this chapter we have examined two very different types of sociological approach to the question of globalization. Castells' work on the network society was shown to be driven by an economistic reading of globalization. The work of Robertson and Albrow favours a multi-dimensional approach to the issue and is built upon an interpretation of globalization as a series of processes working over a long duration. This forms the platform for an important and innovative reading of the relationship between globalization and modernity. The other key element of the work of Robertson and Albrow is the way in which they conceptualize the relationship between the global and the local. Their work is very different in many respects but shares these two key features, the full significance of which will be drawn out in the concluding section to this chapter. First we must turn to the chief rival of the "inclusive globalization paradigm": the work of Held and his collaborators centering on the book *Global Transformations: Politics, Economics and Culture* (Held et al.: 1999).

Held et al. (1999: 16) define globalization as:

a process (or set of processes) which embodies a transformation in the spatial organization of social relations and transactions – assessed in terms of their extensity, intensity, velocity and impact – generating transcontinental or interregional flows and networks of activity, interaction, and the exercise of power.

Various elements of this definition require further elaboration and comment. The authors are of the opinion that it is important to specify "precisely what is 'global' about globalization" (Held et al. 1999: 15), and in their view this centers on the idea that globalization equates to the linking of human activity over huge distances. What is distinctive about globalization is the way social interaction can proceed across continents without hindrance. The degree of interconnection and networking is measured according to four factors: extensity, intensity, velocity, and impact. By extensity the authors are referring to the way social, political, and economic activities are stretched across national frontiers. The importance of this is that occurrences or policies in one part of the world can make a difference to the lives of people in another. Activity and decision making no longer have to be proximate: action at a distance becomes possible.

Transnational connections are not just random, but regular and systematic. The authors see an intensification of interconnectedness, "patterns of interaction and flows which transcend the constitutive societies and states of the world order" (Held et al. 1999: 15). Not only do distant events shape our lives but they do so routinely. Global connections are the norm rather than the exception. What is more, global interaction is rapid. Communication technology is capable of transmitting information around the globe in such a way as to facilitate the interaction of people in far-flung places. These processes combine in such a way as to make "the global diffusion of ideas, goods, information, capital and people" a reality. Another consequence is that the boundary between domestic and global affairs is no longer clear-cut. The global and the local are implicated in a new relationship, one in which distant events can have local repercussions, and localized events can have global consequences.

The approach developed by Held et al. avoids any simple reductionism and prefers to see globalization as a phenomenon which has been a long time in the making and the product of a variety of forces: economic, political, cultural. There are two main areas in which their model differs from the "inclusive globalization paradigm": modernity and its relation to globalization, and global/local relations. We will explore these and assess their importance for the way in which the impact of globalization on the EU is conceived. As the authors make plain, much of their book concerns itself with the question of the impact of globalization on the sovereignty and autonomy of nation-states (Held et al. 1999: 427). This places their work very squarely within an academic frame of reference demarcated by the concerns of modernity. To approach globalization from the standpoint of the extent to which state power has been transformed by globalization is to fall into the trap signposted by Albrow: modernity works to fix the transformations wrought by globalization within its own logic. Albrow also flags up another important related issue, namely Held et al.'s conclusion that what is global about globalization is the degree of transnational connectivity. He comments that "we need to distance ourselves from a time-frame which views the nation-state as the normal, abiding state of society and the transnational as something new and derived from globalization" (Albrow 1998b).

The consequences of Held et al.'s theoretical framework can be seen in their approach to the ways in which globalization is acting upon the EU. In keeping with their non-reductionist approach they see no simple correlation between the rise of globalization and a reduction in the importance of the nation-state or even the erosion of state power. They assert the continued importance of the nation-state in a globalized system of international relations and also find evidence of "a transformation or reconstitution of the powers of the modern nation-state" (Held et al. 1999: 436). What this means is that the nation-state has been subject to pressures from new, mainly supranational levels of authority. They subscribe to the view that contemporary globalization has been responsible for creating "multiple power centres and overlapping spheres of authority" (Held et al. 1999: 441). What this has led to in Europe is a form of supra-national regionalism alongside a "number of subregions and regimes which stack up on top of each other to produce a patchwork effect" (Held et al. 1999: 76). Theirs is a variation on the theme that globalization has created the need for greater European integration. The emergence of global production networks and trading systems have "made global competitiveness a new standard of national and corporate economic efficiency, and encouraged the reorganization of the state and private sectors to maximize national competitive advantage in the context of global economic order" (Held et al. 1999: 440). The need for greater competitiveness in the global marketplace has forced the EU member states to bind more closely together in order to regain at the European level some of the autonomy lost at the nation-state level. EMU is one example of this: "national autonomy in monetary policy has been so compromised that the only means of recovering it is at a European – regional – level" (Held et al. 1999: 443).

The global and its relation to the local is another area where Held et al.'s work diverges from the "inclusive globalization paradigm."

Rather than seeing the local and the global existing in a relation of mutual implication they see the local and the global at opposite ends of a linear scale. "Globalization can be located on a continuum with the local, national and regional. At the one end of the continuum lie social and economic relations and networks which are organized on a local and/or national basis; at the other end lie social and economic relations and networks which crystallize on the wider scale of regional and global interactions" (Held et al. 1999: 15). On this view processes of globalization and localization do not exist as a "globe-wide cultural nexus" as they do for Robertson, but form distinct spheres of activity which operate at different levels. Local networks operate at the local level but are distinct from global or supranational networks which do not have to work within the same spatial restrictions. As we shall see throughout the rest of the book this view of the relation between the global and the local pervades the literature on globalization and the EU.

Global Capital, Local Workers

The relative merits of these positions on globalization can be demonstrated by an examination of the pervasive idea that "capital is global, labor local," which not only summarizes a popular fear of globalization but at the same time represents a brand of neo-liberal rhetoric, and serves as an example of how the dynamics of globalization can be fundamentally misunderstood. In all three cases it must be challenged. There is no doubt that in many circles the word globalization signifies rampant and unfettered capitalism and a threat to local and national jobs. This perception of globalization as a threat to jobs is neatly captured in the following terms. "For an increasing number of workers, even in managerial jobs, it means the possibility that somebody who lives half the world away will dump you on the dole" (Micklethwait and Woodbridge 2000: 10). The perception of globalization as a threat also mobilizes national-popular sentiment, as in the idea that economic management is increasingly beyond state control, out of national hands and that transnational companies are intent on exporting jobs to those parts of the world where labor costs lowest and government legislation weakest.

While many people fear that a global economy represents a threat to European jobs, neo-liberals are able to mobilize the same sort of concerns in an appeal for more freedom and less regulation. Here the fears associated with the idea of the power of global markets are orchestrated in an appeal for greater freedom and flexibility in order to throw off the "shackles" of trade union legislation and national regulation so as to become competitive in the global market place. In this version, globalization can lead to a positive outcome only if the state gives the entrepreneur a free and unfettered hand. Employment protection and trade union bargaining rights represent barriers to investment and need to be reduced or eliminated if investment is to be attracted and jobs secured.[16]

The idea that unemployment is a problem that cannot be solved by the national state is widely accepted by academics and policy makers alike. For example, Held et al. (1999: 53) commentating on the G7 "summit for jobs" held in London in 1997 note that the meeting planned to review how international coordination of national economic strategies might assist job growth across the G7 nations. They conclude that this "represents an attempt to manage or 'govern' those aspects of political life which escape the control of any single state." The idea that the nation-state is vulnerable in this way in the face of global forces is what Weiss (1997: 15–16) terms "the political construction of helplessness." Politicians in thrall to the neo-liberal dream have "played a large part in contributing to this view of government helplessness in the face of global trends." Such ideas not only place the blame for high unemployment on external forces (globalization), but deflect attention away from a concerted attempt to reduce labor costs throughout Europe. Mass unemployment (and the threat of it continuing) has become the means through which labor costs (and non-wage labor costs) can be reduced. A rise in temporary contracts, subcontracting and relocation have been the result (Crompton and Brown 1994: 4). Despite a number of highly publicized rhetorical flourishes to the contrary, tackling the problem of unemployment is not the number one priority amongst Europe's business and administrative elites.[17] The target of reducing wage costs has been the driving force behind "greater flexibility" and has met with a fair degree of success. The *First Cohesion Report* (European Commission 1996a: 45) states that there has been a "fall in the share of total income (GDP) accruing to labor in the form of wages and salaries (pre-tax) in virtually all Member States, while the share accruing to capital has increased." Expressed in different terms, we can say that member states have redefined the idea of wealth redistribution: away from labor and towards capital.

There is another, more sociological, interpretation of the nostrum that "capital is global, labor local." This is the idea that the state is no longer able or willing to constrain capital, or that capital and labor inhabit different worlds and are no longer in conflict (Castells 2000a and b). Whereas in the past the state could play a useful role as mediator in disputes between capital and labor, in the current context globalization has shorn it of this capacity. It no longer has the necessary economic autonomy to dictate terms to capitalists whose interests do not coincide with those of the nation-state. As Turner (1992: 40) explains, "while capital operates on a global scale, labor tends to operate within a local national market." There are many reasons to disagree with such a view, most immediately because it sacrifices sociological rigor in its attempt to capture the importance of innovative social and economic processes. It can also be criticized for over-dramatizing the power of global capital in its pursuit of profit and for underplaying the ability of agencies within the nation-state to exert an influence over processes originating beyond its borders. In effect, it reproduces the logic of non-sociological arguments routinely used to account for the need for ever closer European integration: globalization as an external threat to which the EU acting in unison, rather than as individual member states, can mobilize and shape: the neo-liberal call-to-arms of post-Maastricht integration.

The idea that capital is global while labor is local rests on the global/local dichotomy which was criticized in chapter 1 for having such an impoverishing view of the dynamics of globalization. There are many ways in which we should consider labor to be global, but this should not be taken to imply that workers normally enjoy global mobility. There are instances when labor can be global though, for example where trans-national corporations have an "internal market" for senior jobs and executives can be relocated in any branch world-wide. Another obvious way in which labor is global is in terms of the way in which labor costs can influence the location of investment.[18] This is normally interpreted as an example of how capital is global and labor local. But when labor costs are a factor in a global investment strategy and multinational firms are able to "export" jobs to more profitable locations, labor should be thought of as global too. Competitive pressures often lead workers to compete with each other to make themselves attractive to inward investment. In such cases, the organization of labor takes a neo-liberal inflexion in order to assert itself in the global economy.

There is a different way in which labor can be thought of as having a global dimension. This is where foreign residents and guest workers have an enhanced status as a result of international agreements and conventions sponsored by bodies such as the UN. Non-nationals working in another European country – if they have the status of permanent residents – "are entitled to full civil rights and have access to a set of social services and economic rights almost identical to those available to national citizens, including public education, health benefits, various welfare schemes, and free access to labour markets" (Soysal 2000: 256).[19] In other words, they are not simply at the mercy of local or national rules and regulations. They are the beneficiaries of the growing number of universal personhood rights which are another important facet of globalization. There is yet another type of argument for labor being global which centers on the growing trans-border linkages between various labor organizations and movements representing the unemployed (Coates 1998: 133).

However, the most important dimension of "global labor" is exemplified by the recent developments in EU, and more especially German, immigration policy. Both have recognized that despite high levels of internal unemployment the recruitment of non-EU workers, particularly skilled IT workers, is necessary to address the problems of an aging workforce with the "wrong skills." In Germany the draft immigration law signals a radical break with previous attempts to preserve cultural homogeneity by downplaying the extent of immigration. "Although Germany already has 7.3m foreigners – the highest proportion of foreigners in any European Union state – its politicians have long refused to recognise the country as having a multi-cultural society" (*The Financial Times*, July 4, 2001). The draft law permits regular immigration – up to 50,000 skilled foreign workers to enter the country every year – and is premised on the recognition that Germany has severe skills shortages and that up to 1.5 million further skilled immigrants may be needed to stay competitive (*BBC News*, August 1, 2000).

Conclusion

At the beginning of the chapter it was claimed that for a political sociology of European integration to be adequate it was essential that it was able to come to terms with globalization. This chapter has sought to demonstrate the truth of that statement. Moreover, I believe that an understanding of the EU grounded in political sociology must place globalization at its very center. In this concluding section I will outline ways in which globalization, and more specifically the "inclusive globalization paradigm," is an essential component of a study of the contemporary European Union.

One common feature of accounts on the impact of globalization on the EU is the assumption that it works to unify the EU, and that the EU's response is coherent and coordinated. This stems from an interpretation of globalization which emphasizes its role in dissolving old institutional structures and the boundaries of nation-states: in short the increasing transnationalization of economic, cultural, and political activity. But there are good reasons to challenge the assumption that transnationalization is automatically the dominant or most important result. The integrative logic generated by many accounts of globalization fails to allow space for a consideration of other outcomes of the relationship between transnational flows and the EU. Globalization animates economic, social and political actors from a distance, and leads to greater internal differentiation and fragmentation. Globalization destabilizes the hierarchies upon which the (national) economy is ordered, it asserts the importance of the local *vis-à-vis* the national and the transnational, it fosters a new set of relationships between regions and nation-states, between sectors and the state, between centers and peripheries.

Incorporating a globalization perspective in our study of the EU enables us to demonstrate the complex and contradictory nature of the contemporary EU. It enables us to go beyond the traditional or common sense appreciation of what the EU is, how it works, and what are the most important processes shaping it at the current time. Some examples will illustrate these claims. The question of what form of state the EU represents looms large in EU studies, dominated as it is by the disciplines of political science and international relations. This field of study has been delineated by the claims and counter claims of the intergovernmentalists and the supranationalists. Either the EU is becoming more like a supranational body or its key decisions are still taken by sovereign nation-states. More recently, the multi-level governance approach has taken center stage and usurped the debate. Globalization is by no means central to any of these ways of thinking but certainly impinges on them. I would argue that the aridity of the whole debate is in no small part due to the poverty of globalization theory which it contains (or implies). To the extent that globalization is incorporated in intergovernmentalist and supranationalist thought it is only in the sense that the EU is the product of the transnationalization of economic relations and the need for member states to work together to remain competitive in the global economy. It is strangely absent from the multi-level governance model, in other respects the most sophisticated version on offer. For advocates of the multi-level governance approach transnationalism stops at the EU's borders. The EU bestows a supranational citizenship on the nationals of EU member states but the idea that there are forms of postnational citizenship which originate beyond the EU and have a more significant impact on the lives of Europeans is not given consideration (Marks et al. 1996). All of these non-sociological perspectives hold fast to the idea that the EU must represent *some* kind of state or combination of state forms, rather than the globalization-inspired idea that the EU is governed by a multi-centered set of state and non-state agencies.

If our understanding of the state is transformed by a sociologically inspired understanding of globalization the same is true for society. There exists a great deal of uncertainty about what society means in the contemporary world, and a great diversity of approaches to understanding it, ranging from attempts to theorize it away – "there is no such thing as society" – through to versions that reduce it to civil society, and attempts to recast it as cosmopolitan society. Under conditions of globalization we must move beyond the idea that society must be integrated and cohesive, and that it is a discrete realm protected by the state. European society increasingly displays evidence of a multiplicity of fragmented and autonomous local and transnational public spheres formed by new modes of contestation, claims-making, and collective action. These public spheres have the potential to both regulate social actors (rule is not only exercised via the state) and to generate conflict and social change. Such an appreciation of the changes which society is going through are only available via an approach to globalization which emphasizes its ability to fracture perceived or existing totalities, and to animate and empower actors in a way which compromises traditional political and economic hierarchies.

So far we have concentrated on the ways in which globalization can help us establish a conceptual framework for studying the EU. We should not downplay the extent to which globalization can also enrich our understanding of a whole range of processes shaping the EU. Throughout the book we will examine areas of EU activity and current policy issues which can be best understood through the framework outlined here. The relationship between social exclusion and citizenship is one area where a globalization perspective can make a significant contribution. It is not uncommon to encounter the view that citizenship is still very much the business of nation-states, EU citizenship rights notwithstanding. In fact, the question of citizenship is intimately linked to globalization as citizens' rights and freedoms are increasingly codified by international organizations such as the UN. Social exclusion is less and less about (non-) involvement in production and more about opportunities for participation in public spheres, not all of which are nationally constituted. Non-citizens enjoy formal rights granted by international agencies, and the nation-state's role is more to ratify and implement universal rights rather than instigate a regime of rights for its citizens, or to deny these to non-nationals.

The important role of Europe's regions takes on a new dimension when considered in the global frame. Rather than representing the local in a global/local continuum or being the beneficiaries of a postmodern form of European integration which advantages them over their member states, the region is better thought of as the EU's accommodation to globalization. The region has become the site upon which the global acts most visibly upon the EU, and the level at which the EU has decided that the forces of globalization can best be accommodated. The idea of European integration – that the EU is bound ever closer and acts in concert – masks a panoply of contradictory and disintegrative forces. This is manifestly true in the case of the EU's periphery, traditionally imagined as relying upon a European core for its development. This model breaks down when we begin to see the core and periphery not in terms of territorial relations between discrete and bounded regions but in terms of relativized networks and flows. As the EU is frequently neither the originator nor the main conduit for these flows the relationships between globalization and Europe's regions and peripheries takes on a new complexion.

All of the areas to be explored in the book benefit from and take a new direction as a result of the incorporation of the "inclusive globalization paradigm." In this sense, globalization is much more than an aspect of the contemporary EU to which this book turns its attention. The claim made for this approach is that it reveals aspects of the dynamics of European integration which are simply not accessible via other approaches. In stating this I am also making the claim that a political sociology of the EU constructed along these lines produces a more insightful view of the EU than that currently on offer from the disciplines of politics or international relations. If demonstrating the contribution of political sociology to European Union studies is one objective of this book, demonstrating the superior claims of a political sociology inspired by the "inclusive globalization paradigm" is very much another.

3 The Question of the European State

Sociological Questions

One of the most urgent questions posed by a study of European integration is "what sort of state does the EU represent?" The way that this question is normally approached presumes that the EU must represent *some* kind of state, a supranational state for example. Alternatively, those who favor an intergovernmentalist explanation for European integration argue that EU decision-making is still predominantly conducted on the basis of agreements reached between sovereign member states. If we follow the logic of the debate between these two positions we are asked to arbitrate on the extent to which integrative measure have constituted the EU as a supranational entity. A third approach sees the EU as a tiered polity characterized by multi-level governance. On this model the nation-state delegates decision-making powers both upward, to the supranational EU, and downward, to the sub-national regions.[1]

But does the EU have to be seen as a state at all? This chapter puts forward the case for concentrating on the forms of government characteristic of contemporary Europe rather than relying on the notion that some degree of state building must be at work. In other words, the important questions are no longer "what sort of state does the EU represent?" and "at which levels does it operate?" but "what forms of government and rule are at work within the EU?" and "through what agencies does EU government operate?" It is suggested that changing the line of inquiry in this way is a very productive and distinctive contribution that political sociology can make to this field of study. The following quotation from Albrow (1998a) illustrates the point very well.

> In the case of Europe we are dealing with a multi-centred set of agencies, working towards what many call "integration," but what is

more reasonably understood as the development of common standards, which rather than separating Europe from the rest of the world, effectively reduce that separation.

Albrow brings together three essential components of a political sociology of the EU in this formulation: a dismissal of the idea that the EU must be a kind of state; a critique of the accepted notion of integration; and an assertion of the centrality of globalization to an understanding of European integration. Let us examine these essential components in more detail. First, Albrow establishes that governing Europe should be thought of in terms of "multi-centered agencies." This is important because it avoids the pitfalls inherent in conventional approaches to understanding the EU as a state: that the European Union is either a form of supranational state, an inter-state bargain, or a multi-level polity incorporating sub-national, national, and supranational levels. As we have already seen this approach focuses on the extent to which nation-state sovereignty has been ceded to the EU. According to Franceschet (1998: 126) the continuing debate between the sovereign nation-state and deeper European integration reflects "the dichotomy made famous in the 1960s by Stanley Hoffman: is the fate of the West European state 'obstinate or obsolete'?" This dichotomous model has only recently been challenged and the multi-level governance approach is the most noteworthy new perspective. However, neither multi-level governance nor its predecessors have managed to break away from the idea that the central issue in EU studies is the level at which state rule is exercised. Albrow's preference for multi-agency over multi-level is a crucial one, as it introduces the possibility that government can be carried out by many different actors and agencies, of which the state, as traditionally understood, is but one.

Secondly, Albrow places the notion of integration under critical scrutiny. The vast bulk of the literature on the EU assumes that integration is proceeding apace, and that the history of post-war Europe is an unfolding path to European union. The word integration carries with it a heavy burden of assumptions, not just to do with the degree to which member states are interdependent or subsumed under a supranational authority, but also about the role of the state, the existence of a political system, and the centralization of decision-making powers. The debate that frames the dominant approach to thinking about the EU as a state – between the supranationalists and the intergovernmentalists – is also responsible for circumscribing the way we have come to understand integration. The key issue has always been the extent and pace of integration, and integration has always been synonymous with supranationalism. On the occasions when the idea of integration is questioned it is invariably with the intention of asserting the opposing, intergovernmentalist, position that integration is overstated or has been curtailed. Milward (1997: 5) provides a very good example of this latter tendency. "What has come to be called the 'integration of Europe' is a notion whose origins were unpropitious, the offspring of American disillusionment with the dangerous political disunity of the European continent and naive progressivist optimism." Albrow chooses not to become embroiled in the integration debate and prefers to see the EU as a space within which "standardization" is occurring, an idea which carries baggage of a very different sort.[2] The EU is cast in more of a regulatory role: the idea that the EU applies standards and works to harmonize practices is a very different thing from viewing it as a supranational state.

The third aspect of the Albrow quote worthy of note is that he makes globalization central to our understanding of the EU. We have already discussed Albrow's important contribution to the sociological understanding of globalization and we need not rehearse those arguments here. It is worth noting however that he distances himself from an understanding of the EU and globalization which sees European integration as evidence that the world is dividing into competitive blocs (EU, ASEAN, NAFTA)[3] – what is sometimes termed regionalism (not to be confused with regionalism in the sense of sub-national regions). Albrow's understanding of globalization highlights the increasing global commonality which is one outcome of progressive harmonization measures. What Albrow's formulation also does is to signal the unboundedness of the European Union. Rather than seeing it as "fortress Europe" busy erecting barriers to the free movements of people and goods from outside its territory, Albrow points to the ways in which the EU and other trading-blocs are increasingly traversed by and inserted into a multiplicity of transnational and global networks. These regulate and harmonize the activities of the EU with other actors around the world through agreements, charters and conventions covering a broad range of activities including trade, aid, cooperation, the movements of peoples, human rights, military operations, weapons testing, and space exploration. In no meaningful sense is the EU is separate from the rest of the world.

I have chosen to begin this discussion of European government and institutions by drawing attention to Albrow's work because in addition to the qualities outlined above it is also very much a *sociological* approach to understanding the EU. One of the central themes of this chapter is the extent to which our thinking about EU integration, the form of state that the EU represents, and the relationship between the nation-state and the EU, continues to be dominated by an academic agenda established by the ongoing debate between political science and international relations. Not only is sociology not obliged to follow this agenda, but it also affords the prospect of a more productive way of conceptualizing and explaining the institutions and government characteristic of the EU. Of course not all sociological approaches manage to do this, and a sociological perspective is not in and of itself preferable to an approach drawn from politics or international relations. The argument here is that Albrow's formulation is preferable to the more familiar models derived from political science and international relations. It not only side-steps the orthodox debate completely by starting from a different set of precepts, but offers a valuable way of investigating the EU which does not reduce it to either integration or governance.

The EU as a Form of State

Approaches to the study of the EU as a form of state normally take one of the following general forms. The first concerns the kind of state-like entity that the EU is thought to represent, the second concerns the changes to the role and sovereignty of the nation-state that integration has occasioned. The EU is often thought to represent a new kind of state – a supranational state, a quasi-federal state, a national-state writ large, a network state – or an internationalization of the state. In diminishing the sovereignty of member states and their power to act independently in the world the EU has usurped the authority of the nation-state, doubly so in accounts where the EU is seen as responsible for privileging a "Europe of regions" over a Europe of nations.[4] On this model the nation-state is challenged both from above (the supranational EU) and below (regionalism).

This points to a more important set of questions concerning the changing relationship between the nation-state and the supranational structures of the EU. Member states are clearly key players in the drive for greater integration, and the shifting fortunes of the nation-state over the post-war period suggests a complex, multi-dimensional relationship. The nation-state, despite many predictions to the contrary has not been emasculated by the process of European integration. At the same time as sovereignty has been ceded in certain areas, new spheres of influence have opened up. We can say that the nation-state has been simultaneously strengthened and weakened by European integration. Much thinking on the relationship between the EU and its member states has gravitated towards the idea that the contemporary EU is characterized by multi-level governance. Rather than replacing the nation-state the EU has developed a system of governance which relies on action taken at a whole series of levels (local, regional, national, supranational) by a variety of state and non-state actors who exist in an integrated hierarchy of decision making. This approach has the merit of breaking with the idea that rule can only be exercised at either the member state or the EU level. On the other hand, it tends to reinforce a very territorialist view of integration and, more fundamentally, fails to address adequately the ways in which the EU governs without the need for a pan-European state. One idea which will be developed throughout this chapter is that in order to understand the way in which the EU works we must look not at the form of the state in the EU or the member states, but at the multiplicity of forms of rule which exist throughout the EU and which work, not at different levels of the EU's integrated state structure, but through multiple agencies, including that of the self.

The very idea of European integration is a product of the political science/international relations, neo-functionalist/intergovernmentalist dominated debate. These approaches have all shared the assumption that integration was what they were studying (Rosamond 2000). The chapter does not attempt to offer a thorough historical survey of institution building from the Marshall Plan, the OECD, and the European Coal and Steel Community in the late 1940s and early '50s and culminating with the current European Union. Rather, it develops the idea that the history of institution building, seen through the frame of the reconstruction of post-war Europe, is also a history of the construction of a particular idea: European integration. Europe became the crucible where a whole array of emerging international organizations concentrated their efforts. The cornerstone of the early post-war attempts to construct European institutions was the nation-state itself, and the post-war reconstruction of Europe initially took the form of the rebuilding of the European nation-state within the wider context of the rapid development of pan-European agencies. The work of Milward (1992) demonstrates the link between the rescue of the European nation-state and the origins of the idea of European unification, and allows us to look at the history of integration in a way which does not reduce it to foreign policy choices, cold war necessities, or economic growth strategies.

It is not common to encounter academic arguments for the EU as a nation-state writ large or a super-state.[5] However, there are approaches which emphasize that the EU's supranational authorities have created a tier of supranational governance alongside more established layers of political authority. The EU may not be a super-state but it is thought of as a "quasi-federal polity" (Stone Sweet and Sandholtz 1998: 1). More often than not the element of federalism is queried but the idea of the EU as a "transnational form of governance" remains (for example, Rhodes, Heywood, and Wright 1997). Even approaches which do not hold to the idea that the EU has become a form of state (for example, Hix 1999), suggest that the EU is a political system which bestows certain state-like attributes on the EU. Where the EU is not assumed to exhibit the core requirements for statehood it is the extent to which it differs from a nation-state which is the focus of attention. In other words, the nation-state is the point of departure for much of the current literature on supranational governance and the political system of the EU.

This is also very true of the work which falls under the heading of multi-level governance. The argument runs that the most appropriate way of understanding the complexity of decision-making within the EU and between the EU and member states is via new levels of political authority which have emerged in addition to and alongside those already in existence. Many approaches to the question of the nature of the EU state or supranational governance, particularly those which emphasize multi-level governance, are closely related to the orthodox interpretations of the relationship between the EU and globalization discussed in chapter 1. These approaches follow the dichotomous logic of the global versus local and assume that the contemporary nation-state is being hollowed out and some of its functions being assumed by a supranational state apparatus and others devolved downwards to sub-national regions. The nation-state is thus both "too big and too small." Too big because it is out of touch with the needs and aspirations of many social groups within its borders, and too small to be effective in a world of global flows.

Alternatively, "too big for small nations trapped inside larger states, like the Scots or the Catalans; it is too small for those who would like to see stronger government at the European level" (Miall 1993: 53).[6]

The adequacy or otherwise of the notion of the state – or more particularly the ways in which political studies have attempted to think about the state in relation to the EU – leads us to the consideration of alternative ways of examining the question of government and rule in modern societies. It is suggested that rather than focusing on the state it is more appropriate to examine the broader field comprising the forms of rule which are at work in the EU. In doing so it is possible to accommodate the ideas that government comprises a decentered assortment of authorities – agencies rather than levels – and also that the state is but one location of political power. A whole range of actors – from citizens and enterprises to regions and social movements – are encouraged to be self-regulating. Contemporary forms of rule, particularly when refracted through the lens of neoliberal economics, empower and autonomize actors as economic individuals to the point where they become project managers and entrepreneurs of the self. This points us in the direction of the work of the governmentality theorists and the need to look at technologies of rule rather than concentrating on multi-level governance.

Government or Governance?

The term governance has been used several times already in this chapter but we have not, as yet, looked at exactly what it means and how it is different from the idea of government. There are important distinctions between government and governance, both in terms of what they signify and the way they have become embedded in academic discourses on European integration. It has become very fashionable to talk about governance, not just in relation to the European Union, but more generally as a way of capturing the multilevel or multi-dimensional aspects of governing in a world characterized by globalization, transnational movements, and a changing role for the nation-state. In very general terms we can say that the term government is associated with what (nation-) states do, while governance is carried out by a broad range of state and non-state agencies. The idea of government is associated with national administration and internal organization, while governance points to a different range of activities both within and beyond the national level – of firms and NGOs as well as independent agencies and multi- and inter-national organizations. Rosamond (2000: 108) explains the distinction in the following way. "Governance is usually defined as being about the exercise of authority with or without the formal institutions of government. In recent years, however, the term has come to be used to note the drift of authority away from government." This is because as Rose (1999: 168) explains political scientists have;

> turned away from themes of state power, state autonomy, state capacities; instead they emphasize governance: good governance must recognize the political importance of the ... complex interactions, negotiations and exchanges between ... social actors, groups, forces, organizations, public and semi-public institutions.

There are several reasons why studies of the EU have embraced the idea of governance. One is the growing tendency to study the European Union as a polity or a political system (Hix 1999), rather than as an outcome of international relations and intergovernmental bargaining. Expressed in slightly different terms, there has been a shift from the study of European integration to governance (Rosamond 2000: 109). Another reason stems from the way in which the relationship between the EU and globalization has been understood. The dominant interpretation holds that member-states have voluntarily handed over sovereignty in order to gain a greater degree of security and decision-making ability in a challenging global economic environment. State power has fragmented and been reassigned to new areas and levels: supranational, sub-national. On this model, the nation-state has been "hollowed out" and multi-level governance is the form of organization best suited to the emerging Euro-polity.

This theme is taken up by Hirst and Thompson (1996: 183–4) who see politics becoming "polycentric." States are "merely one level in a complex system of overlapping and often competing agencies of governance," in which the nation-state has an ongoing role. The difference between governance and government, for Hirst and Thompson, is that government is identified with rule over a territorial community: the sovereign nation-state claims a "monopoly of the function of governance." Governance, on the other hand, is not just the business of the state. "Rather it is a function that can be performed by a wide variety of public and private, state and non-state, national and international institutions and practices."

From the way it has been outlined so far it would be possible to draw the conclusion that governance is a useful term which has a wide applicability to a study of the European Union and the way that it governs, particularly as it takes us away from the idea that the EU is in any sense a super-state. The governance model permits a view of the EU in which power centers are multiple and forms of rule various, rather than a concentration of supranational powers. Governance lays emphasis upon the ways in which a political system is patterned according to the complex interplay of a multiplicity of individuals, groups, organizations and agencies – including the state. No single actor, even the state, can control all of the outcomes and dominate the system. The control, steering, and coordination mechanisms of any society involves "much more than the state" (Scholte 2001). Moreover, there are many institutions and agencies which exercise authority but who do not have access to state power.

There are, however, some problems with the idea of governance from the point of view of it being a suitable tool with which to develop a political sociology of European integration. We can identify two main problem areas. First, there are strong associations between the idea of governance and neo-liberal economic and political values. The World Bank talks of "good governance" by which it means a society in which there exists a plurality of power-sharers and political actors. To this end it encourages an end to state-centric government, the privatization of publicly owned utilities, and the transfer of authority to non-state organizations (Rose 1999: 16). Governance is closely associated with the idea of "downsizing government," deregulation and replacing monopolies with markets. As generally employed in relation to understanding developments in the contemporary EU, governance denotes the organization of rule most attuned to the needs of a European space structured by the twin dynamics of neo-liberalism and (economic) globalization.

The second problem area is that governance, while signalling a diffusion of state power, still depends upon the conceptual language of national society. It embodies formal distinctions between state and non-state, public and private, state and civil society, and, as such, its potential is limited when it comes to explaining the complex forms of rule which exist in the EU. Similarly, it makes assumptions about the boundedness of the societies about which it speaks, seeing them in terms of aggregates of groups, regions, and networks with systemic properties. The idea of governance also draws legitimacy, and, in part, is responsible for generating the idea of a global civil society.

The two share some common assumptions: that global governance exists independent of state regulation, and, in working transnationally INGOs, multi-national firms and other non-state actors are the harbingers of cosmopolitan democracy.

At the same time it has to be acknowledged that there are problems associated with opting for the continued use of the term government rather than governance. Government suggests formal rule via the apparatuses of state and the business of managing the affairs of the country. This situation is made more complex by the fact that the business of national government is increasingly conducted by enlisting groups, societies and networks "in a transformation of government into governance" (Albrow 2001). Governance, it would seem, is not distinct from the traditional activities of government but increasingly signifies the way in which governments choose to govern. This is certainly true in the case of the EU (see chapter 4). Nevertheless, there is one decisive reason why government is the preferred term in this account. The work of the governmentality theorists which informs the analysis developed in this chapter utilizes the idea of government in a way which does not reduce it to national or state management. Government can work within or outside formal mechanisms of authority and through diverse actors. For this reason, plus the neo-liberal connotations of the term governance, and a desire to distinguish the present account from the dominant usage of the term in current discourse on European integration – multi-level governance – government is judged to be the term best suited for a sociological study of political rule beyond the state.

Having said this, it is not possible to deny the sheer weight that the idea of governance possesses in EU studies (and the EU's own discourse) at the present time. Thus, we need to engage directly with the multi-level governance approach to understanding political authority in the EU. The multi-level governance approach is interesting not least because it combines two elements that we have previously been critical of, namely governance as a way of conceptualizing non-state forms of rule and the idea of state and non-state actors working at different levels within the Euro polity. In fact, multi-level governance is the best example of the turn towards governance identified by Rosamond, and represents a determined effort to break out of the intergovernmental/supranationalism dichotomy. Multi-level governance posits that multiple levels of authority – European, national, and subnational – are interdependent and that while subnational involvement has increased and regions empowered, the state retains an important role. Authority has been "recalibrated in a way which has changed the relative roles played in the EU policy process by sub-national actors on the one hand and the 'nation-state' on the other" (Jeffery 1997). Moreover, within the EU the different levels – subnational, national, and supranational – are locked together in a way which opens up the European arena for domestic actors (Hooghe 1996a: 18).

Multi-level governance is more than a theory about how the Euro polity is split on three different levels. It offers an explanation for policy making outside the traditional system of national government or intergovernmental bargaining. It also draws attention to the way the European Commission can act as a "policy entrepreneur," bypassing national governments in its aim to strengthen its own position and to institute non-state-centric policy-making structures. The promotion of private interests and sub-national actors is interpreted as Commission-led (Hix 1999: 274). The result is that authority is diffused between different actors and agencies and "there are significant variations in governance patterns" (Rosamond 2000: 110). In other words, some sectors, regions and countries are characterized by multi-level governance to a greater extent than others. While the fact that authority is dispersed is central to multi-level governance thinking it is also emphasized that the boundaries between the various levels of governance will become less clear cut (Rosamond 2000: 111).

This is certainly true in the EU's own understanding of governance in which supranational, national and regional agencies are not thought of as the only, or most important governmental partners. The European Commission, in particular, under the leadership of President Romano Prodi has gone to great lengths to ensure that promoting new forms of European governance is a major policy commitment (Prodi 2000a). At the core of the Commission's understanding of governance is the need to integrate a broad range of sub- and supranational authorities, including NGOs. It is in this sense that we should understand Prodi's (2000b) statement that "Europe is not just run by European institutions but by national, regional and local authorities too and by civil society associations such as NGOs."

Institution Building

The growth and development of what is now the European Union is commonly, but in many respects inaccurately, understood to have involved the progressive usurpation of the powers of the nation-state. The European Union, the culmination of fifty years of institution building, has, in incremental stages, acquired supranational powers in direct proportion to the loss of sovereignty experienced by member states. This transfer of sovereignty is not the result of coercion. Rather, member states have voluntarily surrendered sovereignty in return for increased security from the threat of communist infiltration and/or expansion, and the threat of globalization (Delanty 1998).

This account has been legitimated by the central cleavage in the study of the European Union: that between the neo-functionalists and the intergovernmentalists. The European Union should be understood as either a nascent super-state, or at least an entity with significant supranational qualities, or as the outcome of intergovernmental bargaining between sovereign nation-states. The key decision-making ability is either retained by the member states or has been passed over to the European Council and other Euro-bodies. Irrespective of which approach has the greater explanatory power (and we might want to distance ourselves from both), the most important consequence of this on-going debate has been that the agenda for studying the EU has been kept on a tight rein. The twin focus of European Union studies has been the changing role of the nation-state over the past 50 years, coupled with a consideration of the extent to which a supranational EU has come into existence. European integration has been constituted by this field of study as being about the building of a Euro-polity. This is a significant point, as we shall see. The issues of European integration and supranationalism are virtually inseparable. It is almost impossible for us, now, today, studying the European Union to think of integration in any way other than meaning the building of supranational authority in the economic or political sphere, or both. In short, integration equals the building of a Euro-state. Where dissent from this view exists it takes the form of a re-statement of the intergovernmentalist thesis that integration was and is the conscious choice of sovereign nation-states to further their own interests.

This chapter (in keeping the rest of the book) aims to re-think the idea of integration and to move it away from the automatic assumption that it revolves around the extent to which the EU represents a new form of supranational authority or a super-state. In order to do so it is necessary to identify the resources in the field of EU studies which may be able to assist us in this regard. Rosamond (2000: 109) draws attention to the shift of emphasis in EU scholarship from a focus on integration towards an understanding of governance. This is a positive step as it introduces the idea of a multiplicity of levels and centers in the exercise of power. More importantly perhaps, it speaks of a different object of study. Not state building or centralized supranational power but the exercise of rule and authority throughout the Euro-polity. While not endorsing the governance view, I want to work within the space opened up by this initiative and pursue the idea that many forms of government are at work in the European Union. In this respect at least the chapter owes a debt to the governmentality theorists who hold that government should be understood as the regulation and ordering of the behaviour of individuals, groups and organizations. However, we need to supplement the governmentality approach with an examination of how the dominant understanding of the relationship of the nation-state and EU institutions has circumscribed our ways of thinking about European integration.

The starting point for such an investigation has to be the fact that the European Community was born into a post-war world in which the United States was the dominant player and was instrumental in establishing many international organizations, including the UN and NATO. "The American government set about imposing rules and protocols that would encourage peaceful cooperation and impose limits on disruptive forms of competition and conflict" (Smith 1999: 241). From this perspective the emergence of the EU cannot be dissociated from the US strategy for countering the Soviet Union in the immediate post-war period and throughout the Cold War. In Anderson's words (1997: 60–1), "American policy was driven by the relentless pursuit of Cold War objectives. A strong Western Europe was needed as a bulwark against Soviet aggression, on the central front of a worldwide battle against communist subversion." The foundation of the US policy was a system of international free trade. The IMF, World Bank, and GATT provided the global institutions of the post-war capitalist economic system. As Waever (1995: 162) has pointed out European integration was American-driven and an essential component of the new western order. "The immediate success of west European growth and reconstruction, as well as the more long-term evolution of west European integration, happened inside US-sponsored global institutions of international finance and trade, such as the dollar regime and GATT." Not only has European integration been dependant upon American backing but the US vision for Europe has circumscribed its scope. Wallace (1996: 442) makes the point that, "Western European integration . . . was firmly embedded in the stabilizing framework of the Western alliance. It's eastern limits were set by the Iron Curtain, its potential enlargement limited by the reluctance of democratic but neutral European states to join such an evidently 'western' institution."

At this point we need to explore in more detail the predicament of the European nation-state at the end of the Second World War, and the origins of integration. There are two main variations on the central theme of the relationship between post-war rebuilding, the nation-state, and integration. The first claims that the nation-state was too weak to guarantee its own sovereignty in the face of the communist threat and therefore needed to find security in grouping with similarly vulnerable states. On this reading the process of European integration has been a supplement to the nation-state. The nation-state has continually been found wanting in the face of a whole series of challenges and crises, and the European Community has taken shape to cover the inability of states to fend for themselves. In other words, the EU has been the answer to the problem of the nation-state, and the resulting loss of sovereignty is the price that had to be paid for maintaining a meaningful role in world affairs. A second reading emphasizes the central importance of the nation-state in EU affairs. In the thesis developed by Milward (1992), rather than overtake the nation-state, supplementing and replacing it, the EU has rescued it. The primary contribution of the EU, at least in the early years, was to bolster and protect European nation-states which could not have authored their own recovery from war-time devastation. Before we turn to Milward's work we must first address the other, more commonly held view that the EU has stepped in to replace a faltering nation-state not capable of holding its own in the international order.

Castells (2000b) provides a good example of the first approach. He argues that the process of European integration over 50 years is the outcome of a series of defensive political projects, and that now, in the contemporary context, the rise of economic globalization and "the affirmation of identity as the source of meaning" have given integration a new twist (Castells 2000b: 339). Europe has experienced a number of crises with which the nation-state was poorly equipped to deal. The first of these problems was the threat of another war. Therefore, Germany was accommodated in the West's post-war order as a partner, and the industries central to any future war effort – coal and steel – were the subject of the first of the European communities. The second crisis inspiring a defensive reaction was the perception of a "technology gap" between Europe, the US, and Japan in the mid-1980s. The result was the Single European Act of 1987 and a giant step on the path to the single market. A third crisis point was the collapse of communism at the end of the 1980s which, following the unification of Germany, necessitated another round of integration. Europe had become unbalanced and German economy needed to be further integrated with that of her European partners. A new equilibrium was sought by means of economic and monetary union, the European Central Bank, and further enlargement.

The EU is a protective shield raised by the European nation-state to defend its weaknesses and vulnerabilities. As well as taking over those tasks which the nation-state, for whatever reason, can no longer dispatch adequately the European Union also works according to the principle of "safety in numbers." However, it would be a mistake to see threats to the European nation-state, or challenges to its competency, as coming only from the international arena. What Castells calls "the network state" – a multi-level basis for the sharing of authority in the Euro-polity – is the result of a transfer of sovereignty from the national to supranational level. Under conditions of globalization this has taken the form of a complex network of European, national and sub-national institutions mixing together federal, supranational, and intergovernmental arrangements for exercising power. On Castells' model, this does not only involve functions at the supranational level, which is the way that this idea is normally understood. Castells sees that the same phenomenon can be seen at work below the national level. He remarks that the EU is able "to link up with subnational levels of government – regional and local – by a deliberate extension of the subsidiarity principle, under which the Union institutions only take charge of decisions that lower levels of government, including nation-states, can not assume effectively" (Castells 2000b: 362). In other words, there are duties which nation-states are ill-equipped to discharge. The EU is better placed to fulfil these responsibilities. However, contrary to what is popularly supposed it is not always at the supranational level that the EU discharges these duties. Increasingly, the EU works at many levels: the sub-national as well as the supranational.

Milward's work is both a refutation of the idea that Europe-building necessarily involves a loss of national sovereignty and a forthright defence of the intergovernmentalist position. He outlines

the case for seeing the European Union as an "international framework constructed by the nation-state for the completion of its own
domestic policy objectives" (Milward et al. 1993: 20). The nation-state
and the EU are not antithetical, the EU is not about to supersede or
replace the nation-state. The relationship between them is rather
different. As the title of his most renowned work has it, the post-war
period has witnessed "the European rescue of the nation-state." He
puts the case that the development of the EU has "been an integral
part of the reassertion of the nation-state as an organizational concept" (Milward 1992: 2–3). The idea of integration has been dominated by the notion that national sovereignty has been systematically
drained by the growth of the supranational dimension. In the face of
such thinking Milward (1992: 18) asserts his central thesis. "Integration was not the supersession of the nation-state by another form of
governance as the nation-state became incapable, but was the creation
of the European nation-states themselves for their own purposes, an
act of national will." On this model, integration is a strategy for
preserving and strengthening the capacities of the nation-state, not
eroding them. The "European project" is all about re-building and
empowering the European nation-state.

Interpreting the European State

In this section we will look at several important non-sociological
approaches to understanding the type of state that the EU has
become, or is in the process of becoming. We will examine the work
of Stone Sweet and Sandholtz (1998) followed by the influential work
of Majone (1996) on the regulatory state. Finally, after considering the
work of Anderson (1996) on new medieval territoriality we will turn
our attention to Dehousse's (1997) notion of the fragmented and
redeployed state.

Stone Sweet and Sandholtz (1998: 1) view the development of the
EU as proceeding from "interstate bargain into a multidimensional,
quasi-federal polity" characterized by supranational governance.[7]
Their thesis is that supranational governance is the product of social
exchange across borders and various forms of transnational activity
(trade, investment, networks, and associations). These have generated
a demand for EU-level rules and policies and the institutionalization
of supranational policy domains. As a result, integration does not
proceed uniformly, and is necessarily more complete in certain

sectors and policy areas than others. This has one further important consequence, namely that it is necessary to disaggregate EU governing processes. It is not possible to employ a blanket characterization of the EU as a supranational regime. The EU is not uniformly integrated or harmonized. Put another way, "there are potentially many ECs" (Stone Sweet and Sandholtz 1998: 9).

Integration and EU state building is not simply a top-down process. There are potentially many routes to integration, including ones which do not necessarily involve intergovernmental bargaining or the building of a super-state. They point out that even during the period of "Eurosclerosis" in 1970s, "levels of intra-EC trade and other forms of exchange soared [and] the amount of legislation and the number of EC pressure groups grew steadily"(Stone Sweet and Sandholtz 1998: 13).[8] Integration still took place during this period, even if it did not occur in the places that many people expected to find it. "Integration always proceeded, in some sectors and from some vantage points, despite . . . the divergence of state preferences" (Stone Sweet and Sandholtz 1998: 13).

Supranational governance – "the competence of the EC to make binding rules in any given political sector" (Stone Sweet and Sandholtz 1998: 1) – arises where supranational organizations "make rules designed to facilitate and regulate the development of a transnational society" (Stone Sweet and Sandholtz 1998: 25). Indeed, supranational governance is held to be the form of institutional arrangement best suited to promote the interests of transnational society. As Caporaso emphasizes (Sandholtz and A. Stone Sweet 1998: 345), when commenting on the work of Stone Sweet and Sandholtz, transnational society may fuel the integration process, but without effective leadership from the EU's institutions giving shape to disparate demands, transnational society would be "inert and ineffective."

The work of Stone Sweet and Sandholtz is particularly relevant to a chapter whose aim is to understand both institution building and the European state. Their thesis is that the path of European integration and the existence of supranational governance are intimately related, so much so that it would not be possible to understand the state-like features of the EU without understanding how integration proceeds. But they make it plain that integration is not necessarily EU-led. This is one of the strengths of their work. There are two other interesting features of their work which we should note. First, they highlight the importance of cross-border transactions and the role of transnational society in the development of supranational governance. Second, they see governance not as state-centered but as consisting of a range of rule-making institutions, both state and non-state.

At the same time their approach suffers from a number of weaknesses. As their critics have pointed out their thinking remains "trapped in a supranational–intergovernmental dichotomy" (Branch and Ohrgaard 1999). Their idea of supranational governance, resting as it does on the idea that integration is driven by transnational society would appear to reproduce the "state equals government, civil society equals governance" thinking criticized above. Transnational society is that which escapes the control of the (national) state, and as such, requires a different form of regulation and control, which can only be provided at the supranational level. This is not to say however that the EU progressively replaces the nation-state in all of its functions (Stone Sweet and Sandholtz 1998: 4). It is more the case that those disadvantaged by national rules and who are already engaged in exchange across national borders, will look to the supranational level to serve their interests.

In their desire to work against the prevailing tide of intergovernmentalism they have opted for a model which plays down the role of the state (regional, national, and supranational) in both integration and governance while at the same time foregrounding the idea of society. Transnational society consists of "those non-governmental actors who engage in intra-EU exchanges – social, economic, and political – and thereby influence, directly or indirectly, policymaking processes and outcomes at the European level" (Stone Sweet and Sandholtz 1998: 9). In highlighting the "European civil society" dimension they are contributing to the intellectual trend in EU studies noted by Rosamond towards a consideration of governance in place of an exclusive focus on the European state. Despite their enthusiasm for the idea of transnational society, Stone Sweet and Sandholtz have an underdeveloped understanding of globalization. There are definite European boundaries to their model and for them globalization is that which exists beyond the EU: "integration of a broader geographical scope" (Stone Sweet and Sandholtz 1998: 15). Where it does have an impact on integration it is in the time-honored way of creating pressures from above. Globalization leads to European integration by stimulating the need for greater competitiveness.

Majone's work on the "regulatory state" is important because it supports the idea that the EU is something other than a supranational state. It also helps clarify the way in which the EU governs. For Majone, the EU works not through welfarism and public ownership (the Keynesian state), or through deregulation (the neo-liberal panacea), but by encouraging the development of a panoply of independent or quasi-independent regulatory agencies designed to correct market failure (existence of monopolies, environmental pollution). The EU, rather than acting as a super-state, has set about creating a space across which regulatory innovation can be disseminated, and within which the regulatory systems of the member states can become harmonized. Community activity has not replaced national activity, but "actually created new regulatory responsibilities" (Majone 1996: 59). The upshot is that "member states have been forced to develop new regulatory capacities on an unprecedented scale."

Increased regulatory powers granted to the EU have also multiplied the regulatory activity at the national level. Policy initiatives in individual members are "increasingly likely to derive from an agenda established at the European rather than the domestic level" (Majone 1996: 266).

Majone's thesis is that regulatory reform has been the defining feature of the decline of the Keynesian, welfarist state. He argues that "the last fifteen years have been a period less of deregulation than intense regulatory reform, where the latter term is used to denote the apparently paradoxical combination of deregulation and re-regulation" (Majone 1996: 2). This regulatory reform marks a "reordering of public priorities" (Majone 1996: 54). Until relatively recently "most European countries attached greater political significance to redistribution and to economic stabilization and development than the correction of market failure through competition and other regulatory policies."

Majone charts the path that the European nation-state has travelled from being dominated by redistributive and stabilizing functions to its reincarnation as a regulatory state. This trajectory is closely related to the emergence of the EU as a major regulatory body: the EU has relatively little capacity for redistributive or stabilizing functions.

There are several important aspects to Majone's work which we need to consider. He offers us a way of understanding how the EU governs which does not depend upon the idea of the EU as a supranational state entity: the EU regulates, it does not rule. In doing so he provides a useful model for understanding the relationship between the EU and the member states and the means by which policy initiatives can be transferred between the two. His approach to the question of how the EU governs also manages to avoid the pitfalls common to approaches which emphasize governance. His working definition of regulation (borrowed from Selznick) holds that it consists of "a sustained and focussed control exercised by a public agency over activities that are valued by a community" (Majone 1996: 276). He sees regulation as being carried out by a whole range of public agencies, professional bodies, and other non-state bodies. In important ways his work shares some similarities with the ideas of the governmentality theorists discussed below. In particular, his emphasis on the way in which regulation requires a "detailed knowledge of, and intimate involvement with, the regulated activity" (Majone 1996: 276). Regulation requires fact-finding, rule making, and enforcement. By way of a criticism we might want to ask how Majone's idea of the regulatory state can explain EU or member state activity which does not involve regulation, redistribution or stabilization. Clearly, there are activities of nation-states, and of the EU, which do not fall under any of these headings and which are still carried out by centralized, state apparatuses: military strategy or diplomacy, for example. Majone does not confront such issues – his is not a theory of the EU state but a theory of regulatory reform.

Anderson's (1996) work on new medieval territorialities is notable for the way in which it problematizes the spaces of government in the EU (the discrete and bounded territories of regions, and nation-states) and the interrelationship between different "levels" (subnational, national and supranational). He advances his views in opposition to the tendency to view the EU as becoming a "Europe of regions," and the reluctance on the part of many commentators to see that "distinctly new political forms are emerging" (Anderson 1996: 133). He positions himself between the prevailing orthodoxies of intergovernmentalism and superstate by arguing that the EU is unlikely to conform to either one of these models of development. It is more profitable, he believes, to think of the EU through the categories of new medievalism and postmodernism. Rather than being a transitional form perhaps the EU will not move further in the direction of a superstate or a federal arrangement. Perhaps "this is it," and "arrested federalism" (Anderson 1996: 147) is the end point in its trajectory.

Building on the work of Bull on neo-medieval political order and Ruggie on postmodern state forms, Anderson develops the idea of the EU as a system of overlapping authorities and multiple loyalties:

regional and local, as well as transnational and global authorities exist alongside those invested in the nation-state. Sovereignty is uncertain and dispersed between different agencies. Sovereignty and territory have been "unbundled": "the growth of 'common markets' and of various transnational (or, more strictly speaking, transstate) functional regimes and political communities not delimited primarily in territorial terms" (Anderson 1996: 134). No longer is the nation-state the automatic container of all forms of power and authority. The concepts of postmodernity and neo-medievalism may be problematic, as Anderson readily concedes, but he is searching for a model which helps us to map the radical transformations to which Europe is exposed.

The importance of Anderson's work lies in the way he attempts to develop a conceptual language with which to grapple with what he rightly sees as fundamental changes in the European political order. Neo-medievalism needs qualification to be of service in apprehending contemporary European social and political change. Medieval hierarchies were nested, they sat one inside the other: manor, lordship, kingdom. Nowadays hierarchies are rarely nested:

> people are often directly members of international networks, not via national bodies; small local groups increasingly deal directly with transnational bodies, not via larger intermediaries; regional groups and institutions deal directly with their counterparts in other states without the respective states necessarily having any involvement. Hierarchies still exist, but not in the same "chain of command" sense as formerly.

He also points out that resorting to a "multi-level" model of political rule is not sufficient, even if it is an improvement on the idea that the state is the only important actor on the international stage: "multi-level thinking can also mislead unless it is appreciated that political processes operate as much between as within the different levels"(Anderson 1996: 151). He also points out the dangers of assuming that institutions of governance at different levels are replicas of the state. In other words, subnational regions are not scaled-down nation-states, nor is a supranational entity a nation-state writ large.

Anderson's aim is twofold. First, to highlight the fact that the political transformation of Europe needs to be better apprehended by social science. Secondly, to begin the task of generating a conceptual apparatus capable of understanding the emergent forms of multiple political authority. He is partially successful in these aims but is constrained ultimately by the political science/international relations traditions with which he is working. The departure point for his deliberations is the need to think beyond the nation-state as a model of political authority, but he remains tied to this model, never managing to think beyond how new forms of authority and rule differ from those of the nation-state. In other words, the nation-state is the baseline from which all other political entities deviate. His conceptual problems are not aided by his rather uncritical acceptance of the way postmodernism has been deployed in his field of study, and a rather economistic conception of globalization.

Dehousse (1997) is concerned to move away from the various state-centric approaches to European integration. He distances himself from both the intergovernmentalist position and interpretations that see the EU as a nascent state: "the European Community is not a state, but a complex form of transnational governance" (Dehousse 1997: 54). In the majority of studies of European integration the role of the nation-state has been seen as central to that process. Dehousse rightly points out that insufficient attention has been paid to "the impact of integration on state structures themselves" (Dehousse 1997: 52). He highlights two interrelated developments which he believes are the key to understanding the role of the state in the contemporary EU. The first of these is the fragmentation of the state, and the second is the development of transnational networks.

States should not be treated as unitary structures. While the centralizing tendencies of integration are well known, the "centrifugal (or fragmentary) forces accompanying them have received less attention" (Dehousse 1997: 40). The ways in which EU politics operates means that different government departments will develop their own approaches to European issues. Decision making at the European level structures the organization of national governments, by requiring national governments to mirror the European Commission's range of activities in their ministerial portfolios, for example. Moreover, European integration has increased the power of national administrations, by giving them greater powers of intervention, while at the same time weakening the structures designed to oversee and control them, namely parliament. In other words, Euro-powers have grown much faster than Euro-checks and balances. The integration process has disaggregated the state and some branches, for example the judiciary, "have clearly benefited from the integration process, while other institutions, such as parliaments, have lost ground" (Dehousse 1997: 53). This is what Dehousse means by "fragmentation," one consequence of which is that we should no longer talk of the state as a unitary whole.

Transnational networks linking agencies, sectors, and judicial bodies have been a crucial feature of integration and have contributed to the dissolution of the unitary conception of the state. Experts in a given area or sector can network with colleagues in other member states thereby reinforcing their common interests and values. Like-minded people find it relatively easy to work together and formulate policy "beyond the control of parliamentary bodies" (Dehousse 1997: 49). This is similar to Majone's idea that EU economic and social regulation increasingly takes place beyond the control of central administration. These transnational networks are "evidence of the state's remarkable capacity to adjust to new forms of governance." We are witnessing the redeployment of the state, not its retreat (Dehousse 1997: 52–3). So in Dehousse's model the state becomes differentiated. State agencies develop new competencies, reinforced by developments at the European level, and government bodies develop linkages with similar agencies throughout the EU. This occurs differentially, not all apparatuses of the state securing the same range of powers or network linkages. The state fragments to the extent that it is replaced by a multiplicity of agencies working through self-constituted networks. In Dehousse's view the state is undergoing a transformation, being redeployed not disappearing.

Sociological Approaches to the EU as a Form of State

But what of sociological approaches to the question of the EU as a form of state? In the course of a discussion on the development of democracy and postnational citizenship in the EU Nash (2000: 210) advances the view that the European Union is "increasingly a supernational state." The EU is assuming the mantle of a state by carrying out functions which were previously the preserve of its constitutive member states. What is happening within the EU is also true more generally: the state is being transformed, becoming at the same time more disagregated and internationalized. Nash (following Jessop) outlines "three main trajectories of change in the form of the state": denationalization, de-statization, and internationalization (Nash 2000: 261). We will look briefly at each in turn. First, the hollowing out of the state – what Nash calls denationalization – wherein the state is reorganized and its functions relocated. Some functions are referred

upwards, for example where member states lose a degree of sovereignty over economic policy, others downwards as with the case of
EU regional policy. Some state power evens leaks away "sideways"
where for example, regions occupy portions of more than one nation-
state. Miall (1993: 53) makes a similar observation about the redistribution of state power. He states that the nation-state is "becoming
porous, granting some powers to international organizations, and
others to local governments and regions." These themes resonate
with Dehousse's idea that the state is being redeployed.

Secondly, we can observe a "de-statization of the political system,
a shift from government to governance" (Nash 2000: 262). The state
no longer monopolizes the management of the economy or social
welfare programmes but works in conjunction with non-governmental (or perhaps we should say non-state) organizations to realize
its objectives. Thirdly, the internationalization of some agencies of
the state. The state no longer acts in a unified fashion but as "a
coalition of bureaucratic agencies each pursuing its own agenda"
(Nash 2000: 263). There is also a blurring of the boundaries that
separate international organizations such as the EU and the internationalized state.

The idea that the state is becoming disaggregated and denational-
ized, that there is a growing disjuncture between state, society and
politics is a feature of many accounts of the changing role of the
nation-state, both sociological and non-sociological (for example
Appaduarai 1990, Wierviorka 1994, Soysal 1994). In Nash's account
denationalization or the hollowing out of the state is a variation on
the idea of multi-level governance which posits that sovereignty is
ceded by the nation-state in the cause of European integration.
Powers are passed upwards to a supranational authority and
devolved downwards to regional administrations. In other words,
denationalization is EU integration by another name and, to pre-
empt one of the arguments developed at much greater length later in
the book, is based upon territorialist assumptions concerning the
nature of the integration process. The idea of de-statization centers
on the notion that government is parcelled out to non-state partner
agencies, resulting in a shift from government to governance. This
rests on the awkward idea that government is somehow the legitimate work of the state and that governance involves a different set
of operations involving non-governmental agencies. It also reproduces the idea that the government/governance distinction corresponds to a division between state and civil society. Finally, the idea

that the internationalization of agencies of the state leads to their involvement in "global governance" rests upon the global-local polarity familiar to us from chapter 1. It was argued that the idea that it is only the international dimensions of the EU which have a connection to the global while the subnational levels correspond to the local was shown to run counter to the best sociological traditions of studying globalization.

This interpretation of the European state can be usefully contrasted with the model developed by Albrow with which we introduced this chapter. Both are sociological approaches but draw upon different traditions. The fundamental difference between Albrow and Nash lies in the appreciation of globalization with which they are working, and they are representative of two very important, but very different, political sociology approaches to the study of the EU generally, and the "European state" in particular. The first approach, represented here by Nash emphasizes multi-level governance, a state-civil society distinction, and a global–local polarization. This approach employs sociological categories constructed in response to the need to understand the nation-state and tries to apply them to understanding the EU. This accounts for the state-like attributes bestowed upon the EU: a super-state or a supernational state. The nation-state gives way to the supernational state while civil society becomes global civil society. The local, national, supranational, and global are discrete levels which operate independently of each other.

This model is held to be inferior to what we early designated as the "inclusive globalization paradigm." A sociology which sets its sights on the study of something beyond the nation state, whether it be globalization, the EU, or world society must have an appropriate set of tools with which to work. The starting point for such an approach is that the EU (inasmuch as it can be thought of a state at all) "is a kind of state, but a new kind, such as we have never before experienced" (Albrow 1998a). One key advance represented by Albrow's overall position is that it problematizes the idea of multi-level governance, viewing it as an inadequate response to the growing dislocation between state and society, and an unsatisfactory attempt to capture the dynamics of EU government. Another key advance is that the global and the local are placed within a framework of globalization which sees the two as interrelated: the global being present in the local, and vice versa. Once established, this conceptualization of globalization undermines the international state/global civil society model, and points to the necessity to rethink forms of rule and mechanisms of government.

Government as a Technology of Rule

This section examines the potential contribution of governmentality theorists to the debate on the fortunes of the state and the nature of rule in the EU. In particular we will look at the work of Rose (1999) and Dean (1999), both influenced by the ideas of the French social theorist Michel Foucault. The term governmentality was coined by Foucault to reflect his interest in "governmental rationality": strategies for thinking about and enacting forms of government. Foucault holds that the emergence of governmentality represents a new way of thinking about and exercising power. "This form of power is bound up with the discovery of a new reality, the economy, and concerned with a new object, the population . . . government of the state becomes a distinct activity, and . . . forms of knowledge and techniques of the human and social sciences become integral to it" (Dean 1999: 19). In other words, the rise of governmentality led to the creation of both government apparatuses for the purpose of ministering to a population, as well as mechanisms designed to generate new forms of knowledge needed for the management of political economy.

For Foucault government means the "conduct of conduct": activities intended to organize or influence the conduct of a person or persons. Government works at the level of the individual as well as at the level of society, and, just as importantly is carried out by a whole range of actors including the self: governing is not the exclusive preserve of the state. According to Gordon (1991: 2)

> Government as an activity could concern the relation between self and self, private interpersonal relations involving some form of control or guidance, relations within social institutions and communities and, finally, relations concerned with the exercise of political sovereignty.

Studying rationalities of government – forms of government and the ways in which the practices of government are conceived – broadens out the subject of political rule considerably. According to Rose (1999: 3), Foucault holds that government, refers to all endeavours to shape, guide, direct the conduct of others, whether these be the crew of a ship, the members of a household, the employees of a boss, the children of a family or the inhabitants of a territory. And it also embraces the ways in which one might be urged and educated to bridle one's own passions, and to control one's own instincts, to govern oneself.

Persons are guided and regulated, by themselves and by others, in such a way as to further particular ambitions or to pursue certain goals. These activities are governmental in "their wish to make themselves practical, to connect themselves up with various procedures and apparatuses which would seek to give them effect" (Rose 1999: 288). Political ideas and policies by themselves do not constitute government; they have to be turned into technical practices. What this conceptualization of government does by focussing on the ways in which regulation and direction of the self and others becomes technical is to focus our attention on the complex interrelationships between individuals and forms of political authority. As Dean puts it, governmentality is to do with "the relation between the government of ourselves, the government of others, and the government of the state" (Dean 1999: 2).

In fact, what Foucault does is to privilege government over the state. The state is but one form of the exercise of power: a technology of rule. According to Miller and Rose (quoted in Barry 1993: 317) "the question is no longer one of accounting for government in terms of the 'power of the state', but of asserting how, and to what extent, the state is articulated into the activity of government." The institutional form of any particular state is the product of the practice of government (Gordon 1991: 4). Governmentality points us away from the idea of the state as the exclusive locus of sovereign power the purpose of which is to discipline a population.

Rose suggests that in the contemporary world the state does not work by increasing centralized power and control. In much the same way that Dehousse saw the state as being fragmented and redeployed, Rose sees state institutions as extending their operations and scope, not by centralizing their operations, but by utilizing new forms of knowledge and making use of global networking. In relation to the EU and its governmental strategies the key issue becomes not what type of state it represents, but how it has constituted "Europe" as a governable entity, and what strategies of government have been devised to govern effectively. We have already seen (in the work of

Majone, for example) how the EU works to regulate and harmonize, not to govern through a super-state. According to Barry (1993: 316) this process of harmonization can "be seen both as a way of imagining and of reordering European space, as well as a technical process directed at establishing this space as a governable entity."

The governmentality theorists are associated with the idea of reflexive government: the governmentalization of government. Reflexive government points to the way in which "government begins to conceive its task as operating upon existing forms of government rather than governing either things or processes" (Dean 1999: 211). Governments are less and less concerned with economic process and the distribution of wealth, and increasingly occupied with attempts to ensure the "security of governmental mechanisms" (Dean 1999: 177): from national budgets to the competitiveness of individuals and institiutions. In other words, the purpose of government is to monitor and reform the performance of institutions and governmental techniques.

Dean puts forward the argument that reflexive government has replaced the government of the state (associated with the regulation of populations and welfarism). The social is no longer constituted as a realm subordinate to and governable by the state. The social is to be "reconfigured as a set of constructed markets in service provision and expertise, made operable through heterogenous technologies of agency, and rendered calculable by technologies of performance that govern at a distance" (Dean 1999: 193). The welfarist state has given way to entrepreneurial government. These changes are driven by the realization that globalization is comprised of a series of processes that are beyond the control of (national) government. Reflexive government is distinguished by its attempts to secure the institutions and mechanisms of government, "in the face of processes that are deemed beyond government control" (Dean 1999: 179).

We are no longer dealing with the territorially bounded, sovereign nation-state of modenity. The European Union constitutes a novel form of economic space, no longer linked to the territory of the nation-state (Rose 1999: 34–5). Rose points not just to a reterritorialization of government away from the nation-state but also to a "detotalization of society." Communities of identity are asserting themselves on the basis of locality, ethnicity, lifestyle, sexuality, and political or moral allegiance. Rose (1999: 135–6) states that "individual conduct no longer appears to be 'socially determined' [but] shaped by values which themselves arise from ties of community identification." Society is fragmenting into a variety of moral and cultural communities which do not necessarily share a consensual basis. In turn, community constitutes a new spatialization of government, based on a new set of governmental strategies.

One such strategy is the governmentality associated with "advanced liberalism," the idea of the entrepreneur of the self. Individuals invest in the life-long project of promoting and enhancing themselves, their skills and their marketability. Advanced liberalism replaces bureaucracies with markets. The idea of advanced liberalism put forward by Rose designates both the economic orientation of the "New Europe" and the ways in which government works through the market, the individual, and the community. The state now empowers entrepreneurial subjects in their quest for self-realization. The subject of advanced liberalism is given unprecedented responsibility for governing his or her own affairs. The task of government shifts from the direction and welfare of the population to establishing the conditions within which citizens can become an active agent in his or her own government.

To ensure economic efficiency independent actors and agents must be "responsibilized and entrepreneurialized" (Rose 1999: 139). The relationship between the individual, groups, agencies, and state has been transformed. We must embrace the idea that there exists a multiplicity of authorities and agencies, often combined together in complex ways, which are capable of governing. Government is less interested in bureaucratic control and direct intervention, rather it acts "indirectly upon the actions of these autonomous entities, by focussing upon results: setting targets, promulgating standards, monitoring outputs, allocating budgets, undertaking audits"[9] (Rose 1999: 146). Responsibilization and entrepreneurialization are closely linked to a third process: autonomization. The term autonomization is derived from the work of Donzelot and enters the vocabulary of the governmentality theorists through the work of Burchell (1993: 274). It refers to the way in which neo-liberalism promotes autonomy amongst its participants, in terms of government, the provision of services, economic actors, citizens. Neo-liberalism promotes the autonomization of society, "through the invention and proliferation of new quasi-economic models of action for the independent conduct of its activities" (Burchell 1993: 274). We will have the opportunity to further explore the usefulness of this concept when we turn our attention to the European Union's regions and peripheries (chapters 6 and 7).

Earlier in this chapter we considered a sociological approach to understanding the EU derived from the work of Albrow. This was preferred to other sociological approaches because it problematized the multi-level governance model of the EU, undermined the pervasive state-civil society assumption, and offered a sophisticated account of globalization. The one area in which Albrow's work is relatively underdeveloped, I would argue, is its failure to adequately address the question of the EU as a form of state: emphasising the novelty of the EU state is not sufficient, not least because it still retains the idea that the EU is some kind of state, no matter how unique.

It is at this point that we see the importance of the work of the governmentality theorists. Their work enables us to refigure completely the terms of the discussion on the Euro-state. The issue is no longer to what extent the EU resembles a (multi-tiered) state, but the variety of forms that government of the European Union takes, and the range of agencies and partners who are involved in the business of governing. The governmentality thesis successfully broadens the debate on the state, sovereignty, and political authority. Looking at the state as one possible form of governing has two consequences. First, it undermines a whole range of state-centric approaches to understanding the EU. Secondly, viewing the EU in terms of a complex set of relations between the individual, society, and the state is the very stuff of political sociology.

The work of the governmentality theorists thus renders the EU more amenable to political sociology and offers a way beyond one of the most debilitating side-effects of studying the EU from a political science or international relations perspective: the impossibility of working outside a frame demarcated by neo-functionalist and inter-governmentalist dogma. In order to more fully assess their contribution to developing a political sociology of the EU there are several outstanding issues with which we must deal. The first of these is the fact that that the governmentality theorists have only made a limited direct contribution to understanding the EU.[10] As no detailed analysis exists and references to the EU in their work are infrequent we can only identify the potential that their approach has for understanding the EU. Secondly, we need to be aware that there are criticisms of their work which might limit its applicability. Barry (2001) points out that the work of the governmentality theorists tends to concern itself with programatic politics. That is to say with policies, their aims and objectives, their application and enactment, rather than with political disputes and struggles of a more spontaneous and less predictable nature. Their interest is in the "top-down" politics represented by official policies and government strategies, rather than in more popular forms of politics, protests, strikes, unlawful actions, and the hurly-burly of everyday political life. In a similar vein, it can be said that their exclusive concern with the rationalities of government leaves unexplored the capricious or emotive basis of much politics. Indeed, by moving away from a concern with how the state exercises power towards a study of the rationalities of government the governmentality theorists run the risk of displacing politics from the picture altogether. It is not sufficient to focus on government decisions, directives, policies, and legal provisions. Politics is a much broader field and is frequently irrational. Governments may accumulate vast amounts of knowledge about the economy or their populations but they do not always put that knowledge to good use.

The Common Agricultural Policy: From State Intervention to Reflexive Government

So far we have looked at various interpretations of the EU as a state, but we have not applied any of them to EU issues. In this section we will examine the case of the Common Agricultural Policy (CAP) which until recently was widely considered to be the most obvious example of statist interventionism in the EU. However, recent agricultural reforms have seen the EU begin to abandon traditional forms of market support and protection in favour of a multidimensional approach in which agricultural support instruments are merged with rural (and regional) policy. These changes in the nature of the CAP appear to resonate with the idea of a shift from government to governance, from market control and protectionism to neo-liberal values, but, it is argued, can be better understood through the governmentality theorists' concept of reflexive government.

To many lay people and commentators on EU affairs the CAP represents the worst excesses of the interventionist Euro-state and Brussels bureaucracy, and a poor advertisement for the benefits of European integration. The negative image of the EU held by many people is in no small part due to the association of the CAP with heavily subsidized (French) farmers, EU profligacy, artificially high consumer prices for agricultural produce, and large agricultural surpluses ("grain mountains" and "wine lakes"). Furthermore, the

CAP has always absorbed a large proportion of the EU budget (currently approximately 44.5 percent, but previously in excess of 80 percent) and has tended to dominate the EU policy agenda despite the fact that agriculture employs just 5 percent of the EU workforce and accounts for only 3 percent of GDP (McCormick 1999: 188).

The basis for a Common Agricultural Policy was enshrined in the Treaty of Rome at a time when the nascent EEC was under pressure to lower barriers to US agricultural exports and align price support with prevailing GATT norms, while also having to ensure adequate food supplies to European consumers. National interests dictated that the EEC should institute its own protective measures and permit the maintenance of differing national models of agricultural support. It is for these reasons that subsidies and price controls have always been strong elements of the CAP. It also goes some way to explaining why agricultural reforms are an ongoing problem for the EU, and such progress as has been made has been achieved in the face of some strong national opposition, notably from France.

Some authors (for example Rieger 1996, Hix 1999) have chosen to view the CAP as an extension of the welfare state, that is to say, to emphasize its wider role in bringing stability to society. Rieger (1996: 102), echoing Milward's idea that the EU was a way of rescuing the nation-state, argues that the CAP has provided a means to integrate "the national farming population into both the *national* society and the *national* polity," and evolved into "something which could be called a welfare state for farmers" (Rieger 1996: 104). In a similar vein, Hix (1999: 252–3) interprets the reforms of the CAP as evidence of a new type of welfare policy which seeks to work in the "general 'public interest' rather than the narrow interests of the farmers." The interpretation of the CAP as a component of a wider welfare regime is certainly not shared by all commentators. For Grant (2001) the disproportionate share of benefits going to better-off farmers demonstrates that if "CAP is intended to be a social policy, it fails in that respect."[11] Equally important, the welfare interpretation of the CAP perpetuates the idea that the EU is a traditional form of state. As Majone has pointed out, the EU does not work through welfarism. It is a regulatory state and the regulatory reform of the past decade or so has taken the form of a reordering of public priorities.

In recent years the EU, as a result of both internal pressures (the single market programme and the prospect of enlargement) and external constraints (GATT negotiations) has embarked upon a series of reforms, of which the most far-reaching were the MacSharry reforms of the early 1990s which began to de-link subsidies from production, moving instead to a system of direct payments for farmers.[12] The Commission's Agenda 2000 programme proposed further reforms aimed at strengthening the competitiveness of the sector and introducing a new framework for rural development, the "second pillar" of the CAP. These changes are not simply a response to the perceived problem of eastern enlargement or a new strategy for cutting the level of farm support. No longer is agriculture viewed as "an industry like no other" and a policy area to be managed by intervention, but as a realm which both impacts upon other key policy areas (regional and environmental policy in particular) with which it must increasingly dovetail, and as a key factor in the growth, competitiveness and development potential of a region or nation.

Much the same outlook is guiding the EU's approach to an agricultural policy for the candidate countries. The prospect of accommodating the poorer agricultural economies of the former communist countries within the CAP has always appeared nigh-on impossible, and the alternative of cutting benefits to those who currently receive them has long been deemed politically unacceptable. There is much concern within EU member states that the candidates' large but uncompetitive agricultural sectors could add to the Union's surplus production and put additional pressure on its already over-stretched budget. For this reason the European Commission has argued against candidate countries being able to increase their agricultural production in key areas upon entry (the higher the cost to the Union budget in direct payments and the lower the incentive to modernize). To the candidate countries these measures amount to little more than an excuse to deny new members the full financial benefits of membership.

When portrayed in this way EU policy appears to coalesce around a debate on the distribution of diminishing resources and the thwarted ambitions of cash-starved farmers from eastern Europe. Significantly, although the EU has not committed itself to making direct payments to new member states Farm Commissioner Fischler has acknowledged that the EU will have to make some payments to farmers in the new member states if the EU is to ensure that they do not increase production to unacceptable levels (farmers would be subsidised to restrict production). In any event, direct payments to farmers will be subsumed under a broader strategy to diversify the rural economy of the CEECs. Farmers will be encouraged to retire from agriculture and move into the tourism and leisure industries or traditional craft industries. According to the Farm Commissioner, "The future in rural areas lies not only on farms but in job alternatives outside agriculture." EU agricultural policy is changing. Put simply, rather than paying farmers not to over-produce, the EU will pay them to stop being farmers.

The changing nature of the CAP can be best explained, not by fixating on the problems and issues with which agricultural policy must come to terms (enlargement to the east, budgetary restrictions, uncompetitive farming, environmental and health concerns, global trade regimes), but by viewing the growing importance of rural development policy through the lens of reflexive government. In other words, it is not simply the case that the EU has chosen to reform the CAP as such, but that the EU has significantly transformed the way that it governs. The above example, where farmers are paid to re-train and move out of agriculture demonstrates this very well: less a shift in the emphasis of agricultural policy, more the bringing to bear of new techniques of government. Agricultural policy gives way to the government of rural development, of which agriculture is one component.[13]

State control (both national and supranational) of agriculture has yielded to new forms of rural government having important implications for the way that we view the EU as a state. As Majone has pointed out, over the past 20 years or so the EU has encouraged the rise of regulatory agencies designed to correct market failure through extending competition. Redistribution and stabilization have given way to regulation. The state has become less unitary, more fragmented and differentiated, or redeployed to use Dehousse's term. Other theorists have mapped these changes as the rise of governance, new "levels" of state activity co-opting organizations within civil society. On this interpretation agriculture has been transformed from a policy area in need of special protection (to the extent that it was virtually taken out of the single market programme) to one increasingly aligned with the mainstream EU concern: competitiveness. To this end it has caught up with the neo-liberal imperative that it is the concerns of the citizen-consumer, not the farmer, that are paramount, and that farm policy can no longer be treated apart from any other considerations. Governance dictates that policy areas must dovetail with strategies for achieving broader goals: citizenship rights and "the needs of society."

These are useful formulations but do not capture the full extent of the transformation. The governmentality theorists' idea of reflexive government is the better term with which to characterize how the EU has changed the way that it governs. Reflexive government directs our attention to the governmentalization of government, or the way that the EU is increasingly concerned to secure the means of government. As Dean points out, this is particularly important at a time when there are processes (such as globalization) deemed beyond government control. The diversity of rural areas, hitherto not addressed under the CAP, is brought within the purview of agricultural policy. The EU aims to act not just upon production levels, prices and exported quantities, but a whole new range of rural economic activities (from environmental protection to recreation). As the Commission explains, the policy for agriculture "is targeted not just at agricultural producers but also at the wider rural population, consumers and society as a whole" (European Commission 1999e: 1). The "second pillar" increases the EU's capacity to govern areas which were previously of secondary or no interest at all: food quality, environmental damage, training for agricultural workers, and the use of non-agricultural land. The aim is for an agricultural sector more competitive and compatible with the dynamics of the single market "in the context of a comprehensive, integrated strategy for rural development" (European Commission 1999e: 3).

The development of this kind of rural policy is indicative of a shift away from protection and intervention towards the government of diverse rural areas, regions, and sectors. The "second pillar" of the CAP resembles regional policy more than it does agricultural policy, traditionally understood. Direct aid to farmers and support for rural development is on the increase while market support and export subsidies are on the decline. Rural areas are increasingly seen as regions with special problems. Moreover, rural policy is explicitly linked to EU attempts to reduce disparities between regions. Emphasis is placed on the "multifunctionality of agriculture." In other words, the value of agricultures lies not simply in what farmers produce but in the services they provide (European Commission 1999f). Consumers are encouraged to take advantage of these services and by the same token farmers are encouraged to become entrepreneurs of the self, consuming training courses, retraining to enable them to exit agriculture, and the services of marketing and unemployment agencies. The European model of agriculture has given way to the "European rural model." In the face of mounting criticisms of a narrow, protectionist and production-orientated strategy, the EU has moved to both link agriculture to wider rural concerns and to apply its technologies of entrepreneurial government to greater areas. To this end rural policy incorporates strategies to enhance competitiveness and employment and addresses environmental concerns, rural diversity, tourism, and other non-farming activities.

Conclusion

Throughout this chapter we have looked at sociological arguments for why a study of European integration should be less concerned with what sort of state the EU represents, and more focused on the ways in which the EU regulates and governs through a variety of agencies. It has been argued that neither assessing the degree to which the EU has assumed a supranational role nor mapping the changing role of the state as a shift from government to governance is sufficient. The former assumes that the EU must have some state-like qualities or else remain an association of nation-states, the latter posits a multi-level state structure. In order to break with this statist thinking it has been asserted that the work of the governmentality theorists makes several important contributions to the question of the European state. First, and most fundamentally, it recasts the question of what form the EU state takes, preferring instead to concentrate on the forms of government at work within the EU. Second, that it allows us avoid the pitfalls associated with the idea of governance, that is to say the idea of a political system working on multiple, integrated levels and within which civil society organizations are co-opted as partners. Third, it breaks down the state–society distinction altogether. Traditionally, approaches to state–society relations assume that the state governs a territory, a population, an economy. Governmentality allows for no separation between the government and the governed: they are often one and the same. Government is not something that happens to society: government takes place in all manner of institutions, organizations, agencies and individuals, not just state-designated civil partners. This erosion of the state–society barrier confronts us with a very large sociological question. What do we mean by society? More particularly, what kind of society or societies exists in the European Union? This is the topic that we will address in the following chapter.

4 European Society

The Idea of Society

The idea of society has been the subject of considerable debate in recent years. Many people appear unsure as to what it means, what it consists of, or even if it exists. And those are just the sociologists. Despite the commonsense notion that sociology is the "study of society," sociology along with other academic disciplines has tended to take society for granted. Within more popular discourses the idea of society has been questioned by the prevalence of a certain type of neo-liberal thinking. Former British prime minister Margaret Thatcher famously declared that "there is no such thing as society."[1] Neo-liberalism is also associated with the idea that society is becoming more fragmented by the shift from a collectivist to an individualist concept of social order, as evidenced by the decline of the welfare state. This idea has been reinforced by a rather economistic interpretation of globalization as a set of processes further undermining the sovereignty of the nation-state. Society is frequently thought of as something that has been lost, as in the idea associated with criticisms of multi-culturalism that unitary society has lost its cohesion and is breaking down. Like the idea of community, society becomes something constructed through nostalgia. On the other hand, society can be thought of in terms of what we do not yet possess. In relation to the idea of European integration, the belief is frequently aired that the diversity of languages, cultures, and traditions make the idea of a truly European society an impossible dream.

This chapter examines the question of what kind of society exists in Europe. Before proceeding with this task we need to establish some coordinates, and lay some ground rules for our investigation. The first point to note is that this question should not be conceived narrowly. It is not the same as asking whether a true Euro-society has come into existence, or whether this is a likely outcome of integrative measures. Nor is it to be equated with a comparison between the different national societies that can be thought of as comprising the EU, or an assessment of which might be the most Europeanized. However, the question does not preclude the possibility that it may be more appropriate to speak of a plurality of European societies rather than a singular, unified European society. The second point to note is that while political science approaches were heavily represented in our discussions about the European state in chapter 3, these same approaches have very little to say about European society. The study of society, for better or worse, is left to the sociologists. The third point to note is that society is still a useful concept. This chapter seeks to reclaim the idea of society from discourses which have either subordinated it to the state and/or made it synonymous with integrated and harmonious forms of collective life. In other words, the concept of society has a life beyond theories of civil society and does not necessarily refer to the aspiration to create or preserve a systemic and consensual social entity. Society can be multiple, fissiparous, partial, and disintegrated. This defence of society may be a little surprising after the usefulness of the idea of the state was called into question in the previous chapter. But state and society are not inseparable, and do not have to work in harness. They can exist independently of each other. Concluding that our understanding of the state would be better served by focusing on forms of rule rather than institutions of state does not mean that society can be summarily dismissed. In fact, the opposite is the case. Society takes on a greater significance once the diffuse nature of the exercise of rule is recognized.

Although this chapter examines various sociological approaches to the question of what kind of society exists in Europe this should not be taken to mean that sociology has ready answers. In general, as with the analysis of the European state, it is the potential for answering this question which will be foregrounded, rather than actually existing solutions. There exists a vast body of sociological work on conceptualizing and understanding the dynamics of contemporary societies in general, rather than European society in particular. As we have already seen, the key issue has become how to think about society as something other than that contained within the nation-state: the "nationally sequestered society" (Robertson 1992).

In thinking more specifically about the question of European society we must bear in mind that the European Union, and the connotations of integration which it has carried in the post-Maastricht period, coupled with a growing consciousness of globalization (in all its disciplinary permutations), has generated both a great deal of uncertainty about what society means in the contemporary world, and a whole host of new approaches to delineating, mapping, and understanding it. As testament to this uncertainty there exists a broad spectrum of contemporary sociological approaches to understanding society, ranging from attempts to theorize it away, versions that reduce it to the idea of civil society, attempts to recast it as global society, and moves to detach it from the (nation-) state. More than with any other central concept in contemporary sociology there exists a lack of consensus on what we understand by the term society.[2]

This chapter identifies four distinct political sociology approaches to understanding society. The first, examines the evidence for the existence of a European society, in terms of an entity corresponding to the European "state" engendered by increased integration. Sociological approaches within this category tend to be sceptical. Delanty (1998) asks "Is there a European society?" and Mann (1998) "Is there a society called Euro?" These questions are invariably answered in the negative. The second approach recasts society as civil society. The idea of civil society has become an important one, its popularity stemming in large part from its appropriation by commentators on the popular democratic movements in central and eastern Europe emerging from within the former Soviet bloc and hastening the demise of communism (Kumar 1994). In the West, the idea of civil society has been taken up by those who emphasize the displacement of class politics by new social movements and NGOs (Non-Governmental Organizations), and the shift from materialism to post-materialism. One of the issues which we need to explore is the ways in which the version of civil society constructed in these accounts tends to be a very liberal one which sees civil society as a realm of freedom distinct from, but protected by, the state. The idea of civil society as a realm in which rule is exercised through consent rather than coercion (Gramsci) is uniformly absent from these accounts.

There is another way in which the idea of civil society has been taken up. The "global civil society" thesis has two variants. First, the idea that global civil society corresponds to the internationalization of the state (Nash 2000). Both the state and civil society are enlarged from the national to the international level. Second, the idea of global or cosmopolitan civil society. This is based on the idea that the existence of UN Charters, international NGOs, and the development of universal personhood rights constitute an emerging global society. It is also linked to the idea of global governance, a self-regulating global civil society which does not have to exist in combination with a corresponding global state. Apart from the objection already mentioned – that they rest upon a rather optimistic and liberal conception of civil society – we might also criticize these approaches for what Delanty (1998) terms the attempt to reproduce on the supranational level a model that has reached its limits on the national level.

What all the civil society approaches have in common is that they emphasize the constitutive role of the state/society nexus. In contrast, there exists a range of approaches to the question of society which seek to understand it without any necessary relation to the state. Within this broad category are two distinctive approaches of which we need to be aware. The governmentality theorists view the emergence of society as coinciding broadly with the period of liberal regimes in western countries. Society is conceived as a solution to the problem of how to ensure social solidarity under conditions in which direct state intervention is not desirable. Society becomes a realm to be understood and managed in order to ensure cohesion and security. On this understanding society is one possible form that the management and organization of the social can take.[3] In recent times, neo-liberal imperatives have led to a completely different role for the social: through the generation and self-regulation of markets, for example.

The globalization theorists have opened up a whole range of new ways of thinking about society. They place emphasis, not on national societies, but on transnational movements and linkages, global networks and flows, and the increased awareness that people have of global threats and opportunities. However, it would not be correct to say that the globalization theorists have a common approach to the question of society. There are two main variants that I want to introduce here. First, the idea that we are living in a post-societal phase (Urry 1999): with the decline of the nation-state under conditions of globalization society necessarily loses the meaning it once had. What is being asserted here is that the idea of society is inseparable from the project of the nation-state, that it "is embedded within notions of nation-state, citizenship and national society" (Urry 1999: 5). Second, the idea that under conditions of globalization society is liberated from the (national) state, a position associated with the work of Albrow (1996). This is not to suggest that positions on globalization are easily polarized. There are a number of nuances and complexities which make a simple positioning of the theorists in separate "camps" undesirable. For example, some globalization theorists hold on to the idea of civil society (Beck 2000, Urry 1999), while others explicitly reject it (Albrow 1998).

The line taken in this chapter is that there is still good reason to talk about society and to use the term in a meaningful and precise way. This does not mean that when we speak of society we are necessarily referring to the "nationally sequestered society." The term society no longer has to refer exclusively to the complex of social relationships contained within the borders of a nation-state. A series of epochal processes – globalization, European integration and the collapse of the bi-polar world prominent among them – have forced us to reconsider what we understand by society. In addition, conceptual and theoretical innovations in the social sciences have revolutionized the way we understand social life, our place within it, and the way we apprehend social change. Announcements of the "death of society" have to be treated with suspicion. Society is a resilient category, it has survived the collapse of communism and cannot be erased by globalization. This chapter aims to demonstrate how a sociology of European integration would be incomplete without it.

European Society in EU Discourse

Before giving consideration to the sociological contribution to the question of whether a European society exists, it will be instructive to examine the way the EU views European society. In recent years the issue of European society has become a noteworthy feature of EU discourses of integration and governance. The EU is increasingly concerned with a whole range of questions stimulated by the recognition that European integration has occurred to a significant degree in the economic and more recently political field but that there has been relatively little activity in the sphere of social integration. Increasingly, the issue of European society is linked to that of EU democracy, and there is concern that the EU needs to become a true polity if the "democratic deficit" is to be reduced (Giorgi, Crowley, and Ney 2001).

Moves towards greater and deeper integration dating from the early 1980s, and enlargement from the early 1990s, coupled with a growing awareness of globalization, which the EU conceives almost exclusively in economic terms (Rosamond 2000), and the increasing dominance of neo-liberal thought over policy making have all contributed to the EU's concern with regulating and harmonizing a transnational European space, distinct from the national spaces of its member states. These developments have coincided with the rise to prominence of the term governance as the preferred designation for the way the EU regulates, harmonizes, and manages transnational space. Society and governance are intimately related, and society (or more frequently "civil society") is seen not as something to be managed and controlled, but as a partner in governance (Albrow 2001).

There are four main ways in which "society" is invoked in EU discourse. First, a "European model of society," an inclusive and democratic form of social organization. Second, "civil society" comprising a "third space" between state and market. Third, "social exclusion," the disadvantages created by uneven growth. Fourth, "information society," an epochal designation of a society based on knowledge technology.

The focus here is on the first and second version of society (the idea of social exclusion is explored at length in chapter 5), and in particular on the construction of society in the discourses of the European Commission and Economic and Social Committee. The latter prefers "social partners" and a formalized civil society organized at the European level. The Commission sees society less as something to be managed and more as a partner in governance. In EU discourse there is a tension between the idea of an integrated EU in control of its economy and society, and the notion of a more fluid "network Europe." The tension finds accommodation in the notion of multi-level governance which proposes a transnational civil society within which European solutions to European problems can be formulated.

The idea of the "European model of society" rests upon the assumption that there exists a specifically European social order, "based on the mixed economy, civilized industrial relations, the welfare state, and a commitment to basic social justice" (Ross 1995: 46).[4] Within the context of a drive for greater economic integration in the late 1980s and early '90s the European Commission developed the idea of the "European model of society" as a way of countering criticism that the EU had discarded its welfarist dimension in favour of an all-out embrace of market forces. The "European model of society" stands for the idea that progressive integration amounts to much more than a single market: the market and the "social" go hand-in-hand. Commission President Jacques Delors took the view that "societies were more than markets, citizenship more than consumption, and government more than an economic traffic squad" (Ross 1995: 46).[5] The relationship between economic development and social protection is spelled out in the following statement.

> The organisation of society in European countries reflects the values of the social market economy. This seeks to combine a system of economic organisation based on market forces, freedom of opportunity and enterprise with a commitment to the values of internal solidarity and mutual support . . . With growing European integration, it is inevitable that the Union should increasingly share responsibility with the Member States for the maintenance of this European model of society. (European Commission 1996a: 13)

On the Commission's interpretation, the European social model is driven by economic growth and the single market, which in turn acts as a catalyst for institutional and social developments. Economic integration will promote a wave of cooperation resulting in social solidarity and harmonization across Europe. In Delors' own words, "competition and cooperation, liberalization and harmonization will go together, creating the conditions for a new regulation of the totality which will be created" (quoted in Ross 1995: 46). Society on the European model was to become as cohesive and manageable as the European nation-states upon which it was based. Significantly, the "European model of society" was conceived as more than an aggregation of national societies, and was based on the assumption that the EU was itself becoming a coherent political entity, a sort of a "nation-state writ large" or a Euro-polity. In other words, the creation of a single market and harmonized economic space would not only lead to an enhanced awareness of the European social model but a new realm over which the EU had increasing jurisdiction.

However, this is not to say that the Delors Commission imagined the EU as a protective, centralized welfare state.[6] The harmonization of European economic space has not come about through traditional (nation-) state means. The EU is a regulatory state (Majone 1996) and encourages member states to develop new responsibilities and capacities in order to align with EU norms and expectations. As we have seen in chapter 3, for Majone the EU works not through welfarism and public ownership (the Keynesian state), or through deregulation (the neo-liberal panacea), but by encouraging the development of a panoply of independent or quasi-independent regulatory agencies designed to correct market failure (existence of monopolies, environmental pollution). The EU, rather than acting as a super-state, has set about creating a space across which regulatory innovation can be disseminated, and within which the regulatory systems of the member states can become harmonized. In recognizing the need for a trans-European dimension to EU policy the Commission has moved away from the traditional version of the "European model of society" towards the more contemporary idea of a "transnational social model" (Barry 1993).

The original "European model of society" survives in the discourse of the Economic and Social Committee, which sees it not only as the basis for social consensus and solidarity but as a means of promoting the EU to the wider world. The "European model of society" has been mobilized within a discourse of European heritage and identity and provides a foundation for the construction of a common European culture. This is particularly important in the EU's dealings with non-member countries, especially in the context of enlargement.

> The European social model is based on a number of tenets which form the common heritage of the peoples of Europe. They include: political democracy and the safeguarding of human rights; social justice in a free society; and the involvement of citizens in the decision-making process. The EU promotes and upholds these principles both within and beyond its borders, not in order to impose its model but simply because they represent the basis for the legitimate exercise of power (Machiavelli 2000).

In summary, we can say that the Delors Commission represented the high-water mark for the idea that economic integration would result in total control by the EU of its own markets, trade, economy. Since this time the conception of a European social model has changed noticeably in certain respects. There has been a retreat from the idea that economic integration will drive a new and better kind of European polity. Neo-liberal policies are considered more of a priority than "traditional" forms of social solidarity, and one impact of globalization has been to undermine confidence in the idea that the EU can easily maintain control over economic processes. Society is less of a passive realm embodying solidarity and community and more of a partner in strategies for economic growth and competitiveness. To understand why this is so we need to look at discourses of governance and how civil society has become the dominant understanding of society in the contemporary EU.

The understanding of civil society advanced by the Economic and Social Committee interprets it as an unconstrained and relatively autonomous social sphere, independent of the state but protected by the rule of law (ESC 2000a: 18), comprising institutions to which citizens freely associate and through which their interests are represented. Civil society is positioned as a "third component" of the state system with an intermediary role between state and market: "civil society is not an opposition to the State but has an intermediary function between the State, the market and citizens . . . Civil society prevents the citizen being reduced to a 'dependent of the State' or to a 'market player'" (ESC 2000b: 34).

The Commission and the ESC share the belief that the expansion of "organized civil society" over the past 20 years or so and the emergence of European NGOs has greatly enhanced the potential for a firm partnership between the EU and civil society in the building of an inclusive Europe.[7] For both, civil society and governance are intimately related. In the opinion of the Economic and Social Committee (2001: 2) "one of the biggest challenges for European governance is ensuring effective participation of organized civil society," but in adopting a rather rigid idea of what form "organized civil society at the European level" must assume, the ESC risks excluding and ignoring the greater – and most dynamic, responsive, and meaningful – part of society.

In October 2000 the European Commission published a White Paper on European Governance entitled *Enhancing Democracy in the European Union*, in which governance is understood as encompassing the "rules, processes and behaviour that affect the way in which powers are exercised at European level, particularly as regards accountability, clarity, transparency, coherence, efficiency and effectiveness" (European Commission 2000a: 4). A complementary formulation defines it as "public administration through the interaction of the traditional political authorities and 'civil society': private stakeholders, public organizations, citizens" (Busquin quoted in ESC 2001: 3). The European Commission emphasizes the role of civil society within EU democratic governance and associates it with European integration. Civil society organizations are deemed to have the following key democratic functions: to provide for a public debate; to function as a democratic "warning light" concerning the malfunctioning of the state; to ensure participatory democracy. Civil society can offset the disadvantages of minority groups by giving them a voice in decision making. Participatory democracy thus complements representative democracy. Civil society reinforces extra-parliamentary democratic structures. This is of central importance as democracy in Europe is based on the "twin pillars" of accountability of executives and involvement of citizens in decision-making (European Commission 2000a: 4).

The Commission has calculated that including civil society in strategies of governance is an effective way of countering the "democratic deficit" perceived by many to reduce the appeal of the EU for its citizens (European Commission 2000c). To this end, the Commission has identified six issues for governance at the European level in which work should be intensified: public debates, producing and implementing EU rules, decentralizing the responsibilities of executives, a "networked" Europe, Europe's contribution to world governance, integration of policies. The idea of civil society is central to all of them. However, it is not suggested that civil society should replace established national and sub-national public authorities. It is emphasized that governance involves an interaction between multiple levels of the exercise of power, and the involvement of non-governmental actors in the policy-making process. The idea that governance comprises a partnership between "EU institutions, national governments, regional and local authorities and civil society interacting in new ways: consulting one another on a whole range of issues; shaping, implementing and monitoring policy together," has been termed "network Europe" by Commission President Romano Prodi (2000b).

The discourses of European society considered here all contain doubts that a cohesive and unitary European society exists. For example, the European social model "takes many forms in the Member States" Diamantopoulou (2000b). In other words, while EU members share common values concerning social protection and welfare, the institutionalization of these values varies across Europe. It is acknowledged that European civil society is embryonic and is not embraced by citizens to the same extent as nationally contained civil societies (Prodi 2000b). The information society exists mainly in terms of its potential for the future integration of Europe, and has the capacity to undermine inclusionary social strategies.

At the same time the EU believes that it can create a European society (increasingly conceived in terms of a civil society). The ESC believes that European society can be constructed through organizing civil society at the European level and promoting the emergence of

genuinely pan-European bodies representing Europe-wide constitu-
encies. For its part, the Commission looks to the creation of a
transnational space within which European responses to European
problems can emerge (Diamantopoulou 2000a).[8] The information
society is pivotal in this regard, creating new economic and communication networks which will stimulate growth, ameliorate the
problems of exclusion and cohesion, and facilitate enlargement.

In their analysis of the EU's information society, Axford and
Huggins (1999: 188–96) make the point that there are two contradictory "logics" at work. The first is the idea that the information society
is a key element in the creation of transnational economic space in
which networks of interaction will redefine "the very idea of a
European polity and civil society." The second "logic" is a residual
European social model view of the EU as a "nation-state writ large."
These two "logics" coexist "through a kind of neo-functionalist
wishful thinking, wherein the growth of information society is seen
as contributing to the creation of truly Europeanised publics." We
can generalize this insight further and say that in all EU discourses
of European society there is a tension between the idea of a tightly
organized, structured, and managed Europe – an EU in control of its
markets, trade, economy, society – and a more fluid, differentiated
and dynamic Europe – Prodi's "network Europe," for example. The
way that this tension or contradiction is accommodated within contemporary EU discourse is in the idea of multi-level governance,
which has rapidly become the preferred term for viewing governance
in the EU. Commission President Prodi (2000b), like many other
commentators, recognizes that it is difficult to talk of European
society. There are very few truly European societal organizations and
fora. There is no Europe-wide media, business and trade union
organizations exist only as federal grouping of national bodies, and
most civil society organizations have local or national orientations.
Prodi (2000b) concludes that the best way to incorporate civil society
organizations into EU governance, "may not be through centrally
organised pan-European institutions, but rather through networking
and issue-based activism." This encapsulates the difference between
the ESC and the Commission view of European civil society, and
suggests that if a European society is to come into existence it will be
because of the networked local and "grass-roots" activities of citizens
and NGOs in partnership with a European Commission responsive
to their needs.

The European Union's interest in and appreciation of society changed markedly during the 1980s and '90s. Put simply, the post-war European social model gave way to a transnational social model, a move which is indicative of a broader shift from government to governance. The shift in social model can be tracked through the transition from the Delors to the Santer Commission. While the Delors Commission defended the idea of a "European model of society," which already contained within itself the seeds of neo-liberal governance, the Santer Commission wholeheartedly embraced the idea of governance. Santer's motto for the post-Delors Commission – "do less, but do it better" – reads like a pledge of good governance.[9] The issue is no longer whether the state should intervene more or less, or whether there should be more or less government, but how to ensure better governance.

In relation to the idea that an inclusive and cohesive social model has been replaced by a neo-liberal one there are parallel developments in other areas of EU activity worthy of note. Hooghe (1998), writing about EU cohesion policy, makes the point that during the late '80s and early '90s there was significant contestation in Europe between advocates of neo-liberal capitalism and regulated capitalism (regulated markets, redistribution of resources, public/private partnerships). The reforms of the Structural Funds carried out in 1988 (under the Delors administration) were intended to institutionalize regulated capitalism in Europe (Hooghe 1998: 459). However, this particular social model soon lost ground, and during the 1990s the neo-liberal governance idea gained in strength.[10] One further consequence of the rise of the idea of governance has been the prominence of the concept of civil society, which allows for the idea that European society is transnational and that social and economic partners are incorporated in the business of governance.

In this context it is instructive to see how former Commission President Jacques Delors now aligns himself with the civil society thesis in preference to the 1980s rhetoric of giving birth to a new form of European society (Delors 1999). In Delors' new vision the European Union is now positioned as an intermediary between the conflicting demands of the nation-state and the global (rather than as an intermediary between member states). In contrast to his earlier emphasis on the EU as a nascent Euro-polity, his idea of civil society emphasizes that we have "struck out from the familiar shores of the industrial society and the framework of the nation-state." As a result, the "entire European model" is in question. Citizens no longer find their bearings through the traditional reference points of industrial society. Our social coordinates have been transformed: women's status, the family, religious life, employment, and community.

In other words, the framework of politics has changed. People now look beyond the formal political (party) system for alternatives, and issues which were previously not "political" now assume a greater importance. It is for these reasons that the idea of civil society has assumed such an important role. Civil society organizations have their finger on the pulse of society and they enable greater political representativeness. Civil society offers a synthesis between the "social" and the market and between collective and individual responsibility. Civil society contributes to better governance and improves the functioning of the European Union. The ESC's version of "organized civil society" is increasingly difficult to reconcile with Delors' image of a European society increasingly removed from "the familiar shores of industrial society and the nation-state." Significantly, the solution offered by the ESC to the socially disruptive and exclusionary tendencies of the information society is to fine tune the "European model of society" and underpin social consensus by enhancing education.

The rise of civil society as the dominant way of imagining European society is linked to the decline of the idea that an integrated Europe would be a "nation-state writ large," and the consequent need to ensure the governance of transnational spaces. As such, the EU's appreciation of key social actors has changed, or more accurately, there are competing interpretations of who constitutes the social actors upon which civil society is constructed: civil society is contested ground within EU discourse. The Commission understanding of civil society as a partner in governance can be accommodated comfortably within the "transnational social model" in which social and economic actors increasingly take responsibility for solving their own problems and work within multiple levels of governance to formulate European solutions to a range of European issues.

The Possibility of European Society

Delanty (1998: 2.4) views the question of whether a European society exists as one inherited from the sociology of modernity. He writes, "the conventional notion of society was one that rested on the belief that society was based on one central integrating principle, namely the nation-state." He believes that the term society is problematic when applied to the European Union and that we need a "new concept of group membership or community to theorize 'the social' in European integration" (Delanty 1998: 1.10). He pursues this further by examining the extent to which the project of European integration could create a sense of community throughout Europe. In order to do this he considers four possible bases for the construction of a political community: the demos, the ethnos, the social, the cosmopolitan.

In terms of the demos (membership of a political community), he concludes that despite formal citizenship rights the EU allows only a low level of citizen participation. In relation to democracy and sovereignty the EU compares poorly with nation-states. In terms of the ethnos (membership of a cultural community) Delanty is dismissive of its potential to form the basis of a European society. He is of the opinion that the only sense in which a European ethnos is emerging is a very negative one: "around the articulation of a European identity based on exclusion" (Delanty 1998: 4.10). The demos and the ethnos are exhausted at the European level. Turning to "the social," Delanty suggests that the project of European integration is market driven. While the movement of goods, services and finance has been facilitated by the EU and labor markets been rendered more flexible, "beyond the world of consumption and work there is little on the specifically European level to compare with national societies" (Delanty 1998: 4.11). In other words, the EU is still primarily a trade bloc without corresponding institutions for managing the social, for example a welfare state. As such, "there can be no European society in the conventional sense of the term 'society' as a social domain" (Delanty 1998: 4.12). On the issue of cosmopolitanism, Delanty finds no evidence that the EU is committed to the creation of a world society via global citizenship.

Delanty concludes that a new conceptual framework is needed if we are to be able to assess the extent to which the potential for a European society exists. A conceptual framework that is not tied to the categories associated with the nation-state. He suggests that the idea of the "knowledge society" might be a more appropriate model for "the social dimension in European integration, but a 'social' with a difference" (Delanty 1998: 6.4). By the "knowledge society" Delanty (1998: 6.4), building on Castells' work on the network society, points to a society with the cognitive capacity to interpret itself, understand itself and to imagine alternatives. Knowledge is no longer dominated by one social actor, the state for example. Expertise is being delegitimated and knowledge is increasingly a medium of cultural experience. We live in a world where many cognitive frameworks coexist and rival each other.

The big problem with attempting to found European society on the bases of the demos, the ethnos, the social or the cosmopolitan is that they are all models of inclusion and consensus. Delanty believes that we should work from a model of dissensus. This allows us to understand the constitutive role of contestation in social life: contested knowledge is a prime characteristic of contemporary culture. There are an increasing number of areas of public life in which contestation forms a critical component. Delanty points to the instances of "AIDS, BSE, radioactivity, biotechnical developments such as cloning, medical ethics, neurology which have all opened scienticized knowledge to public scrutiny bringing together discourses of nature, science, law and politics" (Delanty 1998: 6.8). In identity politics as with scientific and technical expertise, a multiplicity of actors vie for domination and/or to demonstrate their authority. He draws the conclusion that "it is the public who is becoming more important as a social mediator in disputes which question the very foundations of a society's cognitive and cultural structures" (Delanty 1998: 6.8). In other words, "knowledge society" opens up a whole new arena of democratic struggle and political contestation in which the public has a constitutive role. This new public space, freed from both the conceptual chains of the nation-state/national society nexus and the hierarchical order of more traditional forms of social and political struggles, is one which European society should aspire to.

There are several criticisms of Delanty's approach that we might want to note. He makes a forceful argument for the futility of "transposing the conventional concepts of social integration borrowed from the nation-state to the European level" (Delanty 1998: 6.5), but at the same time tests out only those categories which he believes are inappropriate. He states at the outset that all of the potential societal foundations to which he gives consideration – the demos, the ethnos, the social, the cosmopolitan – are unsatisfactory. As such, it is no great surprise when they are found wanting. He demonstrates a strong correlation between the idea of society and the nation-state of modernity, but is sceptical as to the possibility that society can exist independently of its link with the nation-state. This is reflected in his unease about the use of the word "society": he uses many substitute words – "the social," polity, community, political community, civil society – and treats them as synonyms for society, when there are good reasons to differentiate between them. For many theorists the terms "civil society," "the social," and "political community" signify very different things.

Mann asks the question: "Is there a society called Euro?"[11] In answer he suggests that a "total society" is an impossibility. This is true of the society based on the nation-state, and is equally true of the idea of global society or Euro-society. "There has never been a singular systemic network of social interaction which might constitute, as it were, a 'total society'" (Mann 1998: 185). In other words, no social system is self contained, bounded, and self-sufficient. Societies, such as they are, are formed out of networks of social interaction that never just stop at national borders. All societies are interdependent, to a greater or lesser degree. In terms of density of network interactions Mann sees these as strengthening in Europe but without attaining the level of a coherent or closed system. In the same way as Delanty saw the EU as being driven by market linkages with little corresponding activity at the social level, Mann (1998: 205) sees financial flows and trade as having no necessary correspondence to internal borders or the development of a coherent society. Euro-networks are the preserve of the "upper social classes and elites" rather than the masses, and exist mainly to serve specialized sectoral and social interests.

Grundmann (1999), writing about the deficit of democracy within the EU, also identifies a deficit in the European public sphere, which he believes is the necessary precondition for a European polity. In addition to there being no European media system, "there are no parties with a European wide range, there are no (or only a few) European political figures, and there is no European public sphere" (Grundmann 1999: 127). Grundmann see two routes towards an enhanced European public sphere: the emergence of a transnational European public and the Europeanization of national public spheres. The latter possibility is limited by the national nature of the European media.[12] Regarding the former, Grundmann (1999: 137) suggests that the emergence of pan-European issues such as BSE and the introduction of the single currency could lead to the "synchronization of national public spheres and thereby strengthen the transnational public sphere." The national orientation of the media is not necessarily an insurmountable problem if national cycles of attention can be synchronized. This would facilitate the emergence of a common European debate about democracy and identity.

One point that emerges from this discussion is that while it may be relatively easy to talk in abstract terms of the existence of a European society, bringing it into existence is a very different proposition. Grundmann's work on the absence of European public spheres shows the extent to which societies remain tied to the nation-state. His assessment of the way in which a true European public sphere could emerge in the future has a strong normative component. He is suggesting that such a sphere would work to link the separate national publics into a common body of opinion, or at least a body that shares a common agenda. This indicates that for Grundmann the idea of a European society is bound up with notions of integration, social cohesion, and harmony. In contrast, Delanty's account emphasizes that dissensus is an acceptable basis on which to construct a European society. His idea of a "knowledge society" is one in which society is able to understand, reflect on, and transform its relationship with the state. Such a society would not be an uncritical and obedient servant of the state. The "knowledge society" would constitute itself as a public space of contestation with no obligation to acknowledge any boundaries that the state may want to place on its sphere of activity.

Civil Society

There are many for whom the concept of civil society is a cornerstone of contemporary political sociology. It occupies a central place in the sociological imagination, bringing together as it does ideas of state, society, citizenship, democracy, participation, stability, and peaceful political change. It is sociological "common sense": democracy needs civil society, it is the prerequisite for freedom, plurality and social harmony. Its applications would appear to be endless, appealing to the left and the right, nationalists and cosmopolitans, and democrats of every stripe. The idea of civil society has been used to explain struggles against communism and, at the same time, finds some of its most subtle expression in Marxist theory. It has a strong liberal economist tradition, yet finds a home in the repertoire of socialist thought. In some formulations civil society requires the protection of a democratic state, in others it presages a post-national democracy. There is plenty of evidence to support the idea that civil society is one of the most flexible and accommodating of concepts. However, the argument advanced in this chapter is that civil society is a concept whose usefulness in relation to understanding contemporary Europe is particularly limited, despite its undiminished popularity in mainstream sociological and political thinking.

There are two main reasons for thinking that the idea of civil society has outlived its usefulness. The first centres on the rather liberal interpretation of civil society that is frequently employed in much current work. Civil society is seen as a realm of democratic freedoms distinct from, but protected by, the state. This understanding of civil society, particularly when applied to eastern Europe, has also tended to see it as the gathering place for a disparate group of pre-existing democratic entities suppressed under communism.[13] It is argued that this model of civil society is an unwarrantedly optimistic, not to mention inaccurate, interpretation of democratic rule. It is assumed that political domination is only exercised via the state, and that a democratic state needs a civil society and vice versa. Against this it is argued that society and the state cannot be separated in this way and that civil society, rather than simply being a sphere of freedom and autonomy, cannot be divorced from the exercise of rule.

The second reason stems from the state–civil society distinction. All the versions of civil society outlined above contain implications as to the form of state that exists in tandem with it. In the previous chapter we argued that there was no European state as such and that it was preferable to think in terms of the variety of forms that government in the European Union takes. If governing takes place through multiple agencies and institutional arrangements, working on many sites, there can be no state as such, and no separate state-protected realm of civil society. This chapter argues that the idea of civil society should be jettisoned if we wish to understand contemporary Europe. However, this does not mean that the idea of society itself has outlived its usefulness. The chapter seeks to demonstrate how society can be reclaimed for political sociology.

In order to begin this task we must examine some of the arguments for civil society and their relevance to a study of the EU. There are two broad categories of civil society theses. First, there are a whole range of arguments that emphasize the importance of civil society to democracy. This is a key theme in much of the literature on the struggle against communism in the countries of eastern Europe and the former soviet bloc. It is also widely employed in the literature on the role of NGOs and new social movements in the democratic development of the western half of Europe. Second, there is a growing field of study centering on the idea of cosmopolitan democracy and global civil society. This necessarily detaches civil society from the (nation-) state and projects it as a realm of transnational democratization. We will examine each of these broad applications of civil society in turn.

Civil Society and Democracy

The literature on civil society as a guarantor of democracy, especially the work on the democratization of the former communist countries, is sustained by a notion of civil society which sees it as an autonomous realm benefiting from the protection of the state. On this model, civil society cannot exist without the presence of a democratic state, which, in return works to secure its democratic foundations. Before looking at how this model has been deployed in interpretations of democratic change in Eastern Europe we will examine its theoretical underpinning in the work of Keane (1988a and 1998b) and Cohen and Arato (1992), writers who conceptualize civil society in very different ways, but who have all attempted to understand the processes leading to the establishment of democracy in the former soviet bloc.

Keane (1988a: 3) defines civil society as, "the realm of social (privately owned, market-directed, voluntarily run or friendship-based) activities which are legally recognized and guaranteed by the state." Keane's definition is close to that advanced by Held (1989: 6), who states that civil society "connotes those areas of social life – the domestic world, the economic sphere, cultural activities and political interaction – which are organized by private or voluntary arrangements between individuals and groups outside the *direct* control of the state." I would describe these as "mainstream" definitions in the sense that they advance an idea of civil society that many writers would assent to. Having said that, it is necessary to add the caveat that not all theorists of civil society allow for the inclusion of economic activity (see for example Cohen 1995, Cohen and Arato 1992, and Gramsci 1971, all discussed below). We will give further consideration to Keane's definition of civil society later in this section. Of more immediate interest is the fact that he is anxious to defend civil society against charges that it has "withered away," or that the concept has no application in the present circumstances. He rejects the argument that the division between state and civil society has become meaningless, replaced "by a 'magma' of overlapping, hybrid institutions no longer describable or recognizable as either 'political' or 'social' entities" (Keane 1988b: 6). When expressed in these terms Keane would appear to be defending the state/civil society distinction from exactly the sort of challenge that was mounted in the previous chapter. Then it was argued that rather than relying on the idea of the state to explain political rule, we should look at the ways in which government is conducted through multiple agencies working throughout "society," of which the state is but one. On the model preferred in chapter 3 there is no formal distinction between state and civil society.

Rather than being eroded or rendered obsolete by changing political realities, Keane (1988b: 7–13) sees the existence of civil society in western Europe (and the state/civil society distinction) being reinforced by three key processes. The first process is the restructuring of the capitalist economy. As a result of privatization and deregulation the economy is increasingly independent of state intervention. "The ability of states to anticipate and control their respective economies has decreased visibly in recent years" (Keane 1988b: 7). The second process is the struggle over the welfare state, increasingly made a scapegoat for any number of economic problems. "These political difficulties of the Keynsian welfare state have been exploited most successfully by neo-conservatism, which emphasizes the negative consequences of state intervention into the private markets of civil society" (Keane 1988b: 9). One result of this has been the creation of markets for goods and services where none previously existed, increased competition, and a redefined role for the state. In other words, "a selective withdrawal of the state from civil society" (Keane 1988b: 10). The third process is the growth of social movements, an interesting phenomenon in as much as they "develop largely outside and 'underneath' . . . institutions of civil society and the state" and work to both expand and democratize civil society as well as "deepen the division between the state and civil society" (Keane 1988b: 12–13). On the latter point, one key characteristic of social movements – whether anti-nuclear protests or movements aimed at securing minority rights – is that they are not concerned with seizing state power. They have an "anti-political" quality and, borrowing Melucci's terminology (see below), are described as constituting "invisible networks of small groups submerged within everyday life" (Keane 1988b: 12).

Keane's defence of civil society should be understood as the corollary of his characterization of the state. Rather than becoming increasingly integrated (a "magma" of institutions) state and civil society are increasingly separated under the conditions obtaining under contemporary neo-liberal politics. The state may be being "rolled back," and restricted in its opportunities for market intervention but this only serves to clarify its role *vis-à-vis* civil society. In keeping with many conceptualizations of civil society he sees it as something which exists in relationship with a (mainly) benevolent and protective state. In his definition of civil society quoted earlier this aspect is made explicit. Civil society is the realm of free association "recognized and guaranteed by the state." The state is defined as a "complex network of political institutions (including the military, legal, administrative, productive and cultural organs" (Keane 1988a: 3). One of its functions is to act as a "referee" in intra-societal disputes: "conflicts of interest generated by civil society could be settled peacefully only by means of laws which are applied universally" (Keane 1988a: 22). The state protects civil society, and the latter depends upon the former for its security: "vigorous political initiatives, funding and legal recognition are necessary for the survival and expansion of civil society . . . sovereign state power is an indispensable condition of the democratization of civil society" (Keane 1988a: 22). This examination of Keane's defence of civil society emphasizes the point that a theory of civil society is by definition also a theory of the state.

Cohen and Arato (1992: ix) conceive civil society in very different terms:

> a sphere of social interaction between economy and state, composed above all of the intimate sphere (especially the family), the sphere of associations (especially voluntary associations), social movement and forms of public communication. Modern civil society is created through forms of self-constitution and self-mobilization. It is institutionalized and generalized through laws, and especially subjective rights, that stabilize social differentiation.

The first point to note is that in contrast to Keane and Held, Cohen and Arato differentiate civil society not just from the state, but from the economy too. They do not wish to see the idea of civil society reduced to a synonym for the market, and they recognize that capitalism can pose a threat to social solidarity and justice. They are striving to make the concept relevant to both former communist and Western countries. In their terms, it is necessary to distinguish civil society from both the state and the economy "to demonstrate the dramatic oppositional role of the concept under authoritarian regimes and to renew its critical potential under liberal democracies" (Cohen and Arato 1992: ix). Cohen and Arato's "sphere of social interaction" shares a good deal in common with Melucci's "invisible networks of groups submerged within everyday life," referred to above. Civil society has a similar "anti-political" quality. The political role of civil society is "not directly related to the control or conquest of power but to the generation of influence through the life of democratic associations and unconstrained discussion in the cultural public sphere" (Cohen and Arato 1992: x). Nor should civil society be equated with political organizations, parties, and governments, what the authors term "political society." Civil society mediates between political society and the state.[14]

One interesting element of their formulation is that they see civil society very much in terms of a realm created by the self-constitution and self-mobilization of public actors. This is a clear advance over the idea that civil society is a "safe haven," a protected space, within which repressed or minority groups can coalesce and organize. It is in this sense that we should understand their statement that civil society "should be seen not only possibly, as a network of institutions, but also actively, as the concept and product of self-constituting collective actors" (Cohen and Arato 1992: xviii). In this way, civil society can be the source of democratization and the driving force behind demands for extensions of political rights and opportunities. Civil society targets the institutions of economic and political society and seeks to make them more inclusive and egalitarian.

Civil Society in Eastern Europe

In the popular imagination the idea of civil society has become very closely associated with the anti-communist and pro-democracy struggles which took place in eastern Europe during the 1980s and early '90s. Writing in 1989, Garton Ash (1989: 174) states that "one could write the history of East Central Europe over the last decade as the story of struggles for civil society." According to Walzer (1995a: 2), the "idea of civil society reentered political debate in the course of the struggle against totalitarianism in Central and Eastern Europe." During communist times, the argument goes, there was no state/civil society distinction. This was the meaning of totalitarianism: civil society was extinguished, absorbed fully into the structures of the state (Keane 1988b: 2–3).[15] Civil society was what was missing from communist countries. According to Hosking (1991: 212), in eastern Europe the idea of civil society became used as a designation for "'what we currently lack', namely political, social and economic institutions independent of the state and the ruling party apparatus." There was no public space where autonomous and independent association could occur. In Cohen and Arato's terms there was no opportunity for "unconstrained discussion in the cultural public sphere."

In much of the literature on the struggles to establish civil society under the unpromising conditions obtaining in communist countries the emphasis is very much upon the creation and defence of a realm of public freedoms in opposition to the state. Understandably, the state is seen as the oppressor and civil society must assert its independence. Garton Ash (1989: 174) writes that whereas through the 1950s and '60s eastern European dissidents and reformers had concentrated their efforts on attempts to reform their national communist parties, during the 1970s and '80s they turned their attention to organizing outside the structures of the Party-state (see also Pelczynski 1988: 361). The disappointment of top-down reforms was replaced by the promise of grass-roots activity.[16] Civil society, as a multiplicity of informal networks, activities and association, became the focus for the democratic opposition in communist countries. The "reconstitution of 'civil society' was both an end in itself and a means to political change, including, eventually, change in the nature of the state" (Garton Ash 1989: 244). However, the reform of the state was to be only an indirect outcome and would occur only if and when it could adapt to a reduction in the areas under its jurisdiction.

Tismaneanu, writing primarily about independent peace movement in the Soviet bloc, inclines to the argument that civil society had long been repressed through state control and that its gradual re-emergence provided a space within which nascent democratic tendencies could prosper. The building of civil society is likened to a rebirth, "a natural process of cultural awakening which restores the individual as a true citizen" (Tismaneanu 1990a: 6). Civil society was never completely eradicated in communist countries, "totalitarianism has never totally annihilated the well-springs of civic autonomy" (Tismaneanu 1990c: 183). There was always a degree of underground activity which managed to evade the attention of the authorities, and the church frequently acted as a rallying point for oppositional sentiment. Dissidents sought both an active disengagement with state authority and autonomous space free of control and ideological manipulation. Refusal to cooperate with the prevailing system of domination was the first step towards rehabilitating the individual and reconstructing social solidarity. This combination of refusal to comply with state demands and at the same time assert an independent alternative has become known by the term "antipolitics," coined by Konrad (1984).

Konrad's "antipolitics" prescribes a way of orienting oneself to the dominant regime: rejecting its values but (out of necessity) living alongside it. Creating something positive out of adversity: "living with one's back to the (Berlin) Wall." Konrad advocates a refusal to share power or reform the state, but not a complete rejection of politics. "Antipolitics" is an alternative form of politics, not its rejection, in the same way as civil society is conceived as an alternative to the state. Being "antipolitical" is not the same as being apolitical. "The apolitical person is only the dupe of the professional politician, whose real adversary is the antipolitician. It is the antipolitician who wants to keep the scope of government policy . . . under the control of civil society" (Konrad, 1984: 227).

Antipolitics is the "political activity of those who don't want to be politicians and who refuse to share in power. Antipolitics is the emergence of independent forums that can be appealed to against political power; it is a counter-power that cannot take power and does not wish to" (Konrad 1984: 230–1). Walzer, (1995b: 22) commenting on Konrad's ideas is suspicious of the "antipolitical tendencies that commonly accompany the celebration of civil society." It is not possible, he asserts, to dispense with the agencies of state power. Civil society cannot be totally self-regulating. Left to its own devices it "generates radically unequal power relationships, which only the state can challenge" (Walzer 1995b: 23). Civil society requires certain forms of state action "to redistribute resources and to underwrite and subsidize the most desirable associational activities" (Walzer 1995b: 26). In other words, it is not possible to choose only civil society. It comes as part of a package which includes the state. On Walzer's account this is not a bad thing. Civil society and the state require each other and are mutually reinforcing. "Only a democratic state can create a democratic civil society; only a democratic civil society can sustain a democratic state" (Walzer 1995b: 24).[17]

Pelczynski's (1988) account of the rise of Solidarity in Poland during the late 1970s views the development of civil society from a

Gramscian perspective. In contrast to Tismaneanu's view that civil society was never completely absent in communist countries, Pelczynski argues the case that prior to the advent of Solidarity there was no infrastructure of genuinely autonomous social institutions, and no civil society. Public freedoms, restricted though they were, only existed as a result of the negligence or laxity of the authorities. "They were the beneficiaries of loopholes in the state structure . . . the application of the civil society concept to Poland before the rise of Solidarity . . . is highly misleading" (Pelczynski 1988: 368). Solidarity constituted true civil society because around it "there crystallized a new 'historic bloc' of anti-state and anti-Party elements in Polish society, elements which now had an organizational base and therefore constituted civil society in a strong sense" (Pelczynski 1988: 370). On this account there is a world of difference between civil society and Konrad's notion of antipolitics. Civil society is here conceived of in direct opposition to the state, and the prime agent of political and economic reform.

Global Civil Society

The models of civil society so far considered vary in many respects but share one important feature, namely that they all assume that the development and deepening of civil society will be worked out within a national space. Furthermore, they envisage a state/society distinction that can be mapped directly onto the territory of the nation state and national society. In the work of Keane (1988b) referred to above and also Melucci (1988: 257) the assumption is that the state/civil society distinction is being rendered more complex by the pressure exerted on the nation-state from both "above" and "below." Keane (1988b: 6) writes, "within any national context 'the state' is becoming less of a unitary agent than in the nineteenth century and . . . it is flanked from above by an interdependent system of transnational groupings and from below by a multiplicity of sub-governments operating their own systems of decision-making." This is closely echoed by Melucci (1988: 257) who sees the state no longer as a unitary agent of intervention. "It has been replaced from above by a tightly interdependent system of transnational relationships and subdivided from below into a multiplicity of partial governments, defined by their own systems of representation and decision-making and by an ensemble of interwoven organizations which combine the public and the private." The key aspect of these formulations is that the greater complexity observed by both commentators is perceived in terms of the ways in which state power is parcelled out and the blurring of the state/civil society boundary that this entails. They are still very much working within a national model of society. There is no sense that a different form of complexity is being created by transnational networks and global flows working to make national boundaries increasingly anachronistic.

In recent years the study of social movements and NGOs has turned its attention to the way these mobilize across national borders, and campaign around issues which are truly global in nature (global warming and nuclear weapons would be two obvious examples). One consequence of this is that assumptions about the nature and extent of civil society have been challenged. The idea that civil society must be coterminous with a nation-state have been displaced by the emergence of the idea of "global civil society." As defined by Nash (2000: 257) the term refers to organizations, associations, and movements which exist between the individual and the state, but crucially which operate across national boundaries. A significant number of INGOs (International Non-Governmental Organizations) now exist – Greenpeace, Amnesty International, the Red Cross, amongst them – and they play a prominent role in constructing global civil society. For instance INGOs may apply pressure on nation-states to adopt UN Conventions on Human Rights, they campaign for changes in the employment practices of multinational corporations, and are consulted by supranational and international organizations such as the EU, the UN, and the World Bank over policy matters.

In a world characterized by multinational firms and global capital flows, the international regulation of which is currently weak or non-existent, it is global social movements and INGOs which offer the best hope of establishing global democratic governance. Global civil society is more suited to this task than nationally orientated political parties and organizations. For Nash, (2000: 259) "Transnational social movements can undoubtedly have some effect on the activities of multinationals which are difficult to control through the politics of the nation-state." She cites the example of how the wave of protests and boycotts which followed the decision by the oil company Shell to dispose of the Brent Spa oil rig by sinking it led to a thorough reassessment of its environmental responsibilities. "In this case, environmental protest in civil society was a good deal more effective than politicians working through government regulation" (Nash

2000: 259–60). According to Giddens (2000: 145), one outcome of the Brent Spa protest is that "Shell and other large oil-producing firms have . . . come to see the management of environmental sustainability as issues to which they should make a positive contribution."

The development of transnational citizenship, global issues around which social movements and INGOs organize, and the transformatory potential of global flows all serve to make the idea of "global society" a meaningful one. However, there is no reason why in an attempt to apprehend the emerging forms of globality we must be limited to thinking within a framework of civil society. Following Delanty we might want to avoid projecting onto the international level a conceptual framework shown to be limited at the national level. The argument here is that thinking about "global civil society" is a limiting way of approaching the question of whether a European society exists. There are two main reasons for this, one concerns the civil society element to this formulation, the second relates to the concept of the global which it employs. First, global civil society retains too many associations with the state to be truly productive. We want to be able to think about global or European society in ways that are totally unrelated to considerations about a world or European state.

The second reason is that the word "global" in the term "global civil society" is used in such a way as to reproduce the idea of a global/local polarity. There is national civil society and there is now global civil society which exists at the opposite end of the spectrum. This gives a wholly misleading view of the relationship between the global and the local or national because it implies that it is only transnational actors (INGOs and global movements) who can participate in global civil society. But "being global" does not just consist of networks and processes that operate across significant portions of the world. Society can be globalized by being fragmented, disaggregated and decentered in particular, often localized ways. This is indeed what has happened to European societies. In terms of the idea introduced in the previous chapter we can say that European society has become autonomized.

Civil Society and Hegemony

One common feature of the diverse body of work on civil society considered thus far is that it is adjudged to be a realm of freedom and autonomy. Civil society works to secure and extend democracy, facilitates the communication of political and oppositional ideas, and enables the creation of political (or antipolitical) movements and associations. The state exercises jurisdiction, intervenes in matters of national importance, upholds law and order, institutes relations with other nation-states, and frames and protects civil society. In none of these accounts is it suggested that domination and rule are exercised directly through civil society. On the contrary, the associations and networks of civil society are seen as independent of the exercise of political power. They are not called upon to regulate and administer either by themselves or in partnership with agencies of the state.

As stated in the introduction to this chapter such a view of civil society and of the state/civil society distinction is rejected here. The way in which the state was conceptualized in chapter 3 does not allow for a separation from civil society. Government is exercised through society just as much as via the state, in as much as that distinction can be maintained. We need to correct the impression that all versions of civil society see it only as a realm of autonomous organization outside of the scope of state intervention. The understanding advanced by Gramsci lays emphasis upon civil society as both the realm of possibility for political change in advanced societies and also as the domain where domination is exercised. Gramsci's Marxist analysis resolves rule into two components: the coercion exercised in political society (the state) and the consent secured in civil society. What Gramsci is suggesting is that rule is exercised just as much through society as it is via the organs of the state. As Simon (1982: 72) puts it, "the social relationships of civil society are relations of power just as much (though in a different way) as are the coercive relations of the state."

Gramsci's understanding of civil society as a complex of private interests through which political rule is exercised is closely linked to his concept of "hegemony."[18] Hegemony, the ability of a class (or class fraction) to articulate the interests of others to its own, takes place in civil society. Political rule is not simply enforced in a coercive way through the activities of the police, the army, and the courts (although these methods are also needed in generous measure). For the ruling (capitalist) class to rule effectively and enduringly (and for it to be able to reproduce the basis of that rule) it must secure the consent of the ruled. "Hegemony is best understood as *the organis-ation of consent* – the processes through which subordinated forms of consciousness are constructed without recourse to violence or coercion. The ruling bloc, according to Gramsci, operates not only in the political sphere but throughout the whole of society (Barrett 1991: 54). It is Gramci's view that hegemony requires that force does not predominate over consent: "the attempt is always made to ensure that force will appear to be based on the consent of the majority, expressed by the so-called organs of public opinion" (Gramsci 1971: 80).

The ruling bloc or class rules by means of hegemonizing society: by offering moral and intellectual leadership, by making society in its own image, and by ensuring the compliance of the ruled. It does this through ideological struggle on the terrain of civil society. Hegemony is achieved not through a series of alliances or pacts between different classes and political groups. The ruling class is hegemonic when its ideas become seen as natural or commonsensical. The ideological domination enjoyed by the hegemonic class "does not seem at all 'ideological' [it] appears instead to be permanent and 'natural' . . . to be beyond particular interests" (Hebdige 1979: 16). An example would be the way in which the idea of a "fair day's wage for an honest day's work" is seen not as an imposition of bourgeois law but as a natural, fair and equitable arrangement. For Gramsci, the "naturalness" of the contract masks the exploitative nature of capitalistic labor relations.

Hegemony is exercised through an ensemble of private and autonomous groupings. Social movements, political parties, media institutions, and organizations devoted to education, religion, and civil rights are all involved in forms of "cultural politics"; struggles over ideas, meanings, and identities. The politics of nationalism works in this way with different social groups attempting to appropriate and recycle cultural raw material: histories and traditions, myths, symbols and emblems, words and images. Examples include the way in which the image of the "British bulldog," for so long an emblem of the neo-fascists in England was reappropriated by Labour leader Tony Blair. There are many other examples of attempts by Blair's "New" Labour to capture elements of nationalism for the left, particularly the ideas associated with "Cool Britannia" and the "re-branding of Britain."[19] Another example is the way in which the song "Jerusalem" is coopted into different political discourses, evoking left-wing utopia, right-wing patriotism, and Women's Institute domestic conservatism.

According to Gramsci the hegemonic class successfully manages to articulate the majority of important ideological elements such as nationalism, democracy, and freedom into a dominant ideology by means of which it secures its domination. It is not possible to rule without first securing the consent of the subordinate groups in civil society. Gramsci (1971: 57) states that "there can and must be a 'political hegemony' even before the attainment of government power, and one should not count solely on the power and material force which such a position gives in order to exercise political leadership or hegemony." In other words, hegemony is not a form of domination which stems from the holding of state power. It is a much more generalized form of domination and its acquisition is a prerequisite for successful rule. This combination of rule through the coercive apparatus of the state and the consent enjoyed in civil society produces a unity of state and civil society which Gramsci terms the "integral state."[20] This leads to his famous formulation: "State = political society + civil society, in other words hegemony protected by the armour of coercion" (Gramsci 1971: 263).

Gramsci also sees in civil society the possibility of radical political change. He develops the concepts and hegemony and civil society to both understand why the working class is not normally revolutionary under conditions of capitalist exploitation, and to theorize how a socialist revolution could be prosecuted under these same conditions. If the working class in western Europe has become enculturated to capitalism and increasingly see their lives as relatively rich and fulfilling (high standards of living, labor-saving devices, legal rights, health and happiness) the old fashioned rallying call for a workers revolution is going to fall on deaf ears. The theory of hegemony is not only an explanation for the sophisticated ways in which the bourgeoisie neutralize the oppositional potential of the proletariat. It is also the blueprint for a socialist political strategy. Gramsci's theory allows for either of the "fundamental classes" to become hegemonic. For the working class to become hegemonic it must engage in a protracted political struggle and aim to capture some of the key ideological elements currently articulated within the bourgeois hegemonic ensemble. Political struggle becomes a "war of position," incremental steps towards securing power, rather than the "war of maneuver," the full frontal revolutionary assault of the Leninist tradition.

The introduction of Gramsci to this discussion has served as a reminder that the dominant contemporary interpretation of civil society is a particularly liberal one. Gramsci points to a much more complex relationship between state and civil society than is allowed in the other versions, and asserts that the state governs through society too. Any attempt to equate the state with rule and civil society with freedom, with the former protecting the latter, is founded on very naive assumptions. Despite these positive attributes Gramsci's work is not particularly useful for understanding contemporary European society. His work is based on a Marxist class analysis which is designed to explain the nature of class rule, and the way in which bourgeois hegemony can be overturned by the working class. Gramsci is often read as a particularly sophisticated Marxist (see for example Mouffe 1979) who believes that the ruling hegemonic bloc is no longer a class as such but a "collective will," a fusion of a fundamental class and its allies.

It is not so much the class basis of his work which makes it unsuitable for our project of establishing a political sociology of European integration. Rather, it is the heavy nationalist assumptions which underlie his thinking that makes his ideas difficult to translate into the contemporary European context. The idea of hegemony is very much tied to political change *within* a nation-state. The "collective will" constructed by the dominant class is thought of as a "national-popular collective will." Gramsci believes that in order for a class to become hegemonic it has to capture the key ideological ground: the popular and the national. In other words, whoever best claims to represent the people and the nation will be the ruling class. His understanding of civil society is circumscribed by his political project: the capture of the national state by the working class, hardly a basis from which to understand European society.

Managing Society

The governmentality theorists provide another example of an approach to society that sees it as a realm where rule is exercised. In his discussion of the liberal[21] forms of government which emerged in Europe in the eighteenth and nineteenth centuries Dean (1999) outlines how liberalism "discovered" society as a means of ensuring security. Liberalism believes that, "to achieve security, it is necessary to respect the liberty of the governed so that the natural processes of the economy and the population might function effectively" (1999: 117). The liberal conception casts security in terms of the effective management of the "'non-political' processes on which government will depend" (Dean 1999: 113): population, civil society, and economy. Liberal thought attempts to restrict the activities of the state in order to encourage economic and individual development, but at the same time keep independent realms such as the economy and society in regular order and to eliminate harmful conflicts. As such, "society" stands for a realm beyond the direct control of the state and for a particular set of problems which must be addressed.

Liberalism requires security and stability but in a form which does not compromise the economic freedoms of individuals and their activities. One way of ensuring security through society is to make it coextensive with the nation, to "place a boundary around the problems of the government of population within a territory" (Dean 1999: 124). In this way, social and economic problems can be isolated and managed more effectively. Achieving security through society is also linked to the economic welfare of the nation. As Rose (1999: 102) points out, the security of the nation-state and its society "came to be understood in terms of their capacity to ensure the security of its national economic well-being." To the liberal mind society is a totality, complete with order and structure, a "relatively pacified totality" (Dean 1999: 110). It is a domain of cohesion and conflict, demonstrating regularity and uniformity, and, at the same time, cleavages formed along lines of class, religion, and ethnicity. According to Foucault, liberals take the view that society is "a complex and independent reality that has its own laws and mechanisms of disturbance" (quoted in Dean 1999: 111).

According to this view there are elements which fall outside the purview of the state but which are also essential to the ends of government and need to be brought within the orbit of state influence. Liberal government separates state and society, public and private. Society is viewed as natural and non-political and thus not to be subjected to state authority. However, it is "governed by processes that are autonomous from the operation of sovereign authority" (Dean 1999: 55). In other words, society is governed, but not directly by the state. There are realms – such as the economy and society – which are not governed directly but which are regulated from within. Liberal government attempts to balance a need for protecting autonomy with the need to shape the conduct of the family, the person, the enterprise (Rose 1999: 101). In this sense liberal government works by "acting on and through relatively autonomous domains of social interaction" (Dean and Hindess 1998: 6). Society is viewed as a "self-regulating domain subject to its own laws and tendencies which depend for their operation on the activities of free, rational and prudent persons."

Governing such an entity poses particular problems. Because society is seen as having a reality independent of formal government, and because it is perceived as "a network of spontaneous orders" it is something that needs to be known by specialist forms of knowledge. In order to govern society more effectively liberalism advocates the development of various forms of expertise. Liberal government needs knowledge of the objects to be governed and has thus spawned the "expert" and a range of academic disciplines, including sociology. Liberalism as a critique of excessive government allows for the generation of new social concerns and the forms of knowledge needed to address them. This is what constitutes self-regulating rule. This concern for the welfare of the population (bio-politics), allied to liberal techniques for governing society would eventually lead (in the twentieth century) to the creation of the welfare state: a way of dealing with the problems of security, coping with social concerns, and "managing the risk of fracture and dissolution within industrial society" (Dean 1999: 130).

The main thrust of the governmentalist critique is that society should not be seen as a natural or indelible feature of human organization. Society came into existence as a response to a particular set of issues. It was the liberal solution to the problems thrown up by the need to create security, reduce harmful conflict, and organize social and economic life under conditions where it was not acceptable to have a heavily interventionist form of state. The autonomy and self-regulation of society was encouraged, as was the ability to deal with what Foucault termed its own "mechanisms of disturbance." Various forms of expertise and actions in the field of social improvements, welfare, and justice predominated. The state could oversee and regulate this behaviour indirectly through the disciplinary mechanisms (repressive, legal, educational, and moral) at its disposal. Providing that societal activity did not spill over into "political" areas or threaten the equilibrium of the nation-state there was little cause for concern. The welfare state became the form that this concern for security took in the post-war period when the spontaneous development of the economy and society was no longer seen to be a realistic option. This way of governing society was dominant for a period in many countries of western Europe but has now been replaced by another set of concerns which fall under the heading of neo-liberalism (or "advanced liberalism").

The idea of the welfare state and the government of society has given way to a "post-welfarist regime of the social ... where the social is reconfigured as a series of 'quasi-markets' in the provision of services and expertise by a range of publicly funded, non-profit and private-for-profit, organizations and bodies " (Dean 1999: 173). There are several key developments within this overall picture. First, neo-liberalism is no longer concerned with the maintenance of the division between state and society. Neither are the public and private spheres distinct: the market is coeval with society. Society is viewed more as a "source of energies consequent upon autonomous action and association, it is at best something to be facilitated and cultivated rather than a problematic and unstable domain to be regulated" (Dean 1999: 152). But there is another significant element to all this. The national state and society no longer have to be united. "*National* government can govern without governing society" (Dean 1999: 172, emphasis added). This implies that national government is concerned with other things, particularly the security of mechanisms of social and economic government itself. Neo-liberalism has bypassed society and it governs "without governing society" (Rose 1999: 88). Government is less and less about governing society and more and more about regulating itself, what Dean (1999: 174) calls the "governmentalization of government." There is also another way that we can interpret the statement that national government does not govern society. It suggests, although the idea is not developed in Dean's work, that society is freed from the nation-state and can be considered to be post- or trans-national. In much the same way that Albrow (1998a) talks of the liberation of society from the nation-state, Dean's work can be read as contributing to the idea that society has become detached from its national moorings.

In summary, we can say that the importance of the governmentality critique is that it presents society not as something natural and universal but as a response to a particular set of problems experienced in European societies in the modern period. Liberalism required order and stability but also a minimal amount of direct intervention. Social forces were recognized as potentially disruptive (to the economic process) and difficult to manage from outside. The preferred solutions were to nationalize the problem (contain it territorially) and create new forms of expertise by which society could become self-regulating. In this way society could remain relatively independent of the state and the risk of fracture and dissolution could be minimized. In contemporary Europe, welfarism has lost its appeal. The economic needs of neo-liberalism are different from the liberalism which proceeded it. Society no longer needs to be managed and organized for the greater good. Furthermore, society and nation do not require each other. In the post-communist world national security and solidarity are no longer the big issues they once were. The independence of the social is now seen as necessary for economic development. Society comprises a series of quasi-markets, and the freedom of society is coincident with that of the market and should be encouraged and facilitated not restricted and compromised.

Globalization and Society

Society is all too often seen as a residual element: that which remains after the more important categories of the state and nation, economic and business life, culture and identity, democracy and citizenship, the family and the individual have been accounted for. Society is frequently seen as that which nurtures and sustains these areas of activity, and in return is accorded a degree of protection. Similarly society is conceived as a realm of freedom and democracy vital to the enjoyment of citizenship and rights. The corollary of this is that the idea of society signifies inner cohesiveness, a relationship between parts: the very possibility for overcoming tension and division. Society may be divided, but it is a divided unity, a whole that may be subject to fragmentation but which can be put back together again by the judicious application of the appropriate remedy for social ills.

The reason why society evokes the ideas of totality and unity is that for a very long time it has been closely associated with the project of the nation-state. This association has provoked a reaction amongst some theorists, particularly those working in the field of globalization, amounting to a rejection of the continuing usefulness of the concept of society. For example, Urry (1999), in his attempt to develop a "sociology beyond societies" investigates the way that the social is being remade, not as society as such, but in terms of mobilities. Society implies fixity and order whereas in a globalizing world we need to look at networks, flows, and scapes. For Urry, society has outlived its usefulness (although he acknowledges the existence of "global civil society") and sociology will have to get by without its central concept.[22] He says of society, "whatever its value in the past, it will not in the future be especially relevant as the organising concept of sociological analysis" (Urry 1999: 1). We have entered a "post-societal phase." Urry is not alone in believing that society, because of its strong association with the study of national societies, has had its day. The rejection of the idea of society is equally explicit in the following formulation. "A central implication of the concept of globalization is that we must now embark on the project of understanding social life without the comforting term 'society'" (Featherstone and Lash 1995).

As has already been stated at various points, one purpose of this chapter is to defend the idea of society and to argue for its continuing usefulness under conditions of globalization. We should note that not all sociologists of globalization consign society to the conceptual dustbin. There are a great variety of positions on globalization and society, many of which argue for its continued centrality. We have already seen how the idea of global or cosmopolitan civil society has accompanied some strains of the globalization thesis, and tend to be associated with the idea of a world state or an internationalized state. The idea of world society (the world as a single place) is of course associated with the globalization theorists, particularly the work of Robertson whose thesis we examined in chapter 2. At the same time other sociologists of globalization dispute the existence of a world society. As we have already seen this is the position of Mann, and is the interpretation favored by Urry, who sees globalization as a series of incomplete processes. However, any discussion of the existence or likelihood of global, world or transnational society is only relevant in the context of this chapter if it furthers our understanding of European society.

The work of Beck (2000) is illustrative. For Beck the idea of global society – our consciousness that the world we live in is one place – is by its very nature a society without a state. When Beck talks about world society he is thinking about the transnational and post-national interconnectedness of the world, not some overarching global form of societal structure. In other words, world society is an inevitability in a world which is no longer structured exclusively around an international system of nation-states. World society does not replace the world system of nation-states, but exists alongside it. The two exist in a relationship of tension. "It is the resulting blockages, breakdowns and unresolved questions which give this situation its political charge" (Beck 2000: 104). He goes on to say:

> The unity of state, society and individual underpinning the first [industrial] modernity is in the course of dissolution. World society does *not* mean world state society or world economy society; it means a *non-state*

society, a social aggregate for which territorial state guarantees of order, as well as the rules of publicly legitimated politics, lose their binding character. (Beck 2000: 102)

The key to understanding society, as was suggested by Delanty earlier in the chapter, is to see it as referring to a non-systemic and dissaggregated whole. Beck's work contributes to the defence of society in this sense. Beck's world society is characterized by diversity without unity. Any absence of integration or fixity should not be taken to mean that nothing below the level of the global or the transnational has any importance. Again, the idea of world society should not be equated with a world without nation-states or other units of political or territorial organization. What globalization does emphasize is the reduced importance of geographical proximity in the creation of social ties. In this context Beck points to the possibility inherent in electronic media to mobilize people and allow them to constitute political movements across frontiers in a way which responds more to shared interests than to networks of kinship or tradition. Beck's work suggests we can employ the term society to refer to something other than a unified and self-reproducing entity, and that society can be thought in a way which does not make it dependent upon the idea of the nation-state.

The work of Albrow, Appadurai, and Soysal also allows us to see the way in which globalization produces societies characterized by on the one hand freedom from the nation-state, and on the other fragmentation and disunity. Albrow (1996: 77) questions the assumption that state, society, and the individual "need to exist in an indissoluble bond and that anything less denotes a crisis." Like Beck, Albrow sees this as a modernist assumption. Albow's reading of the impact of globalization on the nation-state leads him to the view that the social is now free from the constraints of modernity. In the nation-state society social relationships were functions of "business, contract, political power, delegation, marriage and so on" (Albrow 1996: 164). The social – the free-play of human association and search for experiences and innovation – was circumscribed by the organizational structure and imperatives of national societies. In others words, nation-states were able to mould and shape their societies, to restrict their interactions with other societies: to put a lid on the inquisitiveness and search for novelty and innovation of which the social is capable. In contrast, the social has now been released by the impact of globalization. In respect of the nation-state the social is "autogenous" – self-generating and independent – and, freed from its constraints, has generated an increasing amount of non-national and transnational activities. "Globalization sets up new poles of attraction for social relations, which threaten older forms of social cohesion" (Albrow 1996: 213).

As evidenced by the earlier quotation, Beck holds that one of the consequences of globalization is that the nation-state can no longer monopolize the regulation and legitimization of public politics. The social cannot be domesticated and neatly parcelled into a unified public space determined by political or economic necessities. The idea that society is something which cannot be contained nor easily be unified or homogenized suggests that we should explore the possibility that it consists of a plurality of discontinuous and fragmented public spaces. Society as diversity without unity. At the start of this chapter we looked at the work of Delanty and Grundmann and their ideas about how European society comprised a series of public spaces. What we need to do now is to think again about the idea of public spheres in combination with insights from thinkers who are working with the globalization problematic.

Appadurai (1996) concurs with the view that under conditions of globalization the nation-state has a diminished claim over the allegiances and imagination of its citizens. The networks and flows of globalization exist as a resource through which individuals can imagine new relationships and membership in new communities. Appadurai's ideas add a global dimension to the suggestion put forward by Delanty that in a European "knowledge society" the state no longer has the monopoly of legitimized expertise. Public disputes are frequently engendered by competing claims to knowledge, as with the case of BSE or the environmental impact of a new motorway. Delanty sees the emergence of multiple democratic spaces of contestation and dissent as the public claim new rights to mediate in "official" disputes. What is not evident from Delanty's work is why such publics should have a European rather than a national basis. Appadurai's work points to the potential of new media forms to create transnational publics. Electronic media provide access to non-national communities, and the consumption of the mass media encourages the acquisition of agency (Appaduarai 1996: 7). Collective media consumption can create transnational sodalities which are potentially communities "capable of moving from shared imagination to collective action" (Appaduarai 1996: 8).[23] Thus, media consumption is empowering in two senses. First, it helps forge collective agency. Second, it encourages the formulation of publics that are not constrained, divided, and weakened by national borders.

Soysal (1997: 518–19) shows how emergent public spaces are both constituted transnationally and contribute to dissensus and disharmony, processes which work to "disrupt national constellations." In her work on the nature of claims making by Islamic groups in Europe she advances the idea that the practice of citizenship is increasingly based on global rather than national norms (see also Soysal 1994). Citizenship rights have been recast as human rights and transformed by the advent of global personhood rights. "In the post-war era, the rationalized category of personhood, and its canonized international language "Human Rights," has become an imperative in justifying rights and demands for rights, even those of non-nationals in national politics"(Soysal 1997: 512). In other words, the rights available to citizens and non-citizens living in a particular country are increasingly determined not by arbitrary national preferences but by global norms, initiated and monitored by international agencies such as the UN.

Those seeking to claim rights do so in the public sphere. But these public spheres are not necessarily contained within national boundaries: they frequently display a trans-national dimension and solidarities are shaped beyond national jurisdictions. Groups involved in claims-making and the appropriation of collective and individual rights, such as the Islamic groups in Soysal's study, operate in and through a great diversity of public spaces, some of them national and others transnational. They "draw upon host-country and world-level repertoires for making claims, and traverse and bridge a diverse set of public places" (Soysal 1997: 511). By constructing transnational communities and exercising their universal human right to collective identity they diversify and reconfigure the public spheres in which they and other groups operate.

One product of this dynamic is a series of public spheres which do not conform to the traditional notions of contestation and plurality. The nation-state version of citizenship presumes a high degree of societal cohesion and that contestation in public spaces should not threaten this nationally induced solidarity. Soysal points out (1997: 518) that the rights claimed by Islamic migrants to Europe do not necessarily conform to this pattern. They "infuse the public realm with 'competing moral claims' and 'inharmonious' difference" and often "appear as a threat to civil society."[24] Soysal emphasizes that the public sphere should be conceived as a place characterized by conflicts and incoherent outcomes. To understand claims making in contemporary Europe we should focus not on consensus building but on contestation (Soysal 1997: 526). This does not mean that interaction in the multiplicity of Europe's public spaces is not possible. What it does mean is that the public spaces most suited to the task of forging understandings and alliances between groups whose traditions are diverse and whose locations are geographically fragmented and dispersed are those spaces which are inclusive, open and responsive to mobility rather than closed, exclusive and commanded by the nation-state (see Rumford 2001b).

Conclusion

In this chapter we have surveyed a variety of perspectives on the nature of contemporary society in general and considered the extent to which these are applicable to an understanding of European society. The range of approaches to the question of what kind of society exists in Europe is truly panoramic. At one pole there are those who argue for the non-existence of society, European or otherwise, although opinion is deeply divided as to the basis on which such a claim can be made. At the other pole there exists a minority who hold to the notion of a European society, a claim normally tempered with the clause "in the making." That adherents to this position are often representatives of the European Commission should not come as too much of a surprise. However, the heyday of the Commission notion of a "European model of society" has long passed and its chief advocate, former Commission President Jacques Delors, now aligns himself with the civil society thesis in preference to the epochal rhetoric of giving birth to a new form of society (Delors 1999). The move may be led more by strategic than theoretical considerations. In Delors' vision the European Union is now positioned as an intermediary between the conflicting demands of nation-state and the global. Under such conditions the development of European civil society provides a means to strike the right balance between collective and individual responsibility, between the "social" and the market. More importantly, it is through civil society that the better functioning of the European Union can be ensured.

This example highlights a weakness common to many accounts of civil society: that its purpose is the creation of a more unified and inclusive polity. The notion of civil society, sacrosanct to many social scientists, finds no place in our political sociology of European integration. There are two important sets of reasons for rejecting the claims of the civil society argument. First, as outlined in the previous section it prevents us from apprehending the nature of European public spheres, and the way in which they facilitate dissensus and encourage public contestations which are irreconcilable at the level of the nation-state. Second, the regnant model emphasizes civil society's role in inculcating freedom, democracy, and progressive change but ignores its complicity in forms of rule and domination. In keeping with this interpretation the state is accorded the role of sponsor and protector, and state and civil society work in tandem and lay the foundations for ever deeper democracy. In Walzer's (1995b: 24) memorable formulation, only a democratic state can create a democratic civil society and vice versa.

One argument developed throughout this chapter is that society is a more serviceable concept that the excessively liberal notion of civil society, but only when we have divested it of any connotations with integrated wholes and functional unities frequently associated with the societies contained within nation-states. Society as a series of non-integrated and contested public spaces is necessarily a postnational or transnational idea emerging from some, not all, of the work falling into the category of the sociology of globalization. It was suggested that this idea of transnational society should be distinguished clearly from both global society and global civil society models on the one hand, and the idea of a unified and cohesive European public space on the other.

If European society can be characterized as transnational it is in the sense that it is increasingly divorced from the nation-state. Furthermore, this nascent European society should be thought of as a series of spaces where multiple forms of rule and domination are exercised as much as a realm where oppositional sentiments and enactments of resistance find expression. When we say that Europe society is characterized by fragmentation and disunity we refer not to an entity which has begun to unravel but which can be put back together with the right social policies (what we might term the "humpty-dumpty" understanding of society). Such a society would be characterized by social cleavages (the verb to cleave meaning both to divide and to unite). European society is in fact characterized by division without unity. It is constituted by the forces of transnational fragmentation acting on its nation-state underpinnings, and by the transformatory impact of non-consensual social fissures which recognize no national limits.

This sketch of European society needs to be fleshed out and substantiated. This is a task which will be carried out in the rest of the book. In the following chapter we examine the closely related topics of social exclusion and citizenship. We have already seen how Soysal's work suggests the forms which citizenship takes under conditions of globalization are not the same as those associated with the nation-state. Also, the nature and extent of social exclusion is heavily dependent upon the definition and understanding of society which is being employed. We will further explore the theme of the fragmentation and disunity of European society in our examination of the autonomized region (chapter 6), the impact of globalization on European peripheries (chapter 7), and EU democratic identity (chapter 8).

5 Unemployment, Social Exclusion, and Citizenship

Social Unity and Belonging

Not only does the sociology of "nationally sequestered societies" treat society and the nation-state as coterminous, it also presumes an underlying unity, a social whole which can resist (or is constituted by) divisive social cleavages which may work to undermine it. Rex (1999: vii) makes the point that in the main, "political sociology in the 50s and 60s dealt with the structure of national societies seen as complexes of functionally related institutions or as the product of class and status conflict." In other words, society was seen as a purposive, structured and integrated order, patterned not necessarily according to a grand design, but in accordance with a consensus formed through the interaction of leading actors, or on the basis of the implementation of pragmatic measures to counter threats and instabilities. The most important division in modern societies was seen to be class, and the antagonism between workers and owners of capital structured social, political and economic life in western societies and, at times, threatened its continued existence. The stability of society depended upon the successful management and containment of class conflict. As Albrow (2001) points out:

> [T]he divide between owners of capital and propertyless workers extended into every life-sphere, and through every collectivity. The welfare state, the New Deal, the Great Society were all responses to that threat. All involved the management of society to greater national ends, the enlistment of citizens in return for broadly conceived rights of security, welfare, education and health.

In such ways, divisions and internal ruptures are made amenable to domestication: they are fractures within a greater whole, cleavages which are equally capable of rending asunder and reuniting. Societies may come apart, or be subject to external forces with the potential to tear them apart, but have the capability to put themselves in good order by applying the balm of social justice, a liberal dose of one-nation rhetoric, or the nationalistic invocation of an external threat.

In the modern age one of the roles of sociology was to identify these cleavages and to inform social policy remedies. But what if, under conditions of globalization, society is freed from its territorial obligations and begins to resemble a footloose amalgamation of public spaces, social groups, and institutions? What type of sociology is appropriate to a European society characterized by division without unity? How can the transformatory potential of transnational social fissures be made amenable to policy solutions? These questions are particularly acute in relation to the problem of unemployment which, in its contemporary form, is often recast as the problem of social exclusion. The term social exclusion itself is significant, simultaneously signalling both the possibility of social division and the possibility of maintaining mastery over the forces playing on national societies. The idea of social exclusion is indicative of the reluctance of modernist social science to come to terms with the nature of contemporary European society, which increasingly takes the form of a multiplicity of fragmented and autonomous globalized public spheres formed by new modes of contestation, claims-making, and collective action. On this reading, the deployment of the idea of social exclusion is an attempt to resist the idea of a vagabond society freed from the (nation-) state, and a desire to reanimate the feasibility of institutionalized social cleavage.

It is also significant that the issue of social exclusion is closely associated with citizenship, the changing nature of which under conditions of globalization has also drawn the attention of sociologists to the contingent unity of state and society. The idea of social exclusion conjures up Marshallian citizenship norms and aims to explain the problems of nation-state society in terms of the shortcomings of government policy. Under conditions of modernity the number one social problem was the threat of internal (class based) revolution. The solution was the institutionalization of this conflict through the extension of representative democracy and social partnerships, and the advent of mechanisms of social inclusion – citizenship and the welfare state. Today, citizenship is released from its dependence upon membership in a national state. Citizenship now belongs to a realm of universal rights and the valorization of difference. Following Soysal (1994) we can talk of postnational rather than national citizenship. Postnational citizenship points not to formal inclusion in a national state but the decreasing correspondence between national membership and access to rights and benefits. Membership in a nation-state and the benefits and status which goes with it are supplemented by the global institutionalization of human rights regimes based on the universalization of personhood rights. Citizenship can now originate beyond the nation-state; one can be a citizen of the EU, for example. Citizenship once provided the bonds of a cohesive social order. Under conditions of globalization citizenship is an index of the extent to which societies need to accommodate difference rather than institutionalized social cleavage.

We must see this change in relation to wider shifts in the role of the nation-state. Following Albrow (2001) we can say that in modernity the nation-state had responsibility for the management of all the potential sites of cleavage: society, the economy, culture, nation. Now the social, economic, and politics spheres have been de-coupled; they no longer coincide. The changing nature of citizenship is one indictor of the ways in which the globe has become the frame of reference for understanding social change and the dynamics of collective organization. Within such a frame social exclusion has to be rethought. It is not sufficient to assume that individuals operate within circuits of inclusion and exclusion limited by the boundaries of nation-states. At the same time as citizenship forged national unity it also divided other communities – ethnic, religious, linguistic – from themselves, resulting in the creation of minorities within nation-states. Like cleavages, minorities can only exist within a nationally embedded social structure.

Unemployment and Social Exclusion

To inquire into the problem of unemployment in the EU is to lift the lid on any number of important issues, some to do with the way in which the EU renders internal problems amenable to policy solutions and others concerned with questions of a more sociological nature, such as the shifting meaning of employment, and the relationship between joblessness and social exclusion. Even the incontrovertible fact that unemployment is high, standing at 8.1 percent in December 2000[1] (European Commission 2001b), invites contending explanations. To take just two examples, Europe is experiencing a form of "jobless growth" in which high employment is no longer necessary for economic development, or suffering from "labor market rigidities" which prevent sufficient new jobs from being created.

As well as being the subject of differing interpretations, the issue of mass unemployment is a highly charged political issue. There are those who see unemployment as a direct consequence of the demise of the welfarist state and proof that in the absence of adequate regulation market forces do not offer adequate social protection. On the other hand, the present high levels of unemployment have been interpreted as conclusive proof that the European economy needs less regulation. On this reading the EU is hamstrung by unnecessarily restrictive employment regulations (such as the minimum wage) which prevent the creation of new jobs. The situation is made more complex still by the fact that the problem of unemployment is not uniform across Europe and there are significant regional and national disparities. This raises the question of to what extent the problem of unemployment remains a national one rather than a European one. After all, it is member states rather than the EU who are responsible for developing and implementing employment policies, and welfare provision is still a national affair. Markoff (1999: 31) reminds us that a key feature of the EU is that in the field of social welfare policy "the formal role of supranational institutions is very limited by virtue of the explicit decision to keep social welfare at the state level and not construct a Eurowelfare state."

There is a raft of other issues occasioned by an inquiry into the problem of unemployment. Some of the most important of these center on what has become known as growing social exclusion. The idea of social exclusion, rather than being simply a synonym for unemployment, points to much wider and considerably more profound forms of disadvantage.

> Social exclusion . . . is not the same as poverty. The majority of those who are poor at any one time would not be ranked amongst the excluded. Exclusion contrasts with being "poor," "deprived," or "on a low income" in several ways. It is not a matter of . . . having fewer resources – but of not sharing in opportunities that the majority have . . . The deprived are losers but the excluded do not even take part in the game. (Giddens 2000: 105)

The idea of social exclusion is an attempt to indicate the broader social impact of unemployment, an increase in the long-term unemployed and the existence of an "underclass." The use of the term suggests that the problem of unemployment is much wider and more far reaching than can be captured by the more straightforward ideas associated with a lack of job prospects and inadequate policy responses to a surplus labor supply. It is also indicative of a society in which the gap between rich and poor, "haves and have-nots," has grown wider. It also points to changes in the social and class composition of national societies which now exhibit a much larger middle class, a diverse ethnic make-up, and where traditional industrial sectors and low-skilled jobs are in decline. Social exclusion is perhaps better thought of as a "multi-dimensional process, in which various forms of exclusion are combined: participation in decision making and political process, access to employment and material resources, and integration into common cultural processes" (Madanipour et al., quoted in Byrne 1999: 2).

There is a strong theme in the literature connecting unemployment, social exclusion and citizenship. Some commentators believe that the unemployed or low paid are increasingly marginalized from many forms of social participation, including full citizenship, and that this leads inexorably to a diminution of democracy. Beck (2000) is one who holds that that social exclusion can undermine democracy. His argument that contemporary capitalism is premised on jobless growth (productivity which does not result in the creation of extra employment) which leads to a growing underclass excluded from citizenship, rests on two assumptions: that employment is the key to citizenship, and that citizenship can only be granted by the nation-state. These assumptions are challenged by much current thinking about globalization, and it is becoming common for citizenship rights to be seen as tied neither to employment status nor national belonging but the product of transnational global and universal rights regimes.

However, we need to be aware that when globalization is normally considered in relation to unemployment it is in the context of the idea that "capital is global, labor local," in other words that the equilibrium between capital and labor which was evident in the postwar consensus and the (national) welfare state has gone, leading to an increasing asymmetry in industrial relations. There are good reasons why this not the way in which we should view globalization and unemployment. For one thing, it is an example of the global/local dichotomy criticized in chapter 2. In addition, it fails to recognize the global dimension to labor markets that should be at the heart of our political sociology approach to unemployment in contemporary Europe. The line taken in this chapter is that to begin to understand why high unemployment should be the basis of such a diverse range of explanations and interpretations, and at the same time prove so resistant to policy solutions, we need to locate unemployment within a wider field of study which encompasses the changing nature of the welfare state, new forms of citizenship, and the relation between employment and industrial competitiveness.

The major sociological perspectives that inform this book allow for very different approaches to understanding unemployment, social exclusion, and citizenship. The group of theories coalescing around the post-industrialist banner see unemployment as a structural consequence of "disorganized capitalism," in which productive economic activity has been delegated to the developing world, while western economies are increasingly dominated by service industries. The theory of reflexive modernity developed by Lash (1994) and Beck (1994) treads this path, and for Beck (2000) European capitalism is capitalism without jobs. Such ideas are frequently supported by strong sociological arguments but tend to be rather productivist in their orientation, seeing high unemployment as being the product of neo-liberal policy preferences and/or the consequence of the decline of manufacturing industry and the concomitant failure of European governments to address the issue.

Governmentality provides yet another important perspective on unemployment and highlights the way in which the problem is now conceived in terms of the lack of competitiveness of the European work force *vis-à-vis* her competitors, rather than as a problem caused by lack of employment opportunities *per se*. Unemployment is acted upon in the name of enhancing (national) competitiveness rather than for the sake of the social good. A corollary of this is that the problem is individualized: the unemployed are relabelled as "job seekers." The individual is recast as an "entrepreneur of the self," investing in his or her own economic capital and taking responsibility for the management of his or her career. In short, the governmentality theorists suggest that we examine the ways in which the problem of unemployment has been reworked within the particular form of economic governance that characterizes contemporary Europe.

In chapter 3 we explored the idea of a European state and concluded that the question of what form of state exists in the EU was better posed in terms of which type of rule is consistent with the harmonization of European economic, political, and cultural space. It follows that there is no European state as such, either at the national or the supranational level, if by the state we mean "the organization of practices and enforcement of a public interest or good by some people on others" (Albrow 1999: 117). In present day Europe it would be a difficult task to identify a public interest or a public good: such a task presumes a high level of social cohesion and the hierarchical and unified means by which interests can be determined. Also, the nature of the public sphere has changed. It is more appropriate to talk of a plurality of public spheres, interests and goods, and a multiplicity of agencies who would have an interest in the organization and enforcement of these. This analysis accords with the consideration of European society undertaken in chapter 4, which emphasized the multiple, fragmented, and contradictory nature of European public spaces. Against this background it is not surprising that the problem of unemployment has ceased to be dealt with in the public interest and has been recast and individualized in accordance with the priorities of the neo-liberal regime of economic government that prevails in most of (although not all) contemporary Europe.

The idea of globalization, when invoked in connection with unemployment in Europe, tends to be very much the narrow economistic variant criticized in chapter 2. In this sense, globalization is seen as a threat to full employment and the cause of fundamental economic restructuring leading to social instability. Globalization either causes polarization (as in the ideas associated with globalized rich and localized poor, global cities and local peripheries), or necessitates an increase in "local" protection to either offset the worst effects of, or to mitigate against, the homogenizing tendencies of globalization. As we have seen this is a very narrow and restrictive interpretation of globalization. A more nuanced sociological approach completely recasts the relationship between the global and local and permits an understanding of the increasing fluidity of previously stable social, political and economic hierarchies which play such an important role in determining patterns of unemployment in the contemporary EU. It also forms the basis for a substantial critique of the idea of social exclusion, taking as its starting point the idea that democratic participation is no longer exclusively based on the model of the nation-state.

The concept of social exclusion raises a number of key issues for sociological study. These include, not unsurprisingly, the nature of the social to which the term refers and the type of exclusion invoked. The former is a significant issue in a globalized world in which society and the nation-state are not necessarily coterminous. The latter is the focus of considerable attention in the literature as there are many possible bases of exclusion: geographical, ethnic, gendered, generational. Social exclusions proliferate.

> The pattern of social exclusion has been modified by the differential engagement of social classes, men and women, migrants and ethnic groups, and those at different stages of the life course, in the redistribution of income, wealth and power which has accompanied changes in European capitalism. (Hudson and Williams 1999: 4)

Social exclusion is no longer a simple affair which can be equated with the formation of an underclass consequent upon long-term unemployment. The situation is particularly complex when different forms of exclusion are combined and concentrated in particular localities such as inner cities. Many accounts emphasize a different dimension of exclusion, and the debate extends to the nature of citizenship in postindustrial economies and the way in which the social bonds of the nation are coming under threat from the phenomenon of "jobless growth."

Jobless Growth

The appropriate entry point into this discussion is the debate about the nature and causes of unemployment in contemporary Europe. Current neo-liberal orthodoxy holds that European labor markets are insufficiently flexible and that this accounts for high levels of unemployment. European competitiveness is the goal and the rigidity of the labor markets is the biggest barrier to achieving this. According to UNICE, the European employers' federation, Europe's economy is held back by high non-wage costs, short working hours, regulatory barriers, and large and costly public sectors.[2] According to UNICE, in Europe non-wage costs add 80 percent to total wage costs, compared to less than 40 percent in the US (*Financial Times* February 13, 1998). However, there are a multitude of meanings attached to the term "labor-market flexibility," and while it "can be associated with the development of progressive work norms in one context, it can mean poverty, exploitation, and insecurity in another" (Peck 1995: 158–9). In other words, in addition to designating changes in employment relations it is frequently employed as a euphemism for job insecurity, short-term contracts, and the eclipse of collective bargaining. Despite rising to prominence in the popular imagination as a useful designation for a perceived shift in the balance of industrial relations, the dynamics of labor-market flexibility are uncertain.[3] Certainly, increasing labor market flexibility has not solved the problem of unemployment. As Standing (1997: 205) points out:

> Since the early 1980s, the conventional view has been that Western European labour markets have been 'rigid' and that the answer to unemployment is to make labour markets more 'flexible'. For a decade and a half, governments have been introducing measures to achieve that, and there can be no doubt whatsoever that on any conventional definition labour markets across Europe are much more flexible than in 1980. Yet unemployment is much higher.

The European Jobs Summit held in November 1997 was notable for the Commission's exaggerated claims for what could be achieved in a relatively short space of time. The Santer Commission unveiled guidelines which they claimed could create up to 12 million jobs within five years (*European Voice*, October 2, 1997). The Commission's proposals were criticized less for being impractical but because they embraced corporatism and the need to shift the burden of taxation away from workers. The Commission's analysis of the problems underlying mass unemployment throughout the EU were described as "feeble" by *The Economist* (October 3, 1997), which identified the root causes as labor market rigidities and over-generous welfare benefits. Neo-liberal discourse on unemployment devotes significant resources to dismissing the idea that a pan-European unemployment-reduction strategy could be feasible. When consideration is given to EU attempts to reduce unemployment much is made of the existence of major national variations in labor market dynamics, welfare regimes and government subsidies to industry. Such variation is thought to render adequate harmonization measures both impossible and undesirable.

Neo-liberal solutions are based around the need to increase labor market flexibility and scale-down the welfare state. In the case of the "Jobs Summit" the Commission was further criticized for opposing the opportunities which deregulation would provide. For *The Economist* the solution was straightforward: "continental Europeans need simply follow America and Britain, where unemployment has tumbled, thanks to deregulation and cuts in taxes, public spending and welfare benefits" (*The Economist*, October 3, 1997). France was singled out for criticism for regressive policies and for its bias towards the needs of labor in its pursuit of a solution to high levels of unemployment. But since this time France has managed a substantial reduction in unemployment levels (from 10.5 percent to 8.8 percent between December 1999 and December 2000). In March 2001 it was announced that the interventionist polices of the Socialist-led French government had managed to reduce unemployment by 1 million since taking office not much more than 3 years previously (*Financial Times*, March 1, 2001).

The idea of "jobless growth," as developed by Beck (2000), aims to explain unemployment as a structural consequence of neo-liberal policy preferences in contemporary Europe. Beck posits a European economy characterized by a form of dynamic growth that does not create employment.[4] This in turn creates an ever-growing gap between the "haves and have-nots" and the "winners and losers" of globalization: "the new rich no longer 'need' the new poor." Moreover, outside of a national setting redistribution of wealth becomes unthinkable and "there is no framework in which this overarching conflict could be represented and regulated" (Beck 2000: 7). The idea of "jobless growth" also contributes to the debate on social exclusion by drawing attention to the way in which the historical link between market economy, welfare state, and democracy is becoming unravelled. The argument is summarized by Beck in the following terms. "Capitalism is doing away with work. Unemployment is no longer a marginal fate: it affects everyone potentially, as well as the democratic way of life" (Beck 2000: 58). We will explore the relationship between unemployment and democracy and what Beck calls the "future of democracy beyond the work society" in a moment, but first we must look at Beck's argument for why "capitalism is doing away with work."

The main reason he offers is that workers are no longer "fully employed in the classical sense of the term." One consequence of the greater flexibility demanded of the labor markets in some EU countries, Britain for example, is that the number of people in full time employment has dropped drastically, from above 80 percent to one third in the last 20 years (Beck 2000: 58–9). Part-time work, short-term contracts, and unemployment have risen, as has employment insecurity and the "hidden reserves of labor." What has happened argues Beck is that unemployment has been "redistributed" and official figures disguise the true extent of the problem. Less people work full-time on secure contracts, more people work part-time, job share, or secure only short-term contracts. The result is that increasing numbers of people occupy the category of neither unemployed nor income secure. Where jobs are created they tend to be low-paid, unskilled jobs which transform the unemployment figures but do nothing to prevent poverty.[5] The impact of jobless growth is not merely experienced at the level of mass unemployment. It is also a problem which strikes at the heart of European democracies: the demise of the work society breaks down the "labor democracy" foundations of European societies. The foundations of democracy come under threat when the state can no longer guarantee a correspondence between economic growth, political participation, and social welfare. Beck asks, just how much poverty can a democracy tolerate? (2000: 153).

Beck raises some important issues concerning the way in which high unemployment appears to erode the foundations of European democracy. However, there are problems associated with the idea of "jobless growth." By way of a criticism we might want to point out that the type of jobless growth described by Beck is prevalent in only a few EU countries, if at all. While characteristic of, say, the UK and the Netherlands, it is more commonly associated with the situation in the US and does not fit with the experience of many European countries. The power of the image constructed by "jobless growth" rests very heavily on the idea that European societies are no longer capable of producing full-time jobs. While the growth in part-time and short-time working is clearly an issue, so is the extent to which the growth of the potential labor force offsets attempts at job creation. The idea of jobless growth is quite weak, sociologically speaking, and does not for example, take into account the ways in which the idea of full employment has changed over the past 30 years or so, consequent upon the entry of women into the labor force.[6] Full employment today means something different to what it meant 20 or 30 years ago. These ideas are developed in the work of Esping-Anderson (1999) whose work will be discussed more fully later in the chapter.

A consideration of the idea of social exclusion is important because it forces us to think about the nature of the social from which sections of the population are excluded. This opens up a whole range of important issues for a political sociology of the EU. For example, Beck's idea that social exclusion can compromise democracy would appear to be based on two assumptions. First, that employment is the royal route to citizenship, and second, that the only meaningful form of citizenship is that offered by nation-states. The first assumption is contradicted by the fact that while workers rights have diminished, at the same time other dimensions of citizenship rights have been enhanced. Full and active participation in society is no longer achieved only through full employment status. Citizenship is increasingly achieved via consumption (Urry 1999). Dean (1999: 161) notes that the unemployed are increasingly expected to act as consumers (of employment services) before becoming workers. The second assumption fails to take into account the phenomenon of post-national citizenship. People participate in global democratic and political networks without necessarily being citizens of a given nation-state. As Soysal points out, in European countries the link between national identity and citizenship rights has been eroded, and there exist many important circuits of inclusion and networks of democratic participation which bypass the nation-state.

The association between employment, participation, and citizenship runs through much sociological writing on the subject of social exclusion and has its origins in the work of Marshall in the 1950s and '60s. Marshall's account was premised on the observation that a central tension under capitalism is the need to reconcile economic inequality with the horizontal equality that citizenship bestows. For Marshall citizenship had three dimensions, civil, political, and social. In Britain these developed over a long period of time. The eighteenth century witnessed the advent of civil rights – access to legal procedures, freedom of speech and such like. In the nineteenth century political rights emerged as a consequence of working-class struggles for participation in parliamentary democracy. These rights comprised universal male suffrage, secret ballots, and popular political parties. The twentieth century saw the arrival of social rights: claims to welfare, unemployment, and sickness benefits (Turner 1992). For Marshall, citizenship is an unfolding process which progressively consolidates a society which is founded on a fundamental contradiction: that between formal equality and an economically derived class hierarchy. "If citizenship is a principle of equality, class, by contrast, is a system of inequality anchored in property, education, and the structure of the national economy" (Held 1989: 190). Citizenship on this model is about belonging, participation and inclusion, it is a function of rights and responsibilities. But it is also very much about *national* belonging within a system of obligations and benefits which stop at the nation's borders. It is also about ensuring a national balance between the benefits accruing from class position and the advantages conferred by citizenship. We will further consider the changing relationship between citizenship and social exclusion later in the chapter.

At the beginning of the chapter it was emphasized that there is considerable debate about the "facts" of unemployment. Are participation rates high? Has unemployment been "redistributed" so as to distort the figures? What are the reasons for Europe's inability to tackle the problem of unemployment? Labor market rigidities? Inadequate policy solutions? In addressing these questions it has emerged that contemporary Europe has both high unemployment and high participation rates, and the pursuit of competitiveness is driving wages down and bringing about new patterns of polarization and inequality. Two further issues suggest themselves. One is the extent to which the problems associated with unemployment and inequality remain national rather than European issues. The other surrounds the extent to which the idea of social exclusion dominates our understanding of disadvantage, and other forms of poverty and inequality are marginalized from EU studies. We will turn to this second issue later in the chapter. To deal with the first issue we must examine the role of the welfare state in European countries.

Welfare Regimes

The European Union's own account of the problem of persistent high unemployment, described as "the main economic problem facing the EU" (European Commission 1999b: 35), is interesting inasmuch as it avoids monocausal explanations and incorporates an awareness of the wider social ramifications of unemployment. Employment is seen as a key element of competitiveness, which in turn is the route to economic growth. At the same time it is acknowledged that economic growth by itself cannot provide the key to solving the problem of unemployment. However, as the need to enhance competitiveness dominates other considerations, the EU falls short of recommending policy-induced employment growth.

There are several aspects of the EU's account of unemployment and the labor market which are worthy of comment. First, unemployment has risen rapidly during downturns in the economy but employment growth has not been sustained during recovery periods. Second, unemployment is rising at the same time as employment is also increasing. "Over the period 1987 to 1997, employment in the EU increased by 5 million but this was not enough to keep pace with 7½ million new entrants into the labour market." The trend is confirmed by the recent *Second Cohesion Report* which states that employment in the EU rose by over 2 million during the 1990s "but this was not sufficient to significantly increase the employment rate" (European Commission 2001c), which remained at around 60 percent. The issue of labor market participation tends to be dealt with in one of two ways. Either as part of the debate on part-time and temporary work replacing "traditional" employment, or, in terms of wider social changes in the composition of the workforce (for example, the way in which women have entered the labor force). Third, wide disparities in unemployment are to be found within the EU. Regional disparities are more pronounced than national ones and within certain member states the gap continues to widen. Fourth, long-term unemployment can lead to social exclusion. The EU has been unable to mount a convincing challenge to the problem of unemployment despite any number of ambitious policy initiatives, but it is the absence of effective national solutions that continues to be the biggest factor in the failure to combat high unemployment. In addition, national variations in welfare regimes continue to exert a great influence upon the problem of unemployment. This latter insight is closely associated with Esping-Anderson to whose work will now turn.

Esping-Anderson (1999) places the rise of unemployment within the context of much higher (female) participation rates and a changing role for the welfare state. In the present neo-liberal climate full-employment and universal social protection would appear to be incompatible. The problem with the welfare state is that it "produces too much protection where flexibility is needed" (Esping-Anderson 1999: 3). However, it is a mistake to focus solely on the shortcomings of the welfare state. For Esping-Anderson (1999: 4) the root of the problem is to be found in "two 'malfunctioning' institutions: the labour market and the family." He positions the welfare state as one key element within a welfare regime which comprises the interaction between the labor market, the family and the welfare state. The advantage of this formulation is that it allows the study of different national welfare states from within the same frame, and avoids criticism that the analysis of the welfare state is geared towards "northern" norms. "Some regimes, in particular the liberal, Anglo-Saxon, are market biased; others, especially the Southern European . . . are powerfully familiaristic. And still others put the accent on state delivery of welfare" (Esping-Anderson 1999: 5). In other words, welfare regimes can take different forms. Some favor the market-led provision of welfare services, others rely on the family to service the workforce, yet another category prefers a universalistic state welfare system. Each combines a welfare state with other forms of provision to produce a nationally distinctive welfare regime.

Esping-Anderson is probably best known for his book *The Three Worlds of Welfare Capitalism* (Esping-Anderson 1990) in which he developed his three-fold typology of welfare regimes: liberal, conservative and social-democratic. The liberal model, centered mainly but not exclusively on the Anglo-Saxon world, promotes market solutions to social problems, conceives welfare narrowly, and seeks to restrict those who should benefit from state assistance. The social-democratic model, associated with Nordic countries, embraces universalism and egalitarianism. It is distinguished by a comprehensive provision of benefits, which are not dependent on prior personal contributions. The conservative model characterizes most of continental Europe. Its key feature is familialism (male breadwinner plus family as the source of welfare).

The social and economic landscape that prevailed when European welfare states were institutionlized during the 1960s and '70s no longer obtains. We now inhabit post-industrial societies without the familiar reference points of,

> an economy dominated by industrial production with a strong demand for low-skilled workers; a relatively homogenous and undifferentiated, predominately male labour force (the standard production worker); stable families with high fertility; and a female population devoted to housewifery. (Esping-Anderson 1999: 5)

Welfare regimes are undergoing change in the transition from welfare capitalism (and its association with social solidarity and democracy) to the fragmentation and differentiation characteristic of post-industrial society. Welfare capitalism "succeeded in unifying social citizenship, full employment, mass education, and well-functioning industrial relations systems" (Esping-Anderson 1999: 13). We might want to add that these welfare regimes all took national forms: the social problems identified and the solutions put forward were organized by and for nation-states.

The causes of unemployment today can be traced to several key factors: economic growth is less dramatic; there is a diminished need for unskilled workers; and, women have become part of the "clientele for a full employment commitment." On this latter point:

> there is mass unemployment because of an explosion in supply . . . the contemporary postindustrial job disease is not necessarily the result of rigidities, or 'Eurosclerosis'. The real problem is simply that Europe is comparatively less capable of managing the postindustrial family in general, and women's desire to work in particular. (Esping-Anderson 1999: 28)

This is in clear contrast with Beck's "jobless growth" scenario. Esping-Anderson rejects as oversimple the argument that the problem of unemployment in Europe is that the capacity to generate jobs has declined: "contrary to what is commonly believed, overall net job creation in the 1980s has not been uniformly inferior to the booming 1960s" (Esping-Anderson 1999: 101). Clearly there have been major changes in the industrial basis of European societies and (unskilled) job opportunities in manufacturing have dropped considerably. There has, however, been an expansion of the service sector (tertiarization) and present-day employment growth is at the level of professionals and semi-professionals.

In response to the question of why unemployment varies so much across Europe, Esping-Anderson (1999: 96) notes that all countries are situated in an environment dominated by "the new global economy, tertiarization, or by falling demand for low skilled workers." Yet countries like Austria and Norway manage to combine relatively low unemployment and low levels of poverty with relatively generous welfare state provision, while other countries suffer high rates of unemployment. In Britain for example, massive deregulation has not led to an employment performance comparable to that of the Netherlands or Denmark. To begin to understand why this is the case he argues, it is necessary to relate the broader global changes to what is happening within the family in different nation-states. "Most contemporary debate is so enamoured with huge processes that it forgets the household" (Esping-Anderson 1999: 97). In addition, national responses to these sweeping changes differ wildly, as do the ability of welfare institutions to respond to a new set of problems. "This means that being unemployed, a lone mother, or a mid-career yuppie will differ if one happens to be Danish, Italian or American."

For Esping-Anderson it is wrong to assume that the consolidation of the nuclear family under conditions of industrialization and modernization meant a loss of its welfare functions. The welfare state was committed to the provision of health care and income maintenance, but it "did not absorb the family caring burden" (Esping-Anderson 1999: 54). It was, and still is, uneconomical to substitute market services for family self-servicing. In other words, because of wage levels the family has no choice but to provide its own caring services. At the same time, with more women being part of the active workforce the welfare state can no longer assume their availability to perform these functions. On Esping-Anderson's analysis the problems that the welfare state faces come mainly from within national socieities: changes to the labor market and declining family stability. The economic successes of European nation-states in the post-war period – full employment and economic growth – were achieved in no small way as a result of a relatively capacious job market in which unskilled and low-skilled workers could find employment, high levels of productivity, and women accommodated in the role of housewife.

The welfare role of the household and the position of women in the labor market will vary from situation to situation and yet have a crucial determining role in shaping the overall national outcome. Going back to his tripartite model of welfare regimes Esping-Anderson (1999: 138) concludes that the conservative (continental) model exhibits a "strong female unemployment bias and low exit probabilities from unemployment." In addition, welfare responsibilities are delegated to families thereby reducing paid employment opportunities for women. The social democratic regime exhibits both flexible labor markets and universal welfare, and tends to be better at putting people to work, thereby encouraging the dual earner family model. The liberal model relies neither on familialism or welfare statism, and while this regime can have a positive impact in reducing female unemployment it is also characterized by greater employment "precarity, inequality and poverty" (Esping-Anderson 1999: 142).

For Esping-Anderson the family is the pivot between the welfare state and the employment market. Not only will different countries have a welfare regime which consists of a particular mixture of these three elements, but they will rely on different institutional approaches to managing the labor market, unemployment, and welfare benefits. Taken together, these factors explain how countries which face similar underlying economic circumstances – even countries that can be placed within the same broad welfare regime category – can produce such differing responses to the problem of unemployment. One strong conclusion that we might be tempted to draw from Esping-Anderson's study is that in a Europe dominated by globalization and European integration it is the national state, more precisely the difference between the traditions and practices of individual nation-states, which determine the degree of unemployment. But the EU level is absent from Esping-Anderson's study and he does not examine the impact of EU policy on national welfare regimes. Not only does this ignore a huge domain of policy-making it also gives a misleading idea of the autonomy of the European nation-state. While emphasizing the idiosyncratic response of each country to a common problem he takes no account of the ways that policy choices and labor market dynamics are increasingly shaped from beyond national borders. This tendency to treat individual countries as discrete actors whose welfare regimes do not interact with one another, accommodate supranational initiatives, benefit from EU regional development funds, or align themselves with EU employment initiatives, is compounded by an under-theorized notion of globalization as an homogenizing market influence.

Social Exclusion and Citizenship

Social exclusion is sometimes referred to as the European equivalent of the US preference for the term underclass (Procacci 1996: 2), but the idea that long-term unemployment, poverty, and cultural marginalization have produced an underclass in Britain and elsewhere in Europe features strongly in the literature. Generally, it is asserted that growing poverty and social dislocation, whether conceived in terms of the growth of an underclass or as social exclusion, undermines citizenship rights. For example, Procacci (1996) argues that the marginalization associated with poverty leads to people becoming detached from society in such a way as to question whether those excluded in this way are really citizens at all. More often than not the underclass is equated with non-citizens, guest workers and the like, who are excluded by not having access to citizen's rights (Crompton and Brown 1994). Competitive pressures on the labor market leads to the "tendency to draw ever sharper lines between citizens and resident non-citizens, denying the latter social protection and full access to opportunities for health, education, and other services" (Falk 2000). In fact this is a very inaccurate portrayal of the processes leading to social inclusion, and, equally importantly, a misleading depiction of the respective citizenship positions of nationals and non-nationals.

The weakness of the concept of underclass is that it deflects attention from the importance of widespread poverty and "reduces it to minorities for which we can propose targeted policies" (Procacci 1996: 5–6). It also posits a group outside of the social structure of society, which is therefore not linked to the processes that are shaping society as a whole. On this reckoning, "the poor find themselves outside the structure of social classes, separated not only from the other poor, but from society as such. They are therefore also 'outside' citizenship" (Procacci 1996: 9). The idea of social exclusion has its weaknesses too. It assumes a society divided against itself, its wholeness somehow destabilized. But by positioning the marginal and poor as excluded they become separated from the very processes that are polarizing society. "The excluded are thus separated not only from society but also from the processes which are responsible for their exclusion" (Procacci 1996: 12).

For Procacci the designation social exclusion has become popular with policy makers and politicians precisely because its masks the conflictual relations and social divisions inherent in society. If the poor are thought of as being excluded then the task becomes how to include them, a process couched in terms of collaboration and collective effort, and "bound to the realization of each individual's potential, instead of linking them to aims which go *beyond* the individual" (Procacci 1996: 12). In this way, the task of including the poor is not bound up in conflicts and struggles which pit one group against others, class struggle for example, but deals with social problems at the level of individual failure. It also effaces questions of inequality and social power and sets an agenda for political action in which the parameters for egalitarianism have been narrowed drastically. To remedy these deficiencies (which are deficiencies of social science as much as social policy) Procacci proposes that the link between poverty and citizenship issues be reestablished in order that a rigorous understanding of the nature of inequality, and the conflicts necessary to realize greater equality, can be appreciated.

Citizenship is itself founded upon a form of exclusion. Rights, benefits and obligations are extended to those who belong, while those who fall outside the group are denied access to the same. Citizenship in modern nation-states combines egalitarianism with exclusivity: nationals benefit in ways which non-nationals do not.

This model of citizenship has begun to change in the post-war period and several developments "have contributed to the expansion of membership beyond the boundaries of national collectivities" (Soysal 2000: 254). The advent of universal individual rights has enabled various actors including minorities, women, and children to claim new forms of rights alongside or instead of citizenship rights. One outcome has been that the gap between the rights accorded to citizens and non-citizens has begun to diminish. Soysal (2000: 257) summarizes these developments in the following terms.

National citizenship or a formal nationality is no longer a significant construction in terms of how it translates into certain rights and privileges, as attested by the status of postwar immigrants. Rights, participation, and representation in a polity are increasingly matters beyond the vocabulary of national citizenship. What we have is a trend towards a new model of membership anchored in deterritorialized notions of personal rights.

There are several points that we should note. First, we can no longer take for granted the idea that non-citizens and guestworkers are the most likely candidates for social exclusion. The circuits of inclusion and exclusion in modern societies are such that such a simplistic correlation cannot be sustained. Secondly, formal citizenship is only one source of rights and benefits: they accrue from diverse, non-national sources and often apply equally to citizens and non-citizens alike. Thirdly, under a regime of global personal rights territorial belonging is increasingly irrelevant. Citizenship rights cease to be an attribute of place and are accorded on the basis of humanity and human rights. "Universal personhood replaces nationhood; and universal human rights replaces national rights" (Soysal 2000: 258).

This is what Soysal designates as "postnational" citizenship. The individual eclipses the citizen, and a "new mode of membership, anchored in the universalistic rights of personhood, transgresses the national order of things" (Soysal 2000: 261). This is not to say that nation-states have been emasculated by these processes. "The material realization of individual rights and privileges is primarily organized by the nation-state, although the legitimacy for these rights now lies in a transnational order" (Soysal 1994: 143). At the same time the newer postnational model of citizenship transcends national borders and permits a plurality of membership in national and supranational polities. Non-citizens, especially those classified as permanent residents, enjoy many rights traditionally associated with citizens and presumed denied to non-citizens. Eligibility for social services and access to political rights (voting in local elections) and the labor market have blurred the distinction between citizen and non-citizen.

We can identify two sets of processes taking place simultaneously. There are a growing number of rights and entitlements granted to non-citizens independently of belonging in a nation-state (with the nation-state being responsible for the application of these rights). National welfare states are "incorporating foreigners into its system of privileges," at the same time as they work to "regulate immigration and exercise border controls as a fundamental expression of their sovereignty" (Soysal 1994: 8). Soysal further argues that these developments point to "a profound transformation in the institution of citizenship, both in its institutional logic and in the way it is legitimated"(1994: 139). It is not simply that the nation-state has developed a sense of obligation to its non-nationals. Postnational citizenship impinges on the nation-state through a range of international conventions and agreements which are sustained by international institutions and a transnational community. The international rules pertaining to the treatment of individuals "are formalised and legitimated by a multitude of international codes and laws. International conventions and charters ascribe universal rights to persons regardless of their membership status in a nation-state" (Soysal 1994: 145). In other words, states are compelled to operate forms of citizenship and treat their non-nationals in particular ways by a plethora of international agreements into which they have entered. The nation-state has been extremely influential in the generation of transnational rights through the institution of an international state system and supranational political structures. In turn, this has had a profound effect on national sovereignty. "In the postwar era, many aspects of the public domain that used to be the exclusive preserve of the nation-state have become legitimate concerns of international discourse and action" (Soysal 1994: 144). What is considered to be the legitimate business of nation-states is increasingly determined at the global level. The European Union confers citizenship of the nationals of EU member states and in doing so further breaks the link between citizenship and national territory. According to Soysal (1994: 148), European citizenship "clearly embodies postnational membership in its most elaborate legal form. It is a citizenship whose legal and normative bases are located in the wider community, and whose actual implementation is assigned to the member states."

There are several points which we might want to consider in relation to Soysal's work. First, her portrayal of the regime of rights into which non-citizen residents are incorporated provides a compelling case for the emergence of postnational citizenship. Her study does not concern itself with non-nationals who are not accorded formal resident status, a (potentially much larger) group to whom less rights accrue and in relation to which the gap between citizens and non-citizens would still be considerable. Second, the basis of EU citizenship rights has traditionally been the four freedoms – the movement of capital, goods, persons, and services – and is therefore based on the idea of "citizen as worker." Political rights such as the right to stand and vote in elections in another member state are much more recent additions. As such, while EU citizenship may be postnational it is also very limited in scope and conservative in conception. Thirdly, Soysal's understanding of the EU as a form of state conforms to the multi-level governance model discussed in chapter 3. The EU is a multi-level polity and sovereignty is shared between various "levels" of the state. Ironically, one weakness of this model was thought to be that it was rather solipsistic, viewing all developments as emanating from within the EU and failing to locate European changes within a global framework.

Citizenship has never been a homogenous category. Historically, inclusion has been for the minority not for the majority. The extension of citizenship to a greater proportion of national populations was one of the defining features of modernity. Even today not everyone who is classed as a citizen will enjoy exactly the same rights even within the same polity. Men's rights differ from those of women, under employment legislation or in terms of retirement ages, for example. Traditionally, "man as worker" enjoyed greater participation than women. Urry (1999: 165) makes the point that in the UK citizens rights have not been distributed evenly: "citizenship rights have been more restricted within Scotland, Wales and Ireland/Northern Ireland (especially for Catholics), as compared with England . . . and there have been extensive struggles to force the dominant-England nation to establish full rights of citizenship elsewhere within the UK."

Soysal (1994) makes clear that the incorporation of guestworkers and non-nationals is dependent upon the different regime systems and institutional pathways to be found in European countries. In some, non-nationals are treated as individuals in line with domestic norms, in others they are addressed as corporate groups organized according to their country of origin. The relevance of this to our present discussion is that we need to be aware that just as different countries have different regimes of incorporation for non-nationals, existing national citizenship modes are likely to determine the ways in which various forms of postnational citizenship are "taken up" locally. In other words, there are many types of possible postnational citizenship and different national practices of citizenship (to what extent full participation is extended to women, various minorities, incorporated territories) will determine how these are appropriated and incorporated into national rights. The ways in which "full participation" in a society is denied to certain sections of the population (for example, young people under the age of 18 who are taxed, able to marry or join the army, but not permitted to vote) will influence the way in which postnational rights are absorbed and applied in practice. Preuss (1998: 146) makes a similar point when he notes that as Community law is implemented by member states rather than agencies of the EU, "the European character of the rights conferred by the Community is rarely visible." Even in cases where citizens' rights and legal provisions emanate from the European Union they will tend to be experienced as if they were national. In other words, although European citizenship is non-national in character and Community law has supremacy over national law, preexisting patterns of citizenship rights determine the experience of European citizenship.[7]

Preuss views citizenship status rather narrowly in terms of legal rights, and sees the existence of a variety of citizenship concepts in Europe as a barrier to the development of a genuinely European notion of citizenship with common rights and duties for European citizens. Because of this he downplays certain features of European citizenship such as new opportunities for claims making and the ways in which transnational rights-asserting movements impact on domestic legal rights. He also downplays the extent to which a diversity of citizenship forms are coalescing around collective cultural participation, consumption, and ecology. Secondly, he assumes that the European Union represents a relatively unified social space within which common citizenship rights could be exercised. This is coupled with the assumption that transnational rights do not also originate from other sources. In fact there are many transnational routes to citizenship and the EU is but one bearer of transnational rights, a fact which is likely to result in greater diversity rather than

harmonization, and the practice of citizenship – the rights, obligations, and benefits – is likely to become less homogenous than it has
been in the past. There are already many variations in the meaning
and practice of citizenship. There are collective rights (for organized
labor, for example) and individual rights. There are regional variations as in the case of Britain mentioned above, gender variations,
ethnic variations (civil and human rights), and age variations. We
have seen how young people begin to participate in different areas
of public life at different times. Even within this group there are
differences, for example where the age of consent for homosexual sex
is higher than for heterosexual sex.

Urry (1999: 167–8) identifies a number of contemporary citizenships occasioned by a world of global flows and mobilities beyond
national borders. It is no longer sufficient to talk in terms of Marshall's civil, political, and social rights. "Citizenship of flow de-
differentiates civil, political and social rights and responsibilities."
According to Urry there are six meaningful ways in which we can
talk of extended citizenship (allegiances to groups or principles which
do not fall exclusively within the borders of a nation-state). First,
there are the rights of different social groups (ethnic, gender, age,
sexual) to full cultural participation. This he terms cultural citizenship. Second, minority citizenship: the right to live in another society
and participate in its system of rights and duties. Third, ecological
citizenship. One has rights and responsibilities as a "citizen of the
earth." Fourth, cosmopolitan citizenship by means of which people
relate to other individuals, groups, and societies throughout the
world. Fifth, consumer citizenship: the right to goods and information
from private and public bodies. There is no longer a clear separation
between private consumption and public participation. Sixth, mobility citizenship. Visitors to foreign places and other cultures have
rights and responsibilities. Transnational and postnational routes to
citizenship, and the way in which existing national forms filter and
refract the introduction of these, will work to make citizenship a
much more variegated affair in the future, and mitigate against the
idea of global or cosmopolitan forms of citizenship which embrace
us all equally.

Of course these new forms of citizenship will not all be equally
important to each individual, and neither are they to be thought of
as unified or mutually reinforcing in the way that Marshall's civic,
political, and social dimensions of citizenship were. The idea of
multiple citizenships resonates with the notion that the nation-state

is no longer necessarily the only or the most important stage on which the politics of inclusion and exclusion are played out. As we discussed in chapter 4, the best way of understanding European society is as a series of contingent public spaces. European society is not to be thought of as a nested collection of public spheres whose complementary characteristics contribute to the overall harmony of Europe as a distinct cultural, economic, and political space. Europe increasingly exhibits a plurality of discordant public spaces, legitimated and regulated by diverse and often non-proximate agencies, which cannot be aggregated into a cohesive whole on either the national or the supranational plane. These public spheres have the potential to be spaces of contestation and conflict. Citizenship too, in its different forms, can be conflictual and contradictory. Antagonistic positions can result from claims and counter-claims as individuals and social groups work to gain influence over the distribution of scarce resources.

Unemployment and Competitiveness

The govenmentality theorists argue that western societies have moved beyond welfarist regimes.[8] They talk of a post-welfarist regime of the social. Rather than governing society, the task of national government is to reconfigure the social as a series of markets and quasi-markets by developing "governmental consumerism" (Dean 1999: 172–3). Neo-liberalism works not just according to free-market principles but also by contriving and constructing markets where they do not already exist (Dean 1999: 161). Neo-liberalism also works to transform the subjectivity of the worker to be flexible in an economy driven by technological change (Rose 1998: 162). Both the worker and the unemployed have become "entrepreneurs of the self." Individuals are encouraged to "capitalize" themselves, to invest in the management, presentation, promotion, and enhancement of their own economic capital as a capacity of their selves and as a lifelong project (Rose 1998: 162). There are several important consequences that follow from these shifts.

The unemployed become "job seekers," a term which is not just a euphemism for being out of work, but signals a major shift in policy objectives. Such policy repositions the unemployed person as an active participant in the labor market rather than a passive recipient of benefits, and it requires them to be actively seeking work in order to qualify for benefits. In addition, it places much greater emphasis on the need for the individual to develop his or her capacities in the search for employment: the unemployed must "work on themselves . . . in order to make themselves ready and available to take up opportunities in the labour market" (Dean 1999: 160). But more than this, the neo-liberally constituted job seeker is encouraged to be a consumer in the emerging market for employment placement services. The job seeker must exercise freedom as a consumer in order to obtain the guidance and training needed to exercise freedom as a worker (Dean 1999: 161). This is an important formulation. Not only does it highlight the ways in which the problem of unemployment has became individuated and the responsibility for solving the problem delegated to the job seeker and his or her ability to compete in the job market, but it also signals a change in the relationship between the worker, the welfare state, and citizenship. Citizenship is no longer centered on the universalist principles of civil, political and social rights as it was for Marshall, for whom the relationship between poverty and citizenship was central. Rather, the model of the active citizen is the "entrepreneur of the self" (Rose 1998: 164). The citizen is recast, not in terms of membership of a society that carries rights and obligations, but as a consumer. The rights enjoyed by the citizen are the rights of the consumer in the marketplace (Rose 1998: 165).

The analysis of the governmentality theorists has many strengths. Under conditions of neo-liberalism (or "advanced liberalism" in Rose's formulation), the government of unemployment works through the individualization of the problem (much in the same way as Procacci forecast), and through the transformation of the subjectivity of the unemployed person. The unemployed, like the worker, is encouraged to be an active participant in the labor market, and at the macro level the "problem of unemployment is reconceived in the terms of the respective competitiveness of different labour forces" (Rose 1998: 162). As was mentioned earlier, under competitive conditions workers (both individually and collectively) are reinventing themselves as key components of a flexible workforce capable of contributing to competitiveness. Workers must make themselves competitive and be prepared to work for market rates of pay. Moreover, they increasingly assume responsibility for managing the mismatch between jobs on offer and the availability of skilled labor, and to this end become consumers of training opportunities.

In general terms this is a very useful way of seeing how the problem of unemployment is managed. There are certain problems with these ideas however which we must now address. In contemporary Europe the competitiveness of the labor force equates to an increase in the productivity of those already in employment. As we have already seen, this form of economic management is part of a strategy geared to a redistribution of wealth in favor of capital. The forms of "active labor market" participation discussed by Rose and Dean are more about reducing the numbers (and costs) of those seeking work than with the need to create a skilled labor force. The second problem concerns the relationship between consumers and citizens. There is much sociological work that supports the idea that citizenship is increasingly achieved via consumption. That the governmentality theorists contribute to this understanding is well demonstrated in the work of Dean outlined above. However, there is a greater degree of ambiguity in the work of Rose. This takes the form of an assumption that the model of the citizen is the entrepreneur of the self, a move which limits consumption to the area of (seeking) work. In other words, consumption is conceived by Rose rather more narrowly than by Dean, and leads to the assertion that "labour alone is to be the means by which the poor can acquire the status of citizens" (Rose, 1998: 164). This leaves Rose in the contradictory position of supporting the idea that there are different paths to citizenship which are not necessarily tied to the (national) state (Rose 1998: 166), and at the same time advancing a rather conservative and productivist notion of the relationship between citizenship and employment.

Conclusion

One of the most pervasive myths associated with globalization is that it disempowers the nation-state. However, the relationship is more complex. Globalization simultaneously undermines and strengthens the nation-state, and it transforms the means through which the state can (directly or indirectly) exercise its power over national territory. When governments choose to bewail their fate at the hands of global forces they are engaging in the "political construction of helplessness," as Weiss so memorably phrased it. In reality they have a range of options, including the power to do something about unemployment, poverty, and inequality within their own jurisdictions. In fact, despite progressive European integration member states have shown a "marked reluctance to cede powers in the area of welfare and social policy" (Amin and Tomaney 1995: 27). What is continually underestimated, Albrow (2001) concurs, is the range of choices open to governments in the provision of social infrastructure.

> Even with fiscal stability, balanced budgets and low inflation, a formidable array of policy instruments is available to government: coercion, mass media, legislation, conventions, licenses, standards, interests rates, public employment, taxation and expenditure on health, education, environment and social security.

Sociology has tended to link unemployment with citizenship, and this nexus has formed the basis for the idea of social exclusion: the wider social impact of unemployment. There is a strong association between the worker and citizenship, and the idea that full social and political participation is attained via employment. This is what we may call the Marshallian paradigm, a reconsideration of which has been necessary in recent times as a result of the growing dissatisfaction with a sociology enmeshed within a national society way of thinking about social problems and citizenship. Some of these critiques, particularly those embracing the postindustrial society thesis and the governmentality approach, make important contributions to the overall debate but are limited by some rather productivist assumptions about citizenship, and their failure to move beyond classical sociology's enchantment with studying "nationally sequestered societies."

A valuable way forward, it is suggested, is to embrace a globalization perspective, which has the advantage of conceiving citizenship in terms other than employment or national belonging. But not, it must be stressed, a perspective which sees citizenship as being diminished under conditions of globalization (Falk 2000), or which seeks to transfer national citizenship rights and benefits to another "level," whether supranational or global. Rather, our globalization perspective stems from the preposition that the economy, society and state no longer have to exist in purposeful unity. Society is unruly and fragmented, no longer obeying the commands of a nation-state from which it is increasingly divorced. One consequence of this is that society is more uncertain, in the sense that it is less homogenous, less controllable, and less readily knowable than it was previously. Under conditions of modernity the nation-state managed society and its inclusive welfare regimes, institutionalized class struggles, and compensatory citizenship worked to keep societies intact. Citizenship and welfare were homogenizing social forces. Now difference is viewed as a political entitlement and an empowering social resource, and the right to difference is a universal human right. Claims and entitlements to political freedoms find expression in a plurality of movements with the aim of claiming or expressing identity, based on ethnicity, gender, generation, religion, lifestyle, or regional belonging.

This valorization of difference has it downside. It can translate into inequality of opportunity, poverty, marginalization, disadvantage and oppression (Albrow 2001) as new modes of claims making and rights-assertion no longer obligate nation-states to ensure the well-being of all its citizens. Diversity and difference are the new standards by which peoples judge themselves and when propelled by neo-liberal demands for growth, easily translate into greater instability and fragmentation. To presage an argument developed fully in chapter 6 we can talk about processes of internal differentiation, fragmentation, and autonomization turning Europe into a loose assemblage of winners and losers thrown up by the neo-liberally inflected process of integration. In fact, the whole idea of "European integration" as a palpable fact of European political life is called into question by the existence of these processes. We must move away from the simplistic notion that a shift in the roles and responsibilities from nation-states upwards to a nascent Euro-polity is defining contemporary Europe. Postnational Europe is a reality but this should not be taken to mean that a new unity is being constructed at the European level. Postnationalism implies fragmentation, dislocation and autonomization: disintegration as much as integration. In their demands for difference and identity rights a whole range of social actors – citizens, regions, cities, enterprises, and social movements – contribute massively to the postnational degeneration game.

We are now in better position to reexamine Beck's idea that the new rich no longer "need" the new poor. That they needed them previously, or at least felt some responsibility towards them, can be attributed to nationalism and the solidarity engendered by the need for a unified and functional national economy under conditions of modernity. Beck holds that outside of a national setting redistribution of wealth becomes unthinkable and, as a consequence, the poor are condemned to suffer ever-greater levels of inequality. However, elsewhere in his book he sees in the European Union the possibility of a response to the forces of globalization which contribute to this economic polarization. His idea that the EU can act as a regulator and shaper of globalization indicates the possibility of a non-national basis for wealth redistribution (although as we have seen the EU currently works against labor in this respect). It also suggests that the EU, or perhaps some of the public spaces which are opening up within Europe, could provide the setting within which the conflict between rich and poor, haves and have-nots, could be represented and negotiated.

The usefulness of the term social exclusion is limited by its association with the idea of a territorially delineated (national) society regulated by the state. Under conditions of globalization exclusion and inclusion no longer mean the same thing that they did under conditions of modernity. The setting within which we now have to consider unemployment and inequality is one in which societies are multiple and fragmented and social actors are motivated and animated by a host of forces and goals which have the potential to place them within any number of inclusionary and exclusionary circuits. That the term social exclusion has its shortcomings should not distract from the prevalence of inequality throughout Europe. Many forms of inequality and disadvantage exist which are not captured by categories such as unemployment and social exclusion: poverty is ever-present; rights unevenly distributed; minorities under-represented; new and not-so-new groups disadvantaged by policy – asylum seekers, workers compelled to retire at an arbitrary age; and a growing number of workers exist between the categories of full-employed and unemployed. Phillips (1999) argues that concern about inequalities has shifted away from wealth and poverty towards an interest in various forms of political equalities: gender, race, ethnicity. A struggle for redistribution has given way to a struggle for recognition.

There are now many routes to citizenship, a category no longer tied exclusively to national belonging. Citizenship now comes in many varieties corresponding to the participation of the individual in many public spheres. Not all of these are complementary and taken together they do not combine to form a new unified community of nationals or of Europeans. The public spheres which carry citizenship rights and duties are also spaces of contestation and rule in which actors seek to establish their identities, form new alliances, further their collective cause, or maximize their competitive advantage.

6 Cohesion Policy and Regional Autonomy

A Discourse of Redistribution

Conventional wisdom holds that the massive economic and social disparities that exist within the EU can be reduced through dedicated redistributive instruments, namely the Structural and Cohesion Funds. The term "cohesion" has come to stand for the attempt to reduce economic and social disparities between richer and poorer regions.[1] These disparities threaten the integrity of the single market and are incompatible with the idea of community which accompanies integration (Dinan 2000). Discussion of cohesion has tended to address the adequacy of the policy response and the wider role of structural and cohesion support: to facilitate the introduction of other EU policies (the single market, for example), or to promote solidarity between the better off member states and the "poor four" (Ireland, Greece, Spain, and Portugal). The effectiveness of cohesion policy is normally couched in terms of the benefits derived from Structural and Cohesion Fund support and the resulting diminution in national or regional disparities. The extent to which cohesion policy is successful is the matter of some debate, and most commentators have concluded that the funds targeted at reducing disparities are ameliorative, at best. This is despite the fact that over the past decade or so an increasing proportion of the EU budget has been devoted to bringing about cohesion.[2]

A more appropriate starting point for a discussion of EU cohesion policy is the acknowledgment that the very idea of cohesion is framed within a discourse of redistribution. Indeed, the word cohesion invokes a strong association with ideas of welfarism and social solidarity. A central contention of this chapter is that when approached from a more sociological perspective the problem of cohesion manifests some rather different characteristics. The most important of these is that cohesion is revealed as an instrument of competitiveness and growth, rather than simply an agent of social solidarity and redistribution. To argue that cohesion is more properly aligned with competitiveness and growth is to confront a central orthodoxy of EU integration studies. To substantiate such a claim it is necessary to look at the ways in which the notion of cohesion has become detached from the discourse of social welfare and solidarity into which it was born and progressively integrated within a discourse of growth and market imperatives. It is argued that in order to properly understand the issue of cohesion we must look at the ways that both social and economic problems, and what have been considered appropriate solutions, have been constructed in EU discourse. Put another way, it is argued that in order to study cohesion we must go beyond an understanding that fixes its meaning in a series of "official" policy objectives. As the governmentality theorists have taught us, there is a difference between "the explicit rationalities of government ... and the more or less implicit logic of these practices" (Dean 1999: 72).

Many EU scholars have failed to confront the full implications of the fact that EU policies do not necessarily lead to greater cohesion, and in many cases actually work counter to the stated aims of cohesion policy. This is despite many European Commission studies having drawn attention to the ways in which cohesion policy continues to have a limited impact on reducing disparities, and that national and EU policies frequently work counter to each other. There is a deep-rooted and pervasive assumption that the Commission's policies are appropriate to the task, and that cohesion will result from EU activity. Indeed, as I have argued elsewhere, a "narrative of cohesion" is at work which both demarcates the field of study and constructs cohesion as an object of inquiry (Rumford 2000a: 6–10). It frames the type of questions that can be asked and determines the form that the answers will take. The narrative of cohesion works as a type of intellectual closure, restricting the field of study and preempting findings.

This chapter works to establish that such a view of cohesion is unwarranted, overly optimistic, and leads to a distorted view of the EU and the way that it works. It is argued that cohesion can only be properly understood within a perspective which brings to bear some of the sociological approaches to globalization, the state, and government introduced earlier in the book. Put simply, the key to understanding cohesion is to examine the role of the region under conditions of globalization. The region is crucial because it has emerged as both the site upon which the global acts upon the EU, and the level at which the EU has determined that the processes of globalization can best be accommodated. Importantly, there exists a tension between the role in which globalization has cast the region, and the region as a central player in the EU's cohesion strategy.

In addition to a sociologically inspired globalization framework the chapter also draws upon the work of Beck on subpolitics, and the idea of reflexivity developed on the one hand by Beck, Lash and Urry, and Giddens who are all associated with the idea of reflexive modernization, and on the other hand by the governmentality theorists, who have developed the notion of reflexive government. These sociological approaches undermine the narrative of cohesion and point to the ways in which the EU is increasingly autonomized. The term autonomization, derived from the work of the governmentality theorists, designates both that economic governance is increasingly delegated to autonomous regions, and that neo-liberal economic policies tend to fragment and divide in their pursuit of growth. It is argued that in addition to integration there are other, equally powerful, processes at work and which are shaping the EU. Rather than assuming a progressive and unidirectional process of integration, one corollary of which is a normative view of cohesion, it is necessary to confront the partial and fractured nature of the European project. Integration implies a relation between parts characterized by systematic harmonization, internal coherence, unity and interconnectedness. Autonomization, on the other hand, signals differentiation as much as harmonization and suggests an EU dominated by conflicting and contradictory tendencies, the absence of a system, an incompleteness or partiality, dispersal as well as concentration, differentiated growth. A dislocated collection of elements organized according to new spatial hierarchies. In this context cohesion is revealed as one example of the way in which the discourse of European integration has been dominated by the need to manage integrative narratives and efface evidence of disintegrative forces.

What is Cohesion?

Cohesion is generally understood to be a priority goal of the European Union but does not correspond to a set of clearly defined policy objectives. There is no cohesion policy as such (Hooghe 1998), rather cohesion is an umbrella term for a range of policies which the EU hopes will ameliorate the conditions which are held to be barriers to economic convergence at the national and regional levels: high levels of unemployment, concentrations of wealth in central or favored nations and sub-national regions, remoteness.

Thus, cohesion is a somewhat loosely defined term which embodies the EU's broad aim to be more than a giant market place. Article 130a of the Treaty on European Union (1992) states that cohesion stands for, "reducing disparities between the levels of development of the various regions and the backwardness of the least favoured regions" (European Commission 1996a: 13). The term cohesion presents itself as both the diagnosis and the cure: it is used to refer to both the problem of regional inequality and the policy solutions offered by the EU. Regional convergence with the EU average in terms of GDP per head and unemployment levels are used as indicators of disparity, masking the fact that the EU has no measure of cohesion as such, and no criteria for adjudging whether cohesion is becoming weaker on stronger. (It should be noted that poverty is not used as an index of cohesion primarily because there is no consistent EU-wide method of measurement). This has led one commentator to conclude that cohesion is best thought of as "the political tolerability of the levels of economic and social disparity that exist and are expected in the EU" (Mayes 1995: 1).

There are two inescapable features of cohesion in the EU. One, enormous variations exist in levels of economic development, both between member states and between regions within member states (Wishlade 1996).[3] Two, these disparities have increased throughout the history of the EU. This situation has not come about because of the failure of EU policy towards the poorer countries and less developed regions as such, but as a consequence of successive enlargements. All previous enlargements have aggravated the problem of disparities between member states, and in doing so have widened regional disparities in the EU. One likely consequence of the projected enlargement of the European Union involving countries from the former communist bloc is that economic and social disparities between member states will yet again increase. Enlargement will once again undermine cohesion, particularly as the EU is unlikely to offer new members the same structural benefits currently enjoyed by the EU's poorer member states.

In terms of disparities between member states a reduction can be observed in recent times, although the scale of the convergence is the subject of some dispute. In relation to the EU average, over the period 1986–96, GDP per head in the four poorest member states (Spain, Portugal, Greece and Ireland) rose from 65 percent to 76.5 percent.[4] The situation with regard to disparities between EU regions is more complicated and less conclusive. Nevertheless, the Commission conveys a positive message about the reduction of regional disparities. During the period 1986 to 1996 GDP per head in the 10 poorest regions increased from 41 percent of the EU average to 50 percent, and in the 25 poorest regions, it rose from 52 percent to 59 percent (European Commission 1999b).[5]

The need for cohesion support and the increasing resources committed to the Structural Funds over the past decade or so has been accounted for in a number of ways.[6] The dominant interpretation is that cohesion is a redistributive policy designed to facilitate the reduction of economic disparities (Dinan 1994), and promote convergence between regional economies (Hix 1999). In a similar vein, Drake (1994) reads regional policy rather romantically as a mechanism for redistributing wealth from richer to poorer areas – what one might term the "Robin Hood" view of the EU. Other commentators emphasize a more prosaic role: to facilitate the successful implementation of the Maastricht projects (the single market and EMU), or, to compensate for the tendency of other EU policies to concentrate wealth and exacerbate national and regional economic disparities (Swann 1995). Cohesion is also accorded a political dimension: a "side deal" to allay the concerns of the poorer member states that greater economic integration would bring disproportionate benefits to the richer member states (Allen 1996). Other authors see cohesion as a throw-back: a concession to interventionism in an EU increasingly dominated by the logic of the market (Amin and Tomaney 1995).

I do not wish to adjudicate between these positions, but rather to draw attention to some other, rather more interesting issues raised by a sociological interpretation of EU cohesion policy. I will focus on three aspects of cohesion. Firstly, the impact of counter-cohesion policies. That is to say, the way in which many EU policies have a negative impact on cohesion: Research and Development policy (R&D) and agricultural policy are two examples. Also, the EU is coming to the realization that "national cohesion policies frequently run counter to European cohesion policies" (European Commission 1998a: 111). Indeed, EU cohesion policies are seriously undermined by a range of EU and national initiatives that work against cohesion.

Secondly, the relationship between cohesion and the region in the EU. It is argued that the coincidence of increasing regional autonomy, emerging forms of economic governance, and neo-liberal growth strategies has created the autonomized region. The idea of the auton-omized region is advanced as an alternative to both the "Europe of regions" and "integration through differentiation" models of regional integration. Thirdly, cohesion as a tool of competitiveness. This refers to the way in which cohesion has become detached from a discourse of redistribution and progressively incorporated in a discourse of competitiveness and growth. Cohesion is less about ameliorating backwardness and more to do with underscoring development couched in neo-liberal economic terms. Before we proceed to examine the potential contribution that sociology can make to this discussion we need to appreciate the way in which EU regions and cohesion policy are treated in the key literature on European integration.

Multi-level Governance

The most influential current approach to studying the role of regions and cohesion policy in the EU is multi-level governance.[7] This approach places the region within a framework which emphasizes emerging forms of government and highlights the increased signifi-cance of regional mobilization in the contemporary EU. The approach is particularly useful in providing a framework for understanding EU integration which does not rely solely on the idea of a suprana-tional state, and for linking cohesion policy to wider issues.

The multi-level governance approach sees cohesion policy as a good example of a new form of governance developing in the EU in which decision making is dispersed among different administrative levels, not concentrated at the EU or national level. One consequence of this is that direct linkages can be created between the regions and the European Commission as subnational governments are able to deal directly with supranational policy-makers (Marks et al. 1996: 42). In the process, the relationship between the region and the national state to which it belongs is reordered. As Hooghe (1996a: 17) explains "subnational authorities are directly involved in EU cohesion policy-making alongside national state actors and the Euro-pean Commission." The upshot is that EU cohesion policy is con-trolled by no one center. Multiple layers of authority collaborate (or possibly engage in contests) within a framework of dispersed power.

Subnational government authorities have new possibilities open to them and the "European arena is not closed off from domestic actors" (Hooghe 1996a: 18). Regional mobilization goes hand-in-hand with the empowerment of European institutions, but member states are not excluded from this redistribution of decision-making power, they retain "significant control over resources."

Multi-level governance posits a Europe comprised of regions that no longer have to work through their capital cities: they can developed a direct line to Brussels. Evidence of this is the large number of EU regions that have representative offices in Brussels. These developments should not be taken to mean that regional opportunities are distributed evenly throughout the EU. The empowerment of regions is far from uniform and varies from member state to member state. In fact, member states can shape the extent to which their regions are incorporated within the EU's regional regime. Consequently, regional mobilization empowers some regions more than others. This is what Marks et al. (1996: 63) and Hooghe (1996b) mean when they talk of a Europe *with* the regions rather than a Europe *of* the regions. Nevertheless, the multi-level governance approach makes a strong claim for the increased salience of the region as a political actor and policy-shaper. One vital component of this is that the region is more and more capable of evading "the control of the traditional 'gatekeeper', the national state" (Hooghe 1996b: 121).

One of the central tenets of multi-level governance theory is that (some of) the EU's regions have been "lured" to Brussels. This has brought about a change not only to the balance of political and policy-making power in the EU, but also transformed the identities of some regions. Regional movements are less concerned with the possibility of independence (only a small number ever were) and more interested in the idea of greater autonomy within the EU (Marks and McAdam 1996: 110). The European level is now considered very important for regions wishing to exert a greater influence over their national governments. However, as Jeffery (1997) points out, the new powers enjoyed by regions have arrived as a by-product of the dynamics of the EU's relationship with its constituent member states. What is largely absent from the multi-level governance perspective is the idea that regions could more actively work to shape the dynamics of the multi-level polity to which they belong. In other words, they are recipients of autonomy rather than innovators of new powers and freedoms.

Multi-level governance places the issues of cohesion and regional autonomy very firmly at the centre of thinking about the EU. In this sense it performs a major service and causes us to rethink not only the relationship between the member states and the EU, but also the nature and dynamics of integration. Multi-level governance breaks decisively with the idea that the EU operates across two autonomous levels and adds credibility to the idea of viewing the EU as "single multi-level polity" (Marks et al. 1996: 41). However, multi-level governance shares some of the weaknesses of more traditional approaches to understanding cohesion. In particular, that cohesion is a redistributive instrument, and that the subnational mobilization of regions contributes to integrative goals. The first point will be examined in some detail later in the chapter. At this point we need only mention that cohesion policy does not fit comfortably within either the category of redistribution or competitiveness, although it is much more strongly associated with the latter.

The second point, that the mobilization of regions contributes to integration, is a particularly important one. The multi-level governance approach carries a strong sense that the region is mobilized *vis-à-vis* the EU and that the new-found powers and freedoms of regional government are provided by Brussels. As such autonomy-seeking regions are enticed away from their national moorings by the promise, not just of financial assistance, but by being given yet greater powers and freedoms and a promise of the sort of participation in policy making which was never offered by centralized nation-states. The resulting multi-level distribution of governance is viewed strictly in terms of a reorganization of government power internal to the EU. There is no suggestion that regions could become free of both the nation-state and the EU, and no sense that the region is as much the child of globalization's "invention of locality" (Robertson 1995) as it is the progeny of the EU. Likewise the EU is reluctant to acknowledge that its own policies can be countermanded by forces outside of EU control, and far distant in their origin (Albrow 1998a).

Sociological Resources for Studying Cohesion and Regional Autonomy

A sociologically-inspired approach to cohesion can move us away from an exclusive association with regional problems and Structural Fund support on the one hand, and a multi-level governance understanding of the relationship between regional autonomy and the EU, on the other. That cohesion is most commonly associated with Structural Funds rather than strategies for growth and competitiveness, for example, can be accounted for by three interrelated factors. First, a slavish adherence on the part of commentators on EU affairs to an interpretation of cohesion policy which emphasises only those policies which work directly to further the reduction of disparities, while ignoring those counter-cohesion policies which are equally potent. Second, the active encouragement given by the European Commission (particularly under the leadership of Jacques Delors) to an interpretation of cohesion which lays emphasis on its origins in traditions of welfarism and social solidarity (Ross 1995). While the EU embodies the values of the market, the legacy of a more redistributive ethic survives in EU nomenclature. Third, globalization is assumed to be responsible for greater European integration and as such has an affinity with cohesion, but its more contradictory influences – on the region, for instance – are less widely understood. At this point it is necessary to explore the sociological ideas upon which the notion of autonomization is constructed and contribute to it being a useful way of both characterising the role of the region in contemporary Europe and forming the basis for an alternative explanation of the problem of cohesion.

As we noted in chapter 2, in relation to European integration globalization is commonly understood to be the driving force, and this integration can take place simultaneously at the supranational, national and subnational levels. Allied to this is the commonsense notion that the nation-state has become both "too big and too small." Too big to deal adequately with local problems and too small to solve global problems. Indeed, this idea forms the basis for a popular interpretation of the relationship between the EU and the nation-state. The EU has taken over many of the former functions of the nation-state, and in doing so has become a more effective global player than the individual member states could ever aspire to be. At the same time the EU has encouraged the rise of the subnational region, in order to more effectively deal with local problems. These ideas resonate with the widely held notion that globalization is also responsible for the increased emphasis on the local. As Giddens (1990: 65) points out, under conditions of globalization there exists "the strengthening of pressures for local autonomy and regional cultural identity." One important consequence of these ideas is that Europeans have become sensitized to the notion of a "Europe of the regions" as a corollary of both integration and globalization.

For the present discussion the most important feature of this vision of the EU is that the region is seen as an essential component of European integration. This chapter advances a critique of this understanding of the region, of regional autonomy, and of the dynamics of European integration. The cornerstone of our critique is a range of ideas drawn from contemporary sociological theory, particularly the idea of autonomization, which is advanced as a preferred conceptualization of regional autonomy within the EU. It is argued that the idea of autonomization (as formulated here), incorporating as it does a more sociological notion of globalization, reveals the rise of the region to be less the result of deliberate policy choices on behalf of the EU and more to do with processes which are beyond the control of the EU. The resulting autonomized region can escape the gravitational pull of both Brussels and the national centre and contributes to an EU characterized as much by fragmentation and division as by unity and cohesion.

It is into this context that we introduce Beck's notion of subpolitics. The idea of subpolitics – new forms of political activity forming in the interstices of the political system of modernity – supports the argument that the rise of the region is a consequence of globalization and that the activities of regions are, to a significant degree, neither directed by EU policy nor regulated by central control. In Beck's terms, the regions are an example of "politics from below." This should not be taken to mean that movements for regional autonomy can simply be equated with "grass-roots" politics, although that is certainly one form that their political activity can take. By "politics from below" Beck refers to the possibility of bringing about social transformations outside of the orthodox politics arena. This idea of subpolitics is developed as part of Beck's more general understanding of reflexive modernization, a process which comprises both individualization and globalization.

The certainties of industrial society are not being done away with, they are being recast. Class, family, work, and the welfare state no longer presume each other (Beck 1997: 95). What we are witnessing is an increasing individualization: "the disintegration of the certainties of industrial society as well as the compulsion to find and invent new certainties for oneself and others" (Beck 1994: 14). Subpolitics is one form that politics can take in an increasingly individuating society. Subpolitics does not work through the political institutions of industrial society, it emerges in non-institutional locations and beyond formal mechanisms. At the same time as formal politics –

defined in relation to the state and its institutions – is losing its creative utopian quality (Beck 1997: 98) and industrial society is becoming unpolitical, sub-politics emerges in the places we least expect it. In Beck's words, "[p]eople expect to find politics in the areas prescribed for it, and they expect it to be performed by the duly authorised agents: parliament, political parties, trade unions and so on" (Beck 1997: 98). But subpolitics "breaks open and erupts *beyond* the formal responsibilites and hierarchies" (Beck 1997: 99). There is a new dimension to politics, one which comes into existence with a diminution in centralist state policies. Subpolitics animates actors who would previously not have been considered as participating in formal politics. Subpolitics breaks down the distinction between public and private. What previously appeared as unpolitical and disengaged can now be interpreted as a new dimension of politics. In Beck's terms, "the political constellation of industrial society is becoming unpolitical, while what was unpolitical in industrialism is becoming political" (Beck 1994: 18).

Beck summarizes the differences between politics and subpolitics in the following terms. A political science understanding of politics is concerned with polity (constitution of political community), policy (programmes for shaping the social), and politics (contestations over power). Subpolitics, on the other hand, works to enlarge the political community so that it is coterminous with the social, signals a reduction of the power of the state to implement policy (Beck 1994: 23), and minimizes the importance of politics as traditionally understood ("high" politics, the politics of capturing state power). Significantly, the agent of subpolitics is as much the individual actor as it is previously marginalized collective agents: citizens, the public sphere, social movements, expert groups. By way of a criticism we might want to question the extent to which all of these particular groups were in fact "previously marginalized" in industrial society. Nevertheless, Beck has developed an important framework for understanding the way in which under conditions of globalization new political actors appear on the scene and politics begins to take new and different forms.

The political terrain of Europe has been transformed by globalization and Beck enables us to see how new movements and political actors emerge from within previously non-political spaces. The region as a political actor very much conforms to this idea of subpolitics. The region in contemporary Europe is subpolitical in that has emerged from a reduction in centralized control and implies social arrangements from below (in the sense that Beck uses the term), but more than this it designates a form of politics which emerges unregulated from unexpected sources. Although it remains underdeveloped in his work Beck does touch upon the issue of subnational regionalism. Globalization is responsible for the production of both macro- and micro-regionalism, and we can talk of "globalization from below": the global transformation the social outside of the normal political channels. Beck's discussion of "globalization from below" concentrates on the issue of global subpolitics – "a new transnational space of the moral and the subpolitical is opening up" – rather than the subpolitics of the subnational region (Beck 2000: 26). Nevertheless, he does acknowledge that the subnational region is an institutional level which at which subpolitics has emerged (Beck 2000: 68).

In order to further contextualize Beck's idea of subpolitics we must explore the ideas of reflexivity advanced in the work of Beck, Giddens (1990), and Lash and Urry (1994), for all of whom reflexivity has a close relation to globalization, and the idea of reflexive government outlined by Dean (1999), one of the governmentality theorists. For Beck the idea of reflexive modernization designates the contemporary period of modernity. Reflexive modernization is distinguished from what Beck refers to as simple or industrial modernization in that it is a period in which modernization increasingly turns on itself: it is the modernization of modernization (Beck 1994: 4), or the radicalization of modernization. Reflexive modernization aims at the "self-modification of the foundations of industrial modernization" (Beck 1997: 26). The word "reflexive" here should be taken to mean self-confrontation rather than simply thoughtful reflection. In this sense reflexive modernization means self-confrontation with the unmanageability of the problems of industrial society, or with what Beck (1994: 4) refers to as the risk society: a society in which the "social, political, economic and individual risks increasingly tend to escape the institutions for monitoring and protection in industrial society." The paradigmatic risk is that posed to the environment (see Beck 1992).[8]

Reflexive modernization entails a process of disembedding and re-embedding. Whereas "simple modernization means the disembedding of traditional social forms and then the re-embedding of industrial ones, reflexive modernization means the disembedding of industrial social forms and then the re-embedding of other modernities" (Beck 1997: 22–3). This echoes Giddens' formulation that disembedding means the "lifting out" of social relations from local contexts and their restructuring across large space–time distances (Giddens 1990: 21). One important consequence of this is that social classes have been replaced "with forms of the individuation of social inequality" (Beck 1997: 26). Individualization is produced when the industrial society ways of life are re-embedded by new ones in which individuals "produce, stage and cobble together their biographies themselves" (Beck 1994: 13). Similarly, the state is being metamorphosed. The state which existed in simply modernity (the nation-state, the welfare-state) has been forced to give up its monopoly of sovereign and government functions. The state has given way to various forms of self-organization. Both the demise of class structure and the "withering away of the state" are consequences of the subpoliticization of society.

Expressed in slightly different terms the disembedding and re-embedding associated with reflexive modernization points to a complete reordering of the coordinates of industrial society. State, society and the individual are no longer required to exist in purposeful unity, society does not have to be coherent or composed of building blocks of groups, institutions, and social forces. The state neither manages society nor is concerned with the welfare of individuals. There are many societies or social spaces, many agencies of government and many forms of subjectivity, none of which necessarily require each other. The "national container" understanding of the state gives way to fragmentation and individuation. In such a situation everything is potentially "sub-political": the mobilization of each and every actor flows from their disarticulation from traditional hierarchies and settings.

For Beck, reflexive modernization, which is full modernization as opposed to the semi-modernization of the earlier period, only comes about when social agents mount a reflexive critique of the elite structures of industrial society. Giddens also talks about reflexivity in terms of the examination and reform of social practices in the light of new information about those very practices (Giddens 1990: 38). Crucially, the transformation of these practices involves the reflexive appropriation of knowledge. Knowledge no longer equates to certitude in a world constituted through reflexively applied knowledge and subject to constant revision. This feature of reflexive modernization also contributes to the emergence of subpolitics, which thrives upon a critique of established forms of knowledge production and expertise. Lash and Urry (1994: 38) have criticized Giddens for his emphasis on the individualistic dimensions of reflexivity. Whereas

Beck favors a reflexivity of social norms and structures, Giddens' focuses on self-reflexivity. Reflexivity of the social gives way to reflexivity of the self. Although it is true that this is the focus of *Modernity and Self-identity* (Giddens 1991), his previous work emphasizes that reflexivity works to change social practices (Giddens 1990: 38). For Lash and Urry (1994: 111) reflexivity involves a freeing of individuals from social structures so they can "reflect upon, and in a transmogrified form once more find meaning in, the various spaces of social life." Thus, their ideas sit comfortably alongside both Beck's and Giddens' ideas of disembedding, re-embedding, and reflexivity. Lash and Urry's notion of reflexivity is based upon a post-Marxist critique of contemporary industrial society. They talk of "disorganized capitalism," the political-economic basis on which postmodernity is constructed (Lash and Urry 1994: 54). Indeed, they outline their theory of the reflexivity consistent with late- or post-modernity in a number of case studies of post-organized capitalist social life: production systems based on flexible specialization, for example. They criticize Beck and Giddens for underestimating the aesthetic dimension to reflexivity. Economic life is becoming much more cultural and aestheticized (Lash and Urry 1994: 109) and identities are constructed through consumption.

As we saw in chapter 3 reflexivity is also a central idea in the work of the governmentality theorists. In particular, they have developed the idea of reflexive government: the governmentalization of government. As with Beck, reflexivity should not be taken to mean simply reflection or deliberation. Reflexive government points to the increasing interest demonstrated by government in securing the means of government themselves, with the aim of policing and improving the efficiency of institutions and governmental techniques.

One feature that these accounts share is an assumption that under conditions of reflexivity there is an increase in individualization. For Beck, as we have already seen individualization is one of the two key components of reflexive modernization (the other being globalization). Essentially individualization refers to the condition we find ourselves in when we have been disembedded from the ways of life characteristic of industrial society and re-embedded into the world of reflexive modernization. Under these conditions the individual must organize his or her life around new sets of values and without the familiar reference points of industrial society: class, family, sexual division of labor. Men and women are obliged to take greater responsibility for the decisions which influence their life chances (whether to marry, to have children, lifestyle choices). Individualization implies not atomization, disconnectedness or the end of any type of society (Beck 1997: 94) but new social relations and interdependencies. There is a strong relationship in Beck's work between individualization and subpolitics: the opportunities that exist for groups and individuals excluded from the corporatist and political elites of industrial modernity.

We have also seen how for Lash and Urry reflexivity involves disembedding individuals from familiar social structures and forcing them to remake their social lives. Social agents are freed from centralized control and monitoring and forced to be self-monitoring and self-reflexive. They emphasize that individualization should be seen as more than the declining importance of social structures such as family and class. For them individualization "entails the replacement of social structures by information structures" (Lash and Urry 1994: 111). In other words, individualization derives not from the absence of social structure but from the presence of new structures built on information and communication. In turn, information and communication flows are integral to reflexive modernization.

In the previous chapter we saw how the governmentality theorists chart the development of the government of the self and the entrepreneur of the self under conditions of neo-liberalism. They also talk of the ways in which various agents – the individual, the family, community – have become "responsibilized." The individual is increasingly expected to manage his or her own risk in a variety of fields: unemployment, ill-health, for example. The entrepreneur of the self takes responsibility for "his/her own self-advancement and care; within the ideals of enterprise, individuals are charged with managing the conduct of the business of their own lives" (Du Gay 1997: 302). Entrepreneurial governance has progressively replaced forms of welfarism in which the citizen had his or her needs catered for by state programmes of social security, welfare, housing, education. According to Rose, the government of the national economy and society is replaced by the government of other "spaces" such as regions, cities, sectors, communities. The aim of such government is to sustain economic circuits, which flow between regions and across national boundaries. The self-regulating capacities of individuals on the model of the entrepreneur of the self can be easily accommodated into the administration of a whole range of entities; supranational, national, regional, as well as the firm, the institution, the organization. Neo-liberalism has forged new relations "between the economic health of the nation and the 'private' choices of individuals" (Miller and Rose 1990: 329).

Autonomization

The common thread that runs through all these accounts is that there is a form of individualization which is common to the condition of reflexive modernization (and reflexive government). This is not an atomistic form of individualization but a phenomenon which is aligned with new forms of social organization, new relationships between actors, and new economic, social, and political hierarchies. I suggest that the term "autonomization" best signifies the restructuring of the social under conditions of neo-liberalism, globalization, and reflexive modernization.

The idea of autonomization is derived from the work of the governmentality theorists and designates the type of government and rule which empowers individuals and makes them responsible for their own government: the idea of the entrepreneur of the self. In the context of the contemporary EU autonomization is best thought of as a series of processes to which the EU is increasingly subject and which generate integration, but also autonomy, fragmentation, and internal differentiation. To understand the dynamics of autonomization we need to examine the ways in which neo-liberal growth, entrepreneurial governance, and globalization are shaping the new Europe and leading to a particular type of EU integration. Autonomization is the corollary of integration for an EU shaped and moulded by the twin dynamics of globalization and neo-liberal growth. Autonomization also points to an EU in which policies are contradictory as much as they are complementary, and in which change is less policy driven than increasingly shaped by forces beyond the reach of EU policy.

Autonomization refers to a different dynamic of integration, to an EU which is less a closed and bounded geographical, economic or cultural space than it is a multiplicity of networks existing in varying densities and extending in different directions. The notion of autonomization helps us to move beyond the rather positivistic and developmental schema of an inevitable and ever-increasing degree of integration. Autonomization also reveals important tensions and contradictions that are not fully acknowledged in standard integrative narratives of the contemporary EU. Autonomization challenges preconceptions about the nature of integration: that it is policy lead, that it is unidirectional, that it leads to mutually beneficial outcomes, and that it is the goal of all interested parties. Autonomization permits an interpretation of integration, not as a goal or a policy objective, but as a resource from which actors empower themselves and acquire new forms of legitimacy. In this sense, integration is less a shared goal or a political vision than a potential for animating interest groups, sectors, regions, and citizens within the European orbit.

From the perspective of autonomization the process of European integration is a framework of opportunities which some groups and agencies are better equipped to exploit. Integration generates winners and losers, creates new hierarchies, and disperses centres of power. Autonomization points to a form of integration in which the actors concerned are not only member states but also sectors, regions and NGOs not all of which have the same goals and aspirations, or are energized by the same integrative capacities. On this model, integration stems from multiple (extra- and intra-EU) sources and creates a plurality and diversity of strategies amongst the actors which it empowers and autonomizes. Integration, such as it is, is the outcome of complex and contradictory processes taking place between agents who work both within and without European circuits, networks, and spaces, which they frequently create for themselves or for which the EU is neither wholly responsible, nor is able to fully regulate and monitor. Autonomization thus denies that the EU is the sole author of its own integration. Autonomization demands a narrative of EU development that does not assume the inevitability of integration and cohesion. Rather, autonomization suggests the existence of an EU not determined and structured in accordance with a particular unifying principle. It stresses openness, contingency, and incompleteness.

The idea of autonomization causes us to think about EU cohesion policy and the role of the region in new and different ways, or at least to supplement the standard account of the role of the region. This standard account sees the region as the focus for a whole raft of EU policies, ostensibly designed to address the problem of cohesion: the wide disparities in wealth and opportunities that exist between member states and particularly between regions. This has led to the idea that the EU is promoting the interests of subnational regions over those of the nation-state as a prelude to a federal Europe or a "Europe of the regions." For the same reasons the idea of multi-level governance – subnational, national and supranational – is now very much part of our thinking about the nature and development of the EU. In contrast, we need to view the regions as key actors in neo-liberal economic policies. Regional growth is a central feature of the neo-liberal policies that predominate in the contemporary EU, both at member-state and EU level. However, regional growth of this type is incapable of being generalized (Allen et al. 1998). Regions compete with one another, and growth in one region is frequently at the expense of growth elsewhere. Neo-liberal economic growth encourages autonomized regions. The autonomized region is the EU's accommodation to a combination of globalization and neo-liberalism.

From a sociological perspective which incorporates the idea of autonomization, the problem of cohesion ceases to be concerned exclusively with conscious policy choices, nor is it framed within a discourse of redistribution and solidarity. Cohesion becomes linked to a series of much broader questions to do with the dynamics of EU integration and the role of the region. Whereas standard accounts of EU cohesion view globalization as a inducement to greater integration, the argument here is that it works to autonomize the region, placing it partly beyond the scope of EU policy. Also, cohesion policy is revealed to be contradictory: many EU programmes work in such a way as to negate the effects of the Structural and Cohesion initiatives. Once the idea of autonomization has been incorporated into our thinking about the dynamics of integration, and the region located at the intersection of globalization and neo-liberal growth it is no longer possible to view cohesion policy innocently as a redistributive mechanism. Rather than being the antithesis of competitiveness and market principles cohesion is in fact aligned with strategies of neo-liberal growth.

Counter-cohesion Policies

EU attempts at cohesion, particularly the programs devised to arrest the economic imbalances between regions, can be easily countermanded by other, non-structural policies.[9] The EU's position in relation to cohesion is contradictory. On the one hand the EU actively embraces cohesion as a goal, but on the other hand it pursues or legitimates policies which result in greater regional and economic disparities. Importantly, EU and national policies are not always complementary and frequently work against each other, and in doing so undermine the overall objective of cohesion.[10]

Despite the introduction of the single market, member states still pursue national economic strategies that can have a serious (negative) impact on harmonious development. Upon inspection of the relationship between EU and member state policies it is hard to escape the conclusion that the project of European integration is frequently sacrificed to national economic and social priorities. The large amount of government funds spent on state aids to industry in some of the richer member states is a case in point. For example, the four cohesion countries account for 8.8 percent of total manufacturing aid, while the "rich" four (the UK, Germany, France, and Italy) account for 88 percent (European Commission 1998a). Member states, while embarking on ambitious projects leading to greater European integration such as Economic and Monetary Union, are at the same time reluctant to relinquish control over key economic mechanisms, particularly national industrial policy. In other words, "Member States policies are the Union's primary instruments for achieving cohesion" (European Commission 1996a: 6). Or, expressed in more critical terms, member state policies are the prime contributor to the EU's failure to bring about cohesion.

There are deficiencies in the EU's overall cohesion strategy. For example, Portugal (one of the EU's poorest members) has been a net loser from the Common Agricultural Policy (European Commission 1996a: 62). Contrary to the needs of cohesion CAP has at times resulted in 80 percent of the funds going to the top 20 percent of the most profitable farms, and in general has benefited larger agricultural enterprises more than smaller ones. In the case of Greece, the single market "may have had negative effects on growth and employment" (European Commission 1996a: 67). Disparities in wealth can even be exacerbated by EU policies. For example, R&D (Research and Development) policy works in such a way as to help make rich regions richer. R&D incentives are of the same value as regional spending but "their spatial distributions are virtually the opposite. Both overall R&D spending and incentives are high in relation to GDP in the more prosperous countries and are concentrated in the richest regions of all countries." Germany and France together account for 60 percent of total member-state spending on R&D. Ireland, Greece, and Portugal together account for 1½ percent of the total (European Commission 1996a: 52).

Another Commission study states: "the contribution of EU governments to private sector spending on R&D was of the same broad order of magnitude as their spending on regional incentive policy," but, "the pattern of expenditures on policies aimed at improving the competitiveness of national economies by promoting R&D is virtually a mirror image of patterns of regional disparity (European Commission 1998a: 109–10). In other words, R&D spending works as form of counter-regional subsidy or counter-cohesion policy: a subsidy for the rich regions rather than the poor. The importance of these counter-regional subsidies to the richer member states is highlighted by Petersen (1996: 232), who makes the point that EU efforts to introduce a Europe-wide framework for R&D subsidies which would have incorporated a redistributive element was opposed by member states: "by the early 1990s the Framework programme was no longer viewed as a clear-cut means for compensating large, richer member states for their net contribution to the EU's structural and cohesion funds." Clearly there is more than one interpretation of what constitutes redistribution within the EU.

It is commonly believed that the Structural Funds are concentrated in the most disadvantaged regions of the EU (Mitchell and Mc-Aleavey 1999: 182). This is not necessarily the case. Although cohesion policy is designed to favor the poorer regions "the rules are such that each member state gets a share of the funds" (Hooghe 1996a: 6). Also, the award of regional funds by member states is determined more by national priorities than by EU criteria. Weaker member states have difficulty matching the sort of payments made in the richer member states. Expenditure per head is higher in the assisted parts of Italy, Germany, and Luxembourg than in the disadvantaged regions of the poorest countries.

According to the Commission (European Commision 1998a: 110) member states' own regional policies have not led to the concentration of resources in the EU regions with the lowest GDP. Across the EU "there is no direct relationship between the prosperity of a region and its status as a contributor to the national budget or a beneficiary from it; similarly it does not follow that regions of equivalent prosperity in a European context will be equal beneficiaries of Member States regional or horizontal policies." Regional policies in member states, although having the potential to promote convergence and cohesion between regions within individual countries, do not automatically address EU-wide disparities. National policies can result in greater, rather than narrower, regional disparities across the EU. Nationally administered regional policy can work to reinforce existing disparities if, for example, government subsidies are diverted to certain successful industrial sectors. National priorities result in transfers of wealth that are not necessarily related to differences in GDP at the EU level.

EU cohesion policy is undermined by the pattern of support that can be observed at the national level. In the richer member states the better-off regions are subsidizing their poorer neighbours (through state aid and other transfer mechanisms). The same method of regional support is also supposed to operate in the poorer member states where the better-off regions are frequently not affluent in comparison to the EU average. More to the point, the poorer regions are much poorer than their counterparts in the richer member states and a comparable system of transfers does not exist. The result is that there is no equivalence in the way regions are treated across the EU, since national programs are not systematically related to differences in GDP on a European scale (European Commission 1996a: 55). Regional policy – in terms of national programs of assistance and support – is not harmonized across the EU.

All policies have an impact on cohesion, and those deriving from member states frequently undermine Commission initiatives. This means that the EU has to both keep the contradictory effects of policies within reasonable bounds and also regulate the activities of its own and member states' institutions. Contradictory policies are one area in which the Commission comes into conflict with member states. Also, as national objectives in the deployment of regional resources do not necessarily coincide with those of the EU there is conflict in terms of securing the mechanisms of government. The Commission attempts to bring national agencies for regional development within the scope of its own administrative control through partnership and planning frameworks. In an environment characterized by autonomization, coherent and complementary "levels" of government constituting an integrated whole are not possible. Where policy priorities fail to coincide and even work against each other, and where multi-agency government is the norm, the EU acts in a way consistent with reflexive government and works to secure its own governmental mechanisms.

Regional Autonomy and Cohesion

The EU views the problem of cohesion as one that can be solved by dedicated policy instruments, but, as we have seen, EU (and national) policy has a counter-cohesion dimension. The argument advanced in this section is that regional disparities are a structural consequence of EU and national economic priorities. Regional disparities are a corollary of the neo-liberal bias towards the interests of the more advanced regions and sectors (Amin and Tomaney 1995). Neo-liberal economic policies do not lead to uniform and even economic growth. On the contrary, they encourage growth in one area only at the expense of creating disadvantage in another. In other words, neo-liberal growth helps create the backwardness that cohesion policy tries to alleviate.

Problematizing the region is an important step towards a more rounded understanding of cohesion. To this end I would draw attention to the work of Allen et al. (1998) who emphasize the differential growth, affluence, and internal structure of the region. They develop the idea of the discontinuous region in which economic growth is not necessarily uniform. The discontinuous region is not discrete and cannot easily be bounded, nor is it uniform or homogenous. Variegated growth patterns and distributions of wealth are not just experienced between regions, but within them too. A region can contain both pockets of growth and areas of underdevelopment. Regional inequalities are viewed not as an unfortunate product of historical disadvantage or lack of opportunity, but as one outcome of neo-liberal growth. Neo-liberal growth creates pockets of disadvantage as surely as it reinforces economic advantage. Allen et al. recast the relationship between the region and the EU. Regional policy is not a mechanism for wealth redistribution; "its underlying principles are concerned with the removal of obstacles to the free flow of labour and capital as well as goods" (Allen et al. 1998: 127). Regional policy should be understood not as a corrective to the single market, but as a mechanism for facilitating its working. In other words, regional inequalities are a barrier to economic integration and their removal, via EU regional policy, contributes to the neo-liberal imperative.

How are we to understand regions as actors in contemporary Europe? Regionalism can be defined as the prioritization of the subnational region over other units of sociopolitical organization, such as the nation-state. Regionalism is often thought of as a threat to the nation-state, seeking to fragment it and replace it with a multiplicity of smaller nation-states, for example. Alternatively, regionalism may attempt to weaken the central authority of the nation-state and replace it with a federal arrangement that allows greater regional autonomy. This is the sense in which the association of regionalism and the idea of "a Europe of the regions" within the EU is generally understood. It is consistent with the view that the EU is somehow promoting the region over the nation-state; the EU is creating a new tier of governance – the region – which, together with the EU itself as a supranational body, is usurping the role of the nation-state.

There is a type of regionalism peculiar to the EU, not the regionalism of secessionism or cultural autonomy (for example, Basque or Sardinian regionalism even though these variants are certainly potent in contemporary Europe), but a regionalism in which the region is a leading economic actor within the framework of neo-liberal opportunities and economic governance present within the EU. Placing the region within a matrix of neo-liberalism and market development provides the basis for a consideration of the region as an economic actor (relatively) autonomous from formal national and EU government. Indeed, the emergence of the region as a relatively autonomous economic actor is the result of a specific set of economic and political opportunities that exist within contemporary Europe, but which are not necessarily driven by EU policy. This requires further elaboration.

When we say that the EU region is autonomized we draw attention to the uneven and piecemeal nature of growth, to discordance and discontinuity, as well as to cohesion and harmonization. Autonomization successfully captures both the idea that neo-liberal economic policies tend to fragment and divide in their pursuit of growth (growth in one region is at the expense of another, for example), and that economic governance is increasingly devolved or delegated to autonomous regions and sectors. Describing the EU region as autonomized is to resit the integrative logic of more orthodox accounts of recent Union development. Autonomization stands in opposition to the idea of "integration through differentiation," which is premised on the idea that the EU is devolving power downwards to the regions at the same time as the nation-state is being hollowed out. On this latter model the region "works" for the EU because regional agencies are well placed to make decisions concerning the application of policies at the local level and the most effective utilization of resources. The idea is that the application of policy at the regional level is often a more effective means of integration than imposing top-down decisions from the central state. In recognizing the specificity and difference of the region, and tailoring the application of policy accordingly, the EU is facilitating integration. Integration can be better achieved through partnerships which are sensitive to local needs (Hirst and Thompson 1996: 167–9). The EU must recognize that not only national differences but also local differences and varying levels of "Euro-preparedness" exist. "Distinctive "policy cultures" influence greatly the translation of EU policies into national contexts" (Cooke, Christiansen, and Schienstock 1997: 203), and so integration must proceed differentially. But of course such a recognition does not remove the member state from the process altogether. Policy implementation is more successful in situations where the member state works with a coordinated regional administration.

Governmentality studies draw attention to the ways in which government increasingly works by means of empowering autonomous actors who then become responsible for monitoring and regulating their own conduct. Rather than simply by means of the state "government is accomplished through multiple actors and agencies rather than a centralised set of state apparatuses" (Dean 1999: 26). Autonomization embraces the idea that neo-liberalism promotes autonomy amongst its participants (Burchell 1993: 274). The EU animates economic and social actors in new ways and encourages autonomized economic actors: citizens, economic enterprises, NGOs, or regions. It facilitates the autonomy of these actors, it empowers them at the same time as exposing them to a degree of risk (the insecurities of the market), and is not concerned with their well-being in the way that the welfarist nation-state is, for example. Autonomization points to a European Union "governed not through the formation of a European state, but through the autonomous economic actions of its subjects . . . who participate in the amelioration of their own social problems" (Barry 1993: 315–16).

The term "autonomized regionalism" is a useful characterization of the ongoing processes of regionalism and economic autonomy within the contemporary EU. Autonomized regionalism differs from what for convenience we can call the "Europe of the regions" version of regionalism and the idea of "integration through differentiation" in two main ways. First, autonomized regionalism, for the most part, is independent of the influence of EU regional policy, not a component of it. Second, both the rise of autonomized regionalism and the importance of the region as an economic (and ethno-cultural) unit in the contemporary EU is closely linked to the development of the single market. In other words, the rise of regionalism in contemporary Europe can only be properly understood as a corollary of the neo-liberal economic matrix constituted by the domestic policies of many western European governments since the early and mid-'80s coupled with the EU's Maastricht projects, the single market and Economic and Monetary Union. It is in this environment of insurgent neo-liberalism that a new relationship between regions, the nation-state, and the EU has been forged.

The politics of autonomized regionalism are centered on the conflict between free market and state regulation. The region enters this political arena on the side of the market. There is a close match between the aspirations of autonomized regions and neo-liberal economic priorities. For both, the welfarist state is a burden and a fetter and constitutes a barrier to economic prosperity. Both neo-liberals and autonomized regions are in favor of reduced central bureaucracy and taxation, less state intervention in the economy, reduced public spending, cuts to redistributive regional economic development; all areas which traditionally fall under the control of the centralized state. Autonomized regionalism is not a movement of the oppressed or marginalized. It is often most developed in what Harvie (1994: 2) has termed the "bourgeois regions," "areas of sophisticated technology, environmental awareness, local democracy, and a culture and civil society which integrated the intimate and the cosmopolitan." Harvie's bourgeois regions are motivated more by their affluence (and desire to preserve it) than by any cultural identity. Such regions are also geared up to extracting the maximum benefits that the EU has to offer. To the autonomized region the importance of the structural funds resides not in their potential to increase cohesion or bring about convergence. They fulfil a different role, "transforming administrative cultures and promoting greater self-reliance in economic development, they are assisting regions to exploit the possibilities that now exist for innovation and flexible specialisation" (Cooke, Christiansen, and Schienstock 1997: 199).

The autonomized region is not a creation of EU policy as such. It is a feature of the contemporary EU but has little to do with EU cohesion objectives. Growth in a region like the UK's southeast is rooted in a particular blueprint of individual success, "self-reliance, personal ambition, an ethic of hard work and the ability to take advantage of what opportunities came your way in a competitive environment, with little or no concern for the inequities involved" (Allen et al. 1998: 9).

Cohesion and Competitiveness

We must now turn to the third aspect of cohesion: the way in which the relationship between the EU, the region, and solidarity has been recast in terms of market imperatives. The EU has, over the past decade, increasingly come to view cohesion not as an objective in its own right, but as a contributor to other aims, notably competitiveness. This is the influence of neo-liberal economics, which in the words of one commentator, "induces cohesion policy makers to frame policy in terms of competitiveness rather than social goals such as equality or solidarity" (Hooghe 1998: 463). Cohesion is not to be understood as the levelling out of disparities through programmes of wealth redistribution. The EU embraces a market economy not a redistributive one. At root, cohesion policy is a series of instruments contributing to the creation of a harmonized European economic space, and enhancing the competitiveness of the EU. The objective of cohesion is the reduction of economic disparities through the generalized benefits of growth. In other words, cohesion is not designed to compensate for the market but to complement it.

The EU's perspective on cohesion is predicated on the need to increase the competitive advantage of regions, rather than to act directly on economic disparities with the aim of reducing them. Cohesion is only nominally about the redistribution or equalization of wealth. The EU makes this explicit: "cohesion is concerned with increasing economic growth and new opportunities in the poorer regions and for disadvantaged social groups and does not imply a reduction in either growth or jobs for others" (European Commission 1996a: 14–15). In this context, a reduction of disparities is held to mean "convergence of basic incomes through higher GDP growth, of competitiveness and of employment" (European Commission 1996a: 13). Cohesion is a pivotal stage in a "virtuous circuit" of development: cohesion underpins the market, which leads to greater competitiveness, which leads to growth, which in turn contributes to greater cohesion.

The idea that there are regional and cohesion factors beyond the control of the EU is not alien to the orthodox discourse on integration. For example, it is understood that cohesion policy has been developed in response to the effects of extrinsic factors – global, cyclical, historical – largely beyond the control of the EU and the product of historical patterns of development. Such uneven patterns of development have resulted in disparities in the infrastructural and human capital endowments of regions (European Commission 1994: 10). It is interesting to note that the disparities are the result of uneven development, not the cause of them. Regional policy is then offered as a way of ameliorating disparities, not, it should be noted, as a way of tackling the causes of uneven development. This allows the Commission to say that cohesion policy is aimed at reducing the disparities *in competitiveness* between regions (European Commission 1996a: 70, emphasis added). This is an example of how the EU has steadily reworked concepts such as harmonization and cohesion away from their redistributive or social market meaning, increasingly aligning them with notions of competitiveness, and stressing their compatibility with neo-liberal growth.

Cohesion policy has been rendered compatible with the EU's wider aims of market development and economic integration. The notion of "harmonious development," inherited from the Treaty of Rome and embedded in the Maastricht Treaty has to be understood in this light. When the EU offers as a definition of cohesion "harmonious development with a geographical dimension" it means something quite specific: that development will come about through greater equality of opportunity, not through an evening out of wealth. It is in this sense that we should understand statements such as "The promotion of social cohesion requires the reduction of the disparities which arise from unequal access to employment opportunities" (European Commission 1996a: 14). This statement is significant in that it pays lip service to tackling social issues ("reduction of disparities") and invokes the problem of inequality without advocating redistribution. It targets the rather vague "disparities that arise from unequal access to employment opportunities," rather than, say, "unemployment." This is another very good example of what the governmentality theorists term reflexive government. The government of the social would attempt to reduce unemployment, reflexive government (the government of government) works to secure the mechanisms that regulate the employment market.

There are other examples of the relationship between growth, competitiveness and the objective of cohesion in which the language of cohesion continues to use the idiom of social solidarity while its substance reveals a very different set of concerns. The European Commission routinely affirms that economic and social cohesion is one of the Union's priority objectives and continues to describe cohesion in terms of "redistributive policies." For example, one Commission publication (European Commission 1997) lists a series of objectives that are said to be designed to contribute to solidarity, but which in fact point to the conclusion that cohesion is becoming increasingly allied to strategies for the harmonization of economic opportunities rather than social solidarity. The list of strategies for solidarity includes: speeding up economic and social development in the less-prosperous countries so that they can play a full part in economic and monetary union; redressing imbalances (in wages, social security systems, productivity) which can lead to distortions of competition; and promoting growth, competitiveness, and employment through infrastructure projects and training. From this we can again see that cohesion is less an objective in its own right and more a tool to further other objectives. Cohesion facilitates EMU by bolstering growth in less-prosperous areas, and offsets the worst shocks that this "discipline" entails. Cohesion policies are designed to "redress balances" so as to prevent market distortions and promote growth and employment. In every case, cohesion is an adjunct of competitiveness not redistribution. Accordingly, economic and social disparities will be reduced only through increased productivity. It is clear that the notions of solidarity and cohesion at work here have been displaced from their social welfare origins. It is also evident that the Commission believes that there is still considerable political capital in propagating the idea that cohesion equals solidarity towards its poorest countries and regions.

Conclusion

A study of cohesion reveals some interesting contradictions in EU activity. The EU makes explicit that it wishes to increase cohesion yet provides no indication of what an acceptable level of cohesion would be. The problem of cohesion tends to be expressed in terms of regional disparities in wealth yet cohesion is in fact determined to a great extent by other, non-regional factors. Numerous programs have been brought forth with the aim of increasing cohesion but the EU has been largely unsuccessful in reducing regional disparities. Given this context it is difficult to understand why cohesion is treated uncritically in the literature.

The orthodox position on cohesion rests upon two central tenets. First, that cohesion is synonymous with regional policy, and second that cohesion embodies ideals of redistribution, compensation, and amelioration of regional disparities. This orthodoxy holds that EU regional policy is the mechanism through which the EU can reduce economic disparities and enhance cohesion (Mitchell and McAleavey 1999). This is an inaccurate and one-dimensional interpretation. Every EU policy has a cohesion dimension and has the potential to increase or reduce disparities. The EU has, by accident or by design, a range of anti-cohesion policies and counter-regional policies which have a far greater impact on cohesion than structural measures. The ortho-dox interpretation of cohesion views the Structural Funds as meas-ured responses to a particular set of problems, and appropriate solutions to the problems at which they are directed. The EU's policy choices are seen as necessary and reasonably effective mechanisms to combat the problem of cohesion; their main limitation being that the funds are insufficient to tackle successfully the enormous range of problems with which they are faced.

The argument presented in this chapter is that attempts to bring about greater cohesion are undermined by key processes at work in today's European Union. These processes do not, for the most part, originate within the EU, and the EU has only a limited degree of control over them. The nature of globalization, it has been argued, is such that it cannot be reduced to a series of transnational processes: movements of capital, goods and services, and so on, which have stimulated the need for greater EU integration. Globalization has a close relationship with EU integration but has also set in motion a number of other dynamics, which act on the EU in contradictory ways, and at many different levels. Globalization has generated autonomization, and the region has been produced at the intersection of a multiplicity of processes. Neo-liberal growth policy and the search for greater EU competitiveness, taken in conjunction with globalization, the growth of reflexive government, and sub-politics have led to the creation of the autonomized region, a combination which has worked to compromise the EU's attempts to bring about greater cohesion. Under the sign of autonomization the region loses its homogeneity and coherence. The region becomes internally differ-entiated and exhibits discordant and non-generalizable growth.

Cohesion in the EU cannot be understood simply in terms of EU policies designed to act upon a range of economic disparities. The problem of cohesion has not been caused by the failure of a particular set of policies. Rather, the problem of cohesion is the dynamics of neo-liberal growth itself. The growth of interest in structural and cohesion programmes, and in the levels of funding for these, has coincided with the onset of the Maastricht project of greater economic integration. The emergence of cohesion – both the concept and the problem – is coincident not only with the means to deal with it, but with the rise of the very neo-liberal economic ambitions that created it. Placing cohesion within the frame of globalization makes manifest its many contradictions. Cohesion is not primarily a means of assisting the less-developed regions. The EU's attempts to underpin the single market by preventing existing economic disparities from becoming wider are contradicted by the accommodation of cohesion policies to strategies for growth in an economic environment circumscribed by globalization.

7   Rethinking Core–Periphery Relations

Europe at the turn of the millennium is constantly surprised
by its periphery. (Leontidou and Afouxenidis 1999: 268)

Regions and Peripheries

As far as the EU is concerned its peripheries are hardly surprising at
all. They might be somewhat problematic, but predictably so. Peripherality has its causes, these can be identified, and appropriate
remedial measures brought to bear. To understand why the quotation
which heads this chapter is an accurate statement of affairs, and why
the periphery can spring a surprise or two, we need to question
many of the assumptions upon which EU thinking about its peripheries are based. One of the most important of these assumptions is
that the periphery exists in a relation of dependence with the core.
Another is that the periphery is a particular kind of region with its
own set of regional problems. In other words, the periphery is
governed by the same "laws of motion" which rule the region, and
the EU has certain expectations about the behavior of its peripheries.
In what ways do they not conform to these expectations, and how
may we understand peripheries? The conceptual tools introduced in
the previous chapter in order to study the region also provide the
starting point from which to "rethink core–periphery relations." The
critique of cohesion advanced in the previous chapter was based
upon a conceptualization of the region as an actor increasingly
autonomous from any center, and it was argued that the region was
a good example of how globalization promotes new kinds of action
at a distance. The autonomization of the region points to a new series
of hierarchies in which regions enjoy new relations to each other,
their national states, and the EU. More specifically, regions are no

longer necessarily defined in relation to their nation-states, nor, by the same token, are they dependent upon a new "center," for example the European Union.

At one level, peripheries can be thought of as either the regions that constitute the EU's border with non-member states, or those regions which are most distant from the northwest European "core" (or both). This is the most common way that peripheries are conceptualized in EU reports and commentaries on regional development. In order to fully understand peripheries it is necessary to begin by extending the idea of the autonomized and discontinuous region introduced in the previous chapter. The idea of the autonomized region offers a powerful critique of more established notions of the relationship between the EU region, the problem of cohesion, and the dynamics of European integration. Nevertheless, the way in which we have discussed the reordered hierarchies of economy and space to which autonomization draws our attention is still very much based on the region, although now it has assumed a new role and offers evidence of a different dynamic. We have replaced one model of the region with another, more critical version. The autonomized region reveals different characteristics, but is still very much a region. Similarly, Allen et al.'s (1998) attempt to "re-think the region" successfully challenged the internal coherence and homogeneity of the region as constructed in EU discourse, but retained the centrality of the idea of the region. They set out to "re-think the region," not dispense with it.

In order to extend the account of the region under conditions of globalization begun in the previous chapter we must now re-think the region in other ways, particularly the extent to which it is taken to be an essential component of the core–periphery model that dominates and structures the orthodox discussion of patterns of inequality in the EU. There are two main components to this exercise. The first, which follows from the insight that globalization reshapes the hierarchal framework within which regions are constituted, is to introduce another way of thinking about the relationship between regions and institutions of government. To this end, the idea of the network will be introduced and examined in conjunction with the region. The idea of the network, with its connotations of horizontal connectedness and fluidity, confronts more established ideas of hierarchical arrangement and would seem to be the natural ally of autonomization. The core–periphery understanding of disparities is premised upon a certain notion of hierarchical relations which are undermined by globalization. The corollary of this is that the conceptualization of the EU constituted by a space of centers and peripheries "is no longer tenable in a globalised world" (Gledhill 1999: 19). The core–periphery model loses any coherence that it may once have had, and needs to be replaced by a model which acknowledges that actors are no longer always animated from a centre, rendering patterns of disparities more complex.

It is argued that the core–periphery model is inadequate to the task of representing spatial inequality in the contemporary EU in general, and the situation of the peripheries in particular. More than this, the core–periphery model encourages the belief that the countries and subnational regions of the EU are united by some overarching nexus of cohesion. Examples of this way of thinking proliferate. For example, the core needs the periphery (for a supply of cheap labor), or the periphery needs the core (as the originator of growth). The idea that the nation-state is composed of discrete and homogenous regions all dependent upon a national (or supranational) center stems from the same logic. In opposition to this it is necessary to assert that "Globalization sets up new poles of attraction for social relations, which threaten older forms of social cohesion. It therefore represents the innovative forces of sociality" (Albrow 1996: 213). In short, to appreciate why Europe is "constantly surprised by its periphery," we need to challenge existing notions of regional hierarchies and locate our understanding of spatial inequality within the framework of globalization and autonomization.

The second component of the critique concerns the model of growth which predominates in discussions about the EU. Describing peripheries as autonomized amounts to more than saying that the spatial or power relationship between center and periphery has been transformed. It refers equally to a critique of the model of economic growth with which the EU works. In many important respects EU policy assumes that growth is more pronounced in the core regions and the benefits of this growth need to be disseminated to the peripheries. In other words, growth in the peripheries is dependent upon growth in the core, and it is the EU's task both to ensure that the wealth creation potential of the core is maximized and that the dissemination of the benefits of growth are transmitted as efficiently as possible to the peripheries. Many EU policies are predicated on this logic: trans-European networks and cohesion policy being two obvious examples.

This chapter is organized in the following way. In the first section the core–periphery assumptions underlying both the EU's model of dependant economic growth and some of its key policies will be outlined. The following section will examine a number of approaches to the relationship between the peripheries and European integration. This will be followed by a detailed assessment of the contribution of contemporary sociological and social theory to the question of understanding core–periphery relations. In addition to the contribution of the globalization theorists, whose work in effect frames the whole discussion, other important sociological work on the network will be explored, focusing on the work of Mann (1998), Barry (1996 and 2001), and Castells (2000a and 2000b). Axford and Huggins (1999) ultilize the idea of networks and flows as a way of thinking about transnational citizenship. Appaduarai (1990) focuses on "flows and scapes" as a way of taking us away from the necessity to study nationally bounded societies and in doing so paves the way for a new understanding of the relationship between globalization and peripheries. In sum, sociological and social theory approaches which problematize the idea of bounded society – particularly where they talk of networks, flows, and fluids – will be shown to have the potential to make an important contribution to understanding the issue of core–periphery relations in contemporary Europe.

The Core–Periphery Model

Spatial inequalities across the EU are normally represented as either regional or national disparities, that is to say variations in wealth between regions or member states, or more broadly in terms of a core–periphery dichotomy. On this latter model an affluent core centered on the industrial regions of northern Europe is surrounded by the less-developed Mediterranean, Celtic, and Nordic fringes. In fact, these two representations of inequality are linked: both the core and the periphery comprise of regions and/or their aggregate: member states. The employment of the core–periphery model as an explanatory tool in EU discourse reveals some important assumptions concerning a whole range of issues: the nature of the relationship between regions and member states, the type of growth experienced within the EU, the dynamics of EU integration, and the form of regional policy appropriate to deal with the problem of disparities in wealth.

EU reports regularly use the term core–periphery to designate the pattern of national and regional inequality that is thought to exist in the contemporary EU. To take one example, "economic disparities between Member States are most evident at the regional level and, in particular, between the centre and the periphery" (European Commission 1996a: 21). Furthermore, the idea of a core–periphery or center–periphery disparity within the EU has taken on a greater significance since the EU launched its single market programme in the mid-'80s. The reason for this is that despite the introduction of designated "compensatory mechanisms" (meaning the Cohesion Fund and increased resources to the Structural Funds) economic disparities have grown, the result of the increased concentration of economic activity engendered by the single market. In other words, the single market tends to exacerbate regional disparities and reinforce a core–periphery pattern of disadvantage.[1]

It used to be said that the rich–poor division in Europe had a north–south axis, exemplified by the north–south polarity of wealth distribution in Italy. This representation of Europe's wealth divide has now been superseded by the core–periphery division. The European periphery consists of the Nordic, Celtic, and Mediterranean fringes, with the majority of poorer regions to be found in the Mediterranean areas. Clusters of poorer regions exist on the northern periphery (northern and eastern Finland and the north and west of the UK). The EU's wealthy core extends from southeast England, through northern France and Paris, the Benelux countries, Germany, and northern Italy. In the "poor four" growth is centered on the relatively prosperous urban centres, particularly capital cities, rather than on the poorer regions. On this model "favored regions" experience more rapid growth than less favored regions and, initially at least, disparities within a country widen. Later, a "second phase" of growth occurs in which "efforts need to be concentrated in the poorer regions to ensure they benefit from national success (from 'trickle down')" (European Commission 1999b: 21).

This dynamic of growth is significant for two reasons. First, the pattern of growth in the Cohesion countries suggests a high degree of internal differentiation, with some regions growing much more quickly than others, and the main loci of growth being the capital cities and better-off regions. This lends support to the idea that the EU's core–periphery relationship is being undermined by the dynamic of growth. In circumstances relatively favorable to growth the periphery is not growing uniformly, but unevenly and in a way that accentuates existing disparities. Peripheral "cores" are developing in relation to local "peripheries." Secondly, and linked to the first point, this is a pattern of growth consistent with the idea of auton-omization; internally differentiated regions, discordant growth, regions benefiting at the expense of others within the same member state. To give an example, in Ireland the growing dominance of multinationals in certain sectors has been achieved without the development of linkages with the other sectors in the local economy (European Commission 1999b: 30). This is entirely consistent with autonomized growth, which by its very nature cannot form the basis for generalized regional development.

Policy aimed at enhancing cohesion and the reduction of disparities in the EU takes the form of a dissemination of the benefits of growth, not the encouragement of a more even spread of growth. In doing so, cohesion policy serves to reinforce existing patterns of disparities, even while its expressed purpose is the exact opposite. It does so in two main ways. First, it links cohesion and competitiveness through a "virtuous circuit" in which cohesion underpins the market, which leads to greater competitiveness, which leads to growth, which in turn contributes to greater cohesion. Tying cohesion to competitive-ness in this way makes the development of problem regions contin-gent upon growth elsewhere and lagging regions become dependent, not just on other, richer regions, but upon growth itself. Second, it prioritizes growth above all else. The EU's cohesion policies encour-age, legitimize, and propagate initiatives that emphasize growth at the expense of redistribution. For example, in Greece where regional disparities have historically been small, "increasing trade and com-petition have begun to have a differential effect between regions, with Athens being favoured, in part because of its better access to the rest of EU" (European Commission 1999b). Growth has been concen-trated in Athens and disparities are opening up with the rest of the country. Disparities are not the result of insufficient levels of struc-tural support or a failure of cohesion, they are caused by particular patterns of growth.[2]

We have seen how EU regional policy (and its national counter-part) is predicated on a model that assumes that the benefits of growth will flow from richer areas to less developed areas and disadvantaged regions. This is very also much the philosophy under-lying the trans-European networks: a modern transport and com-munication infrastructure is indispensable if the benefits generated in the core of the EU are to be more easily spread to the periphery. Trans-European networks are intended to complement the EU's range of policies for economic and social cohesion, and to assist with the development of the single market. The trans-European networks work as the unifying principle for an array of disparate projects associated with enlargement, cohesion, growth, and competitiveness. In addition, enhanced communications can reduce peripherality, or at least its more negative aspects. The accessibility of a region is held to be a critical determinant of its competitiveness and growth. In general, the more peripheral a region the lower its GDP per head is likely to be (European Commission: 1996a, 1999b). It is because regional disparities are closely linked to accessibility that infrastructural development is fundamental to any prospect of greater cohesion, and a central plank in the EU's pre-accession support for applicant countries.

The trans-European networks are nominally mechanisms of competitiveness and cohesion but work to reinforce a model of growth, which leaves backward regions heavily dependant upon more developed ones. Less developed regions can only grow by sharing in the growth potential of richer regions. Growth is passed on or handed down from richer to poorer regions, it is never independent of the richer regions. Such patterns of growth can only lead to continued regional unevenness. TENs are an instrument through which the EU aims to ameliorate the problems of peripherality but "it remains the case that the centrality or peripherality of a region's location can be improved but not fundamentally changed through transport" (European Commission 1994: 114).

TENs are a crucial component of the EU's self image – modern, mobile, and efficient – but the idea of the developmental contribution of high-tech infrastructural networks is not matched by their actual contribution to EU cohesion. This is one reason why the rather over-optimistic estimations of the benefits of TENs which the Commission sometimes feels compelled to make are counterbalanced by more sober judgments. Many of the benefits claimed for TENs center on the lower transaction costs that they can entail.[3] But overall the Commission's claims for the impact of TENs on the peripheries are rather restrained. In addition to bringing about the possibility of lower costs, efficient transport systems contribute to a reduction in *"the perception of distance"* (European Commission 1996a: 76 emphasis added), a rather less tangible benefit for the EU's peripheries.

Criticisms of the EU Model

The European Commission's discourse on peripherality has three main characteristics. First, peripherality is inherently a bad thing, a cause of poverty and backwardness, and must be acted upon and, if possible, eliminated. Second, peripherality is caused by a combination of the absence of growth (and/or dependence upon growth in another place – the core), and distanciation. Expressed slightly differently, peripherality is the product of lack of integration with the single market and lack of infrastructural development, measured in terms of distance from major centers or travel time by road, rail or air (European Commission 1994: 112). Third, peripherality is a problem for European integration and hence the target for remedial support (although it is claimed that a reduction in disparities can be better achieved via growth rather than targeted redistribution).

There are two rather obvious weaknesses in this way of thinking about peripheries. The first, is that the EU is working with a very productivist model. Leontidou and Afouxenidis (1999: 261) highlight this tendency to reduce peripherality to an absence of positive productive qualities: "the friction of distance, impaired accessibility, economic disintegration, including both stagnant production structures and de-industrialization or failure in productive restructuring." The second weakness is that the EU's notion of peripherality is predicated upon "northern values," the norms of the northern member states. We have seen in relation to national programs of regional support how there is the expectation that the better-off regions subsidize the poorer ones. This may work in the richer members states but runs into problems in the case of the richer regions in the "poor four," which are not rich at all in comparison to the corresponding regions in the better-off countries.[4]

We will explore this criticism of "northern" bias in more detail by looking at the work of Hadjimichalis (1994) who argues that the European Commission is aware of the fact that greater integration is likely to produce an increase in regional inequalities.

Hadjimichalis (1994: 23) argues that:

> Dominant approaches in the Union acknowledge the fact that regional and social disparities are likely to deepen with the prospect of market unification. They see it as a necessary price to be paid towards a united

Europe, however, and as something that can be controlled socially through EU programmes, especially regional policy.

He supports the contention that cohesion policy works according to the principal that "growth is the best form of cohesion" and that the EU views market forces rather than targeted intervention as the best way to reduce regional disparities. The Commission insists on maintaining a policy of allocating resources "towards strengthening competition and market forces as the main mechanism to bring benefits to peripheral regions" (Hadjimichalis 1994: 19). Given the evidence that market forces lead to a concentration of growth in already rich areas Hadjimichalis describes the EU's stance as a contradictory, "some may even say cynical" way of dealing with the prospect of increased regional inequalities.

There are two main problems facing the southern regions of the EU. First, the south is disadvantaged by the fact that "EU policies have a north-central European socio-economic bias incapable of appreciating southern peculiarities" (Hadjimichalis 1994: 20). Second, the single market stands to benefit the large urban centres at the expense of the southern regions. However, in reinforcing this second point he is not merely restating the orthodoxy that the single market has reinforced core–periphery distinctions. He is concerned that economic expansion away from the traditional centres, which was a feature of growth in the late 1970s and '80s, will be disrupted by the rigors of the single market regime. "Capitalist development started to flourish, not around the poles of induced development as a planned trickling-down effect, but rather spontaneously in other regions and localities" (Hadjimichalis 1994: 20). This type of growth does not fit with EU expectations, which assume a "rather linear and economistic view of the regional development process" (Hadjimichalis 1994: 21), in which lagging regions are assisted in order that they can be expected to catch up with more developed ones. This view of development is also a "northern" one in as much as it assumes a social context which does not conform to the southern reality. Southern Europe does not easily conform to the model of "man-as-worker (or officially unemployed), with a Fordist definition of work, and with a family supported partially by the state" (Hadjimichalis 1994: 22). That the south does not conform to this model is considered deviant, the "northern" route to capitalist development being the norm against which this is measured.

The outcome of this pattern of single market driven development, favoring as it does the northern core of the EU, is an increasing unevenness in integration. On the one hand, there are highly integrated regions which benefit from being included in European and global networks. On the other hand, there are disintegrated and fragmented regions, "the larger part of which are to be found in southern Europe" (Hadjimichalis 1994: 27). While some of this argument resonates with the idea of autonomization, Hadjimichalis has a very different appreciation of the way in which globalization impacts upon regions and peripheries in the EU. He sees the single market as a force which will widen the gap between the "two extreme poles, the global and the local," and that in a polarized EU it is the northern core which comprises the global, and the southern fringes which are accorded the inferior status of the local. It is to the issue of globalization and its relation to the EU's peripheries which we must now turn.

Globalization and Core–Periphery Relations

We know that the relationship between globalization and the EU is frequently assumed to be one in which the former has stimulated the integration of the latter. There is another common assumption about the relationship between globalization and the EU which is relevant to our present discussion. Globalization is credited with stimulating the role of the region in the contemporary EU. As outlined in the previous chapter there are two main variants of this argument: (a) the idea of a "Europe of the regions," and (b) the idea of "integration through differentiation." We will consider how each of these conceptualizes the periphery, and then outline an alternative interpretation of the relationship between core and periphery based on the understanding of globalization, the region, and the process of autonomization developed earlier in the book.

The "Europe of the regions" model of integration proposes a Europe integrated less on the basis of the pooled sovereignty of member states and more along the lines of a federal Europe in which the key actors are subnational regions. This version of European integration gained ground following the Maastricht Treaty and the apparently enhanced role allotted to regions in the drive for economic integration – the idea that Brussels had bypassed the nation-state and had struck a deal direct with Europe's regions. Increased spending on regional problems, the idea of subsidiarity, and the creation of the Committee of the Regions fuelled support for such an interpretation.

The region is in the ascendancy, it was argued, because globalization and the EU's supranational institutions have rendered the nation-state obsolete. Subnational regionalist movements – whether seeking secession, cultural freedoms or economic autonomy – were also taken as evidence that the time of the region had come. Whichever way you looked at it, from the top down or the bottom up, the future of the EU was in the hands of its regions.

In terms of core–periphery relations the "Europe of the regions" model of integration posits a solid relationship between the regions and the centre – now Brussels rather than the national capital – and between each other. Regions are able to revel in their newfound freedoms and are being empowered by Brussels in a way that they never were within the framework of the nation-state. There are two points to note concerning the "Europe of the regions" idea in relation to peripherality. First, the EU is assumed to be generating and controlling the regional initiative. Such freedoms that the regions enjoy have been made possible by the EU, loosening the regions' ties to the nation-state and granting additional powers from Brussels. But this does not necessarily alter the position of the peripheral regions to any fundamental degree. Regions are still locked into a centre–periphery relationship; it is just that the location of the center is somewhere different. Second, the regions are assumed to have a greater degree of equality in this new relationship. Peripherality within the context of the nation-state and traditional patterns of advantage and disadvantage are not necessarily mapped onto the pan-European level. In addition to general regional policies the EU has also launched a number of cross-border programs designed to offset the problems associated with peripherality and being located on the external borders of the EU.

The "Europe of the regions" model of integration is another example of the way in which accounts of the relationship between globalization and the EU assume an integrative dynamic. Other possible interpretations of this relationship suggest themselves. According to Albrow (1998a) a key feature of Europe in the Global Age is the autonomy of locality. In the case of the old local versus central government; "if the central entered the local that was the end of the local." In other words, the center could determine, regulate, and dominate the local or the peripheral. Under conditions of glob-ality however, this cannot be said of the relationship between the global and the local. When entering the local "the global actually differentiates the local, even produces it." We must remember that such ideas develop from an understanding of globalization which assume a complex relationship between the global and the local, and which move us away from a model of globalization which posits a spatial continuum with "the local" at one end and "the global" at the other. The latter is the model upon which Hadjimichalis bases his view that the polarization "global/local" would exacerbate the core–periphery problems inherent in EU growth. On Albrow's understanding of the production of locality, the local is not increasingly dominated or polarized by the global. The local is animated from a distance not from a proximate center. This is consistent with the idea that the global does not possess a center and its relations with localities are "infinitely various." It is not simply that regions are freed from central government constraints: "The new localities in their globality are as independent of Brussels as they are of Rome or Paris" (Albrow 1998a).

The idea of "integration through differentiation" also presupposes the hidden hand of globalization. The premise, shared to some extent with the "Europe of regions" approach, is that the EU is devolving power downwards to the regions at the same time as the nation-state is being hollowed out. The region "works" for the EU because regional agencies are well placed to make decisions concerning the application of policies at the local level and the most effective utilization of resources. This centers on the idea that the application of policy at the regional level is often a more effective means of integration than imposing top-down decisions from the central state. In recognizing the specificity and difference of the region, and tailoring the application of policy accordingly, the EU is facilitating integration.

This approach shares much with the multi-level governance approach. On this model globalization organizes different levels of integration which fit snugly inside one another like Russian dolls. The regional "fits" the national, which in turn is contained within a supranational framework. The global encompasses them all. Importantly, the levels are viewed as harmonious and non-conflictual. Regionalization is a sensible and rational way of organizing EU activity, building integration from the bottom up as well as facilitating top-down structures. It is also a model which perpetuates the idea of the "global–local continuum" criticized above. There are several other criticisms of this model that we should consider. First, that it tends to render peripheries invisible, treating regions as rather uniform throughout the EU. It also diminishes the importance of intra-regional disparities, in a way so common to EU regional studies. Second, it rather optimistically presumes that the regions, their member states and the EU exist in a state of mutual cooperation, and assumes that each level requires the others for integration to take place.

Neither of these approaches offers an adequate model for understanding why "Europe is constantly surprised by its periphery." In order to begin to understand the nature of peripheries within the contemporary EU we must first of all shift the emphasis of our study away from the region. We have already seen how the idea of the discontinuous region undermines the idea of the region as a coherent and bounded entity. We have also seen how the idea of autonomization forces a re-assessment of the dynamics of integration, and the role of the region within that process. We must now move forward and examine ways in which we can conceptualize European Union space which does not depend upon a straightforward cartographical notion of the EU as an assemblage of nations and regions.

Networks and Flows

In order that we might better understand peripheries and find different ways of conceptualizing them it is suggested that we examine some recent writing on networks and the EU. We have already encountered Castells' conceptualization of the EU as a "network state" in chapter 3, and here we will look at his ideas in the context of the EU as a space of networks. The EU understood as a complex of networks is also developed in different ways by Barry (1996 and 2001) and Mann (1998), while Axford and Huggins (1999) equate the coming of the network society with the EU as a "postnational polity." The relevance of all these writers for our present discussion is that they all seek to problematize what Axford and Huggins (1999: 174) call the "territorialist assumptions" about integration which dominate thinking on the EU.

For Castells (2000a) networks allow for a conceptualization of the EU which emphasizes openness, unboundedness, and fluidity. Networks do not have centers (nor, by extension, peripheries). Instead they comprise nodes which can be linked in any number of relationships.[5] Networks do not preclude power inequalities between participants and, as such, hierarchies of power exist but, importantly, "the nodes of the European network state are interdependent" and "no node, even the more powerful, can ignore the others, even the smallest, in the decision making process" (Castells 2000b: 363). No doubt many will find this an unusually optimistic interpretation of EU policy-making structures. That aside, while promising to reveal the existence of a dynamic, open system at the heart of the EU, Castells' network society cannot fully dispense with the territorialist apparatus: the local, and regional link up with the national and the supranational.[6]

To understand Castells' ideas on Europe and networks it is first necessary to appreciate the extent to which they are shaped by his interpretation of globalization. Networks arise from the need to accommodate various centers of national and regional political authority across Europe and, at the same time, to respond to the forces of globalization. According to Castells, the originary and dominant networks are those of the "new economy" which is "organized around global networks of capital, management and information" (2000a: 502). The networks which constitute the EU stem from the networks comprising of global flows of capitalism. Castells' appreciation of globalization is undoubtedly an economistic one in which global movements of capital and technological knowledge are the key indices.[7] The network "works" for capitalism and is a sensible arrangement under conditions of globalization. Castells writes, "the network state . . . is the response of political systems to the challenges of globalization. And the European Union may be the clearest manifestation of this emerging form of state" (Castells 2000b: 364).

Castells work exhibits a tendency to reduce globalization to technologically engendered capital flows.[8] It also fails to break with many "territorialist assumptions" about the nature of political rule and integration in Europe. In Castells' hands the idea of the EU as a "network society" is little more than an alternative way of formulating the familiar idea that government in the EU is now organized on different levels, and that the regions are important players alongside nation-states. The EU represents a new form of state – the network state – consisting of new institutions of government "created at the European, national, regional, and local levels" (Castells 2000b: 339). This is disappointing end destination to a journey starting so promisingly with the image of the network as "a highly dynamic, open system, susceptible of innovating without threatening its balance." What Castells offers subsequently is a minor variation on the care-worn theme of the EU as a multi-level state system and a geometrically variable sovereignty.

Axford and Huggins link the emergence of network society to the possibility of a postnational polity in Europe and work from the premise that Europe is a "space of flows rather than a super- or supra-statist entity" (1999: 173). They are well aware of the tensions that exist between "a Europe of networks and spaces and a Europe of places," a tension which Castells' network model was unable to resolve. For Axford and Huggins (1999: 174) the European network polity in prospect is "de-spatialised, multi-layered and multi-nodal," and "local, regional, national, European, and global in scope." This represents a clear advance on Castells' version, emphasizing as it does the rejection of a territorial basis for EU integration, and allowing networks to extend across different spatial systems without seeking to connect them or arrange them in a hierarchy. Borrowing Axford and Huggins' terminology we might say that Castells' net-work society is a space of places integrated by a network. For Axford and Huggins, on the other hand, network society has a more open texture and comprises a space of flows without any necessary order or regulation.

For Axford and Huggins the EU is a post-national polity, a space of flows, "communities without unity, increasingly pluralistic, open and founded on networks" (1999: 184). This is a very useful formulation. The idea of Europe as a loose collection of communities without overall unity but connected via networks has affinities with the idea of autonomization outlined in the previous chapter. Axford and Huggins' approach is also able to incorporate the idea that the EU is characterized by forms of government which do not rely upon the state (which they designate by the term governance). This leads them to the conclusion that the European network society model "captures the indeterminate nature of the European Union as a system of rule" (Axford and Huggins 1999: 185). The strength of their analysis is that they never assume that Europe is unified or integrated in a simple or straightforward way or indeed that current processes will inevitably lead to such unity. Elements of a transnational polity characterized by governance without government and founded on networks may be discernible, but this should not blind us to the fact that the configuration of the European Union is far from simple. Different Europes coexist. "United Europe partakes of some elements of state-centred co-ordination, a whiff of supranationalism and a growing amount of non-hierarchical, cross-border networking" (Axford and Huggins 1999: 186).

This idea that there are many Europes, or more precisely, a multiplicity of European networks, is the starting point for Mann's investigation of whether "European society" exists. He asserts that rather than total systems, societies always consist of "multiple, over-lapping, intersecting networks of interaction each with differing boundaries and rhythms of development."[9] He sets out to examine the "degree of internal coherence and external closure of European social networks." In the case of the EU there are five main spatial networks existing at different levels: subnational, national, inter-national, transnational, and global.[10] Not surprisingly Mann finds that the various power networks have reached different degrees of closure and coherence. In terms of economic and military power he concludes that the networks certainly have global reach but this does not mean that these global network are internally coherent and systematic. He states that "outer global closure is perfectly compatible with multiple inner networks each embodying limited degrees of closure and cohesion" (Mann 1998: 205). The growing salience of the global should not be taken to mean that the local or national are not maintaining their importance. What it does mean is that the recog-nition of the multiplicity of networks which overlap, intersect, and conflict is an essential step in apprehending the complexity of glob-alization. Globalization does not imply cohesion and conformity and to say that there exists a global economy does not mean that the EU fits harmoniously into this scheme or that there are not tensions and conflicts at the national or subnational level. "Euro" itself lacks "overall internal cohesion and external closure."

While Mann's work offers a productive way of thinking about the EU's internal and external relations in terms of a multiplicity of networks, it fails to dispense with the more territorialist aspects of thinking about EU space. For example, when giving consideration to economic networks Mann notes that "Euro" has "become a substan-tially bounded network of trade interaction." One consequence of this economic integration he notes, has been a widening of inequali-ties between regions. The cost of integration has been tensions between core and periphery (Mann 1998: 195), with the core prosper-ing at the expense of the periphery. Mann sees no potential for subnational, transnational or global networks to significantly amelio-rate what, in his analysis, is a by-product of increasing national economic interaction across "Euro" networks. In terms of offering remedial measures Mann can do nothing more than point to the cost to economic efficiency that would be incurred if the powerful forces leading to core–periphery patterns of wealth were challenged (Mann 1998: 195).

In Mann's work there is no sense that regional networks could have a relationship to global networks independent of those operating in national or "Euro" space. Furthermore, the subnational (and the national) are precluded from the category of transnational actors. For Mann, the local or subnational is separated analytically from the transnational ("relations freely crossing through national borders"). In other words, the local can only operate subnationally and never transnationally or globally. The global comprises transnational or international relations which span the globe, but do not act locally. The local and the global operate in distinct spheres of influence and never the twain shall meet. Such a polarization stems from the frequently encountered assumption that the global and local exist at opposite ends of a linear scale. The equation of core–periphery inequalities and global–local dichotomies, which we encountered in our assessment of the work of Hadjimichalis, also underlies Mann's work.

According to Barry (1996 and 2001), within the European Union the model of the network has come to provide a dominant sense of political possibility. The network is not, as it is for Castells, primarily a mechanism through which capitalism can become global. The network should not be thought of as simply a supplement to the workings of the market. Rather it can form the basis for thinking about EU government in a way which does not reduce it to an opposition between state and market: "the network is both more organised than the market and yet less centralised and less bureaucratic than the state" (Barry 1996: 28). Similarly, the idea of the network can be employed to transcend the political conflict between welfarism and neoliberalism (Barry 1996: 33). The European Union should be understood as a manageable space constructed "through a whole series of specific competitive and co-operative networks" (Barry 1993: 321).

Thinking about the EU in terms of "the European network" has many advantages. As Barry notes, it enables us to better understand how the EU governs not by acting on and managing bounded spaces (whether the region, the nation or the community) but by working through networks which are not necessarily coterminous with national or EU boundaries. The EU's influence extends, via networks, beyond EU borders in the case of the single market, for example. Indeed, the EU extends its sphere of influence through networks, externally as well as internally (Barry 1996: 35). In addition, networks should not be thought of simply as a communication framework: they can be actors too.[11] They are capable of animating social and political actors in a way which frees them of a dependency on the state. In Barry's hands the network becomes a potential means of empowerment for political agents and his formulation complements the notion of autonomization developed in the previous chapter. In contrast to Mann who sees networks as delineating the field in which actors can work, Barry sees networks as much less circumscribed. Networks create independence amongst their constituents and animate rather than regulate.

Despite the undoubted importance of the idea of the network to an understanding of the EU, Barry has certain reservations as to its ultimate value. While representing a clear advance on more traditional spatial mappings of the European space the metaphor of the network has its own limitations. It "may convey an illusory sense of rigidity, order and of structure; and it may give little sense of the unevenness of the fabric and the fissures, fractures and gaps that it contains and forms" (Barry 2001). As we have seen, by itself a theory based on networks does not necessarily lead to a view of the EU as unbounded and contingent. In the work of Castells and Mann network society can be rigid and inflexible in its own way and conform to a rather one-dimensional and deterministic view of the impact of globalization and the EU. The generic advance offered by the idea of the network – generated by the universal agreement that networks are spatial arrangements without a center – does not necessarily translate into more flexible thinking about center–periphery relationships unless it is accompanied by a thoroughgoing critique of the territorialist assumptions which dominate thinking on EU governance and integration. As Hetherington and Law (2000: 128–9) point out, networks are not the only or best way of thinking about the spatiality of relations: "it is clear that the metaphor of the network is too limited in its assumptions about connections, regions and centres of calculation – nodes that come to sum up the relations of the network."

We have already encountered the idea that the EU should be envisaged as a "space of flows." Axford and Huggins' idea of network society seeks to challenge the territorialist assumptions of integration by viewing the EU as a space of flows rather than a space of places. In order to explore this idea further it will be instructive to look at Appaduarai's (1990) much cited paper *Disjuncture and Difference in the Global Cultural Economy*.[12] Although Appaduarai does not deal with the EU as such and is more concerned with modelling the complexity of the global cultural economy, his ideas do have a relevance to our study of EU networks and flows, and after a brief consideration of some of the most important elements of his work we will turn our attention to exploring the ways they can be applied to EU regions and peripheries.

The global cultural economy, he asserts, can no longer be understood in terms of traditional core–periphery models, even ones that allow for multiple centers and peripheries. The global cultural economy is now much more complex and, importantly, there are "fundamental disjunctures between economy, culture and politics" (Appadurai 1990: 296). To investigate these he proposes that we study the "relationship between five dimensions of global cultural flow which can be termed: (a) ethnoscapes; (b) mediascapes; (c) technoscapes; (d) finanscapes; and (e) ideoscapes." There are two initial points that should be made before considering what each of these scapes signify and how they are related. The first concerns the word "disjuncture," the second the word "scape." Disjuncture designates disjointedness or separation, dislocation. Appadurai uses this term both to signify that he does not endorse a simple deterministic version of Marxism, and to distance himself from the suggestion that in studying the global level he is positing another kind of unity: the world as a global economic or cultural system, for instance.[13] The designation "scape" is used to indicate that these facets of global cultural flow are "perspectival constructs" rather than objective relations. In other words, different actors (governments, businesses, and individuals) will have different perceptions as to the meaning of, and their place within, global flows.

Appadurai recognizes that under conditions of globalization social and political actors inhabit not just the imagined communities of nation-states (Anderson 1983) but also imagined worlds. These worlds consist of shifting landscapes which are not integrated or unified, but exhibit changing structures and relationships. It is important to register that Appadurai is looking at key aspects of global cultural *flow*. The importance of this can be seen in his conceptualization of ethnoscapes, for example. Ethnoscapes comprise groups and persons in motion – tourists, immigrants, guestworkers – who influence "the politics of and between nations to a hitherto unprecedented degree" (Appadurai 1990: 297). The stability of societies and networks is constantly undermined by human movement. Technoscapes are formed by high-speed communications moving across "previously impervious boundaries." Finanscapes refers to the flows of global capital and speculation on commodities which are increasingly difficult for nation-states to regulate. Mediascapes refer to the global reach of news, television and film, as well as the images of the world which they produce. Ideoscapes also comprise images but center on conflicts between state ideologies and counter-ideologies and contestations around the meaning of key terms such as democracy, sovereignty, and freedom. The critical thing to understand about these scapes is that there are disjunctures between them all (Appadurai 1990: 306). In particular, "the global relationship between ethnoscapes, technoscapes and finanscapes is deeply disjunctive and profoundly unpredictable" (Appadurai 1990: 298). It is at this point that the importance of the disjunctures becomes clear. Disjunctures have become central to the politics of global culture. It is the disjunctures which facilitate global flows which in turn, *occur in and through the growing disjunctures between ethnoscapes, technoscapes, finascapes, mediascapes and ideoscapes*" (1990: 301).

Appadurai's scapes are characterized by disjunctures and their fluid and uncertain relationships. He is offering us a model of global flows which emphasizes not global integration and interconnectedness but "global fragmentation, uncertainty and difference" (Appadurai 1990: 308). He directs his attention to the ways in which the disjunctures he has outlined are leading to the disunity of nation and state in the contemporary world.[14] One consequence of this is that ethnicity can no longer be restrained by the "national container" of the nation-state and has "become a global force, forever slipping in and through the cracks between states and borders" (Appadurai 1990: 306). This is a very good example of the important spaces which disjunctures open up, and also the way in which he conceives of a "world in motion." Stable communities, in as much as they exist, are always undermined by movement and flow.[15]

Appadurai provides the means by which the study of social relations and cultural and political change can be approached without being bound to the idea of the nation-state. He draws attention to the global vision of many groups and agents in society, and to the ways in which different actors have different perspectives of what the global is, and what possibilities it offers them. This is the way in which we should think of applying his work to an understanding of the EU. Global flows are not constituted out of pre-existing, static entities, which can be conveniently linked up into networks. Global flows stem from disjunctures, not the other way round. As we have already seen, in the work of other thinkers a "Europe of the network" is commonly imagined as a new set of connections between regions, enterprises, and suchlike. Networks bypass existing relations and subvert dominant hierarchies (as they work to impose their own).

The most relevant aspect of Appadurai's work from the point of view of understanding regions and peripheries is that networks and flows do not arise from a desire to organize existing elements in a new way. Appadurai takes us beyond this network model and shows us how disjunctures free-up actors and enable them to reimagine their relationships along global lines. Where there are no disjunctures, or where actors choose to imagine their community as national rather than global, there will be no global flows. To understand the EU's peripheries and the dynamics of integration we should, following Appadurai, direct our attention to the disjunctures between economy, culture, and politics, which exist at both the member-state and EU level. Nowadays it is widely accepted that the bond between nation and state has been undermined and nation-state no longer provides the dominant frame of meaning for its citizens. In the case of the EU we can say that such disjunctures empower diverse actors – including peripheries – by making it possible to both see themselves in a different way and embrace the idea of globality, thereby creating for themselves a whole new range of opportunities.

The implications of Appaduarai's work for a study of the EU are quite profound. Not only does he make a clear break with the territorialist assumptions identified as such a problem by Axford and Huggins, but he successfully undermines the model of the EU as a network of connected places patterned according to some overarching logic. Under conditions of fragmentation, disjunction, and unpredictability there can be no core–periphery relationship. The global is not something distant and removed from the local, rather global flows allow for the emergence of localities and other actors hitherto rendered invisible or marginalized. The disjunctures between economy, culture and politics, which deprive the nation-state of its unity, also work to destabilize the integration predicted by the EU. Appadurai enables us to see that the EU is inserted within, and to a large extent dominated by, a complex of global flows which have their origins not in the processes leading to deeper integration, but in the failure of the EU to constitute itself as an economic, cultural, and political polity. In other words, Appadurai suggests that it is the extent to which EU integration is incomplete which drives globalization, thereby reversing the orthodox interpretation of the relationship.

Conclusion

The difference between networks and flows inheres in the extent to which the former are structured, patterned and formally interconnected, while the latter are fluid, dislocated, and unpredictable. We have seen that there are two main limitations in the way that the idea of networks tends to be deployed in an attempt to understand EU peripheries. The first concerns the relationship that is assumed to exist between globalization and the network. When the global and the local are assumed to be polar extremes and globalization is seen to be responsible for exacerbating core–periphery distinctions (as was the case with Hadjimichalis), disparities are the price to be paid for greater European economic integration, and regional policy, networks and other cohesion mechanisms are merely palliatives. Networks connect peripheries to the core but in doing so institutionalize existing wealth differentials.

The second limitation concerns the relationship assumed between regions and the network. In the main, the idea of a "Europe of the network" designates the way in which different administrative levels are connected to each other in new ways. Europe as a network of places in which the region is accorded an increasingly important status. The network is thus attributed with an important role in European integration: transport and communication networks facilitate the workings of the single market and bind non-member countries and peripheral regions of the EU ever more tightly to the European core. This version of the network sits easily inside both the "Europe of the regions" and the "integration through differentiation" approaches to understanding unification. In other words, the European network is a metaphor for European integration.

Flows do not have the same connotations as networks, nor do they suffer from the same limitations. Flows are not weighed down by the baggage of territoriality, and they allow for a more nuanced understanding of the way in which globalization works within and without the EU. Flows emphasize unevenness and disorder, rather than regularity and structure, autonomization rather than integration. In a useful contribution to this debate Urry (1999) differentiates between scapes and flows. Scapes are structured connections along which important financial, economic, and news information flows. Scapes comprise transport and communication networks, which, once established, attract individuals and businesses who, in wishing to become included, form nodes on these networks. Organizations like the EU (also the World Bank, the UN, Microsoft, CNN) are involved in the globalization of these scapes. In contrast flows – whether of people, information or finance – "move within and especially across national borders and which individual societies are often unable or unwilling to control directly or indirectly" (Urry 1999: 36). Flows and networks work according to different logics. Urry sees flows as having no necessary link to a given society: they work independently of nation-states (and their regions). In a passage which echoes Appaduarai's language of disjuncture Urry states that flows cannot be contained within given societies. "This generates, within any existing 'society', a complex, overlapping, disjunctive order, of off-centeredness, as these multiple flows are chronically combined and recombined across times and spaces often unrelated to the regions of existing societies" (Urry 1999: 36).

To break with the network image altogether Urry distinguishes between global networks and global fluids. A sociology of fluids (as opposed to networks) emphasizes the heterogeneity, unevenness, and unpredictability of mobilities. The idea of global fluids captures "the remarkably uneven and fragmented flows of people, information, objects, money, images and risks across regions in strikingly faster and unpredictable shapes" (Urry 1999: 38). Urry's work confirms the limits of the network metaphor and points to the need to think about peripheries in relation to global flows. In doing so it contributes, along with the work of Axford and Huggins, Barry, and Appaduarai, to breaking the association of networks with the idea of integration. It does this by emphasizing the non-EU origins of global flows and the irregular and contradictory ways in which the global acts upon the EU.

From our discussions of networks, scapes, flows, and fluids – and their relationship to globalization and the idea of the region – we have emerged with a conceptual framework capable of a more complete understanding of core–periphery relations in the EU. A central plank of this understanding is the outright rejection of the region and the periphery as discrete entities, and as currently understood in EU discourse. If we are to dispense with the core–periphery model how are we to understand Europe's periphery? And of what does it consist? Where does this leave us in our attempt to understand the EU and its dynamics of integration? By way of a conclusion to this chapter we will turn our attention to these matters.

It has been argued that the core–periphery relationship is an inappropriate metaphorical tool with which to understand the pattern of inequalities within the EU. We have already noted some criticisms: the presumption of fixed spatial relationships between regions;[16] the assumed homogeneity of regions; the high degree of naturalness accorded to the periphery;[17] the dependent model of growth (and the cohesion mechanism) which stems from core–periphery assumptions. The dominant understanding of EU disparities is based on this core–periphery model, and, with its "northern" and productivist assumptions is both distorting and debilitating, inhibiting consideration of other patterns of disadvantage and exclusion.

At the center of this territorial model of core and periphery stands the region: the EU's self-conscious accommodation to the global marketplace, and the keystone of integration. The sheer mass of the region, as both an object of statistical inquiry and as a "level of governance," imposes itself on any study of the EU. We may theorize an alternative set of relationships within which to position the region and the peripheries, but we cannot easily dispense with them in the form that they are currently thought to exist. Not only is the region discursively constructed and homogenized through the data collected about it, but problem regions and peripheral regions are made manifest. The centrality of the region to the debate about the "democratic deficit" and its role in making the EU more relevant to the needs of its citizens makes it difficult to displace from popular interpretations of integration. The centrality of the region to policy solutions directed at any number of social and economic problems again consolidates its position. That complex social and economic problems require solutions at the regional level is now axiomatic. The option of mobilizing national programs of development as a way of eradicating backwardness and underdevelopment – which was of course the preferred method in the early days of the EEC – has been completely discredited. The shift from national development to regional initiative is not simply an index of the hold which non-interventionist, neo-liberal thinking has over EU policy, it is also a measure of the extent to which the region is central to the EU's understanding of itself.

The idea of the region, and the "presence" of the region, is so dominant that it obscures the global flows which have begun to act upon, energize, and disrupt the EU in new and unpredictable ways. Nevertheless, when placed within a matrix of globalization and de-territorialized flows the region and the periphery reveal new characteristics and provide a focal point around which a new understanding of integration can coalesce. An approach to EU integration centred on a sophisticated understanding of the relationship between global-ization, networks and flows, and the discontinuous and autonomized region permits a different view of the peripheries. Peripheries are simultaneously challenged and re-invigorated by the opportunities which accrue in the spaces created by the EU's attempts to connect with global flows and scapes. Following Appadurai, we can say that the EU is distinguished not by its level of integration but by the disjunctures between its economy, politics and culture, and those which exist within its member states. It is these disjunctures which permit a whole new set of relationships – as yet somewhat tentative, partial and fleeting – between global flows and the local, the regional, and the peripheral.

8   Europe and Democracy

European Identity

Questions of European identity have become a central feature of the study of the EU. Indeed, the question of what Europe's identity consists of and how it can be legitimated have become very closely associated with the project of economic and political integration and enlargement to the east. It has been suggested by Picht (1993) that this search for identity has become equated with the "health" of the EU: the European Union is troubled by its identity problems and a remedy has so far proved elusive. One particular aspect of the identity issue is the way in which democracy and identity have, in a relatively short period of time, become interwoven. The "democratic deficit is closely associated to an identity deficit" (Giorgi, Crowley, and Ney 2001: 74). The success of the European project is increasingly seen as depending on the consolidation of a viable model of European identity (Castells 2000c: 364), and such a model is unlikely to emerge until the "democratic deficit" in the EU is addressed and its institutions become more accountable to its citizens (Smith and Wright 1999). For Siedentop (2000: 24), the crisis of European integration is the issue of political democracy.

It was not always thus. In the early days of the European Community "democracy was never an inherent part of the European unification project" (Rich 2000: 195), and democracy, in as much as it was an issue during the Mediterranean enlargements of the early and mid-1980s (Greece, Portugal, and Spain), centered on whether these countries had functioning parliamentary systems. Since this time the idea of democracy with which the EU identifies has become more sharply defined and given a much higher profile, particularly in dealings with applicant countries. Democracy is center stage and the EU demands compliance with the political elements of the Copenhagen criteria as a condition of entry.[1] Democracy is now an implicit part of the EU's *acquis communautaire* (Markoff 1999: 34).

To many, the idea of European identity is frequently associated with exclusion. We can identify two main variations on this theme. The first is the idea that Europe is thought to possess an exclusive identity based on common history, traditions, and religion. This is an insidious theme which is embraced by a broad spectrum of academics and politicians. Famously, Huntington (1993, 1996) divides the world into primordial and incompatible cultural blocs. His thesis is that in the post-cold war period the world is divided along civilizational rather than ideological lines. Civilizations are basic divisions within humanity, defined as large-scale cultural entities decided according to religion, values, customs, ethnicity. Thus, "Europe ends where Western Christianity ends and Islam and Orthodoxy begin" (Huntington 1996: 185). Center-right politicians such as Germany's former Chancellor Kohl have utilized similar ideas in their attempts to delimit Europe in terms of a Christian heritage and a historical legacy stretching back to the ancient worlds of Greece and Rome. This notion of Europe has been mobilized to oppose Turkey's membership of the EU, for example (Glos 2001). Sociologists too, have embraced the idea that European identity must consist of a coherent collection of shared beliefs, traditions and cultural practices, modelled after national identity.

> Roman law, Judeo-Chrisitan ethics, Renaissance humanism and individualism, Enlightenment rationalism and science, artistic classicism and romanticism, and above all, traditions of civil rights and democracy, which have emerged at various times and places in the continent – have created a common European cultural heritage. (A. D. Smith quoted in Schlesinger 1994: 320)

Others are more sceptical. Delanty (2000: 84) argues that "there is no European identity as such. Europe does not have a shared cultural community which could be the basis of a common cultural identity. There is no common language nor ethnic commonalities upon which a European identity could be built."

The second variation is the idea that Europe, or rather the EU, is constructing a "fortress Europe," the better to control immigration and protect itself from the intrusion of the "third world."[2] These ideas were particularly strong in the early 1990s at the time when the initiatives covered by the Single European Act – especially the creation of the single market, or "1992" as it was termed – were beginning to take effect. The dominant idea was that in choosing to deepen its economic integration the EU was creating new barriers (both physical and metaphorical) to the outside world. "A key point about 1992 and the creation of a single Europe is that it will mean the virtual closure of the EC to non-EC nationals, the creation of what has come to be called Fortress Europe" (Gordon 1989: 11). Europe was in the process of defining and delineating itself in no uncertain terms, with important consequences for those falling outside of its borders. European consolidation and convergence was also an exercise in boundary policing. For example, Hall (1991: 18) was of the opinion that the creation of the single market would entail a major boundary-marking exercise.

> Now that a new Europe is taking shape, the . . . contradictory process of marking symbolic boundaries and constructing symbolic frontiers between inside and outside, interior and exterior, belonging and otherness, is providing a silent accompaniment to the march to 1992.

The uncertainty aroused by a growing number of nationalist ideas and political movements emanating from the collapse of communism, coupled with the changing relationship between the EU and its constituent member states occasioned by the advent of the single market, heightened awareness that the EU – in common with a plethora of emergent national states and nascent ethnic nationalisms – was in the business of establishing and regulating its borders. Moreover, after a generation of living with borders that were rigid and firmly demarcated – particularly those which separated east from west – Europe was experiencing a degree of disorientation. Familiar borders had disappeared, new ones were being established in unexpected places, and the issue of borders, whether demarcating rival ethnic groups, newly constituted nation-states, or delimiting Europe itself, appeared high on everyone's agenda. In the EU context, internal borders were becoming less important while the external ones were taking on a much greater significance. Schlesinger (1995: 324), writing in 1992, concluded that, "fears of an incipient Fortress Europe appear to be borne out by current developments in terms of governmental concerns about the defence and policing of the outer frontiers as the inner ones become less salient."

This cluster of ideas portraying Europe as a fortress, erecting new barriers following the collapse of the Berlin Wall, or deciding upon the "limits to Europe" can be seen as one consequence of the dominance of the idea of unification and unity in EU discourse. European integration has been founded upon the idea of unity and security in much the same way as the nation-state was. That we have come to think about Europe almost exclusively in these terms is because the logic of modernization (Delanty 1995) which infused the post-war European project privileged the nation-state, both in terms of bolstering its legitimacy and by viewing it as the building-block of European unity. The development of the EU has been conceived as a Europe of integrated nation-states (and only latterly in terms of subnational regions). What Delanty refers to as the logic of modernization running through the post-war European project has privileged the nation-state in another very important respect. The practices and institutions of democracy are premised upon those associated with the nation-state. When critics talk of the democratic deficit in the EU they are most commonly referring to the gap between the practices of representative democracy at the nation-state level and the difficulty in instituting comparable procedures at the European level. In Habermas's (1992: 1) view, the EU's democratic institutions and practices "lag hopelessly behind the supranational form taken by economic integration."

Markoff (1999: 34–5) reminds us of the ambivalent attitude to democracy characteristic of the EU. Freedom to organize and express interests is secure and the EU has no coercive apparatus of its own. It is in terms of representative democracy that the EU is deficient: "the only central institution whose members are elected by citizens is weaker by far than the parliamentary counterparts within any of the member states." This perception of the democratic-deficit within the EU, coupled with an interpretation of globalization as a threat to the autonomy and sovereignty of the nation-state, has contributed to the idea that the nation-state is the guarantor of democracy. Undermining the nation-state will lead to a diminution in democracy. Self-determination and sovereignty, electoral representation and participatory democracy are all closely associated with the nation-state. How will these democratic rights be guaranteed if the nation-state has been weakened? Beck (2000: 93) is also aware of this problem.

A guarantee of basic rights, it would seem, presupposes the national state. So how is it possible to establish and secure a cosmopolitan legal relationship between different states and citizens which reduces the importance of the nation state as guarantor, without at the same time becoming lost in the false alternative of either striving for a world state (to take the place of national states) or placing basic rights in a space without laws or states?

As we shall see, the idea of cosmopolitan democracy aims to offer a way out of the dilemma posed by Beck. The stark choice between a world state or international anarchy is rejected in favour of an arrangement which aims to bring nation-state power under democratic control. But we do not need to be an advocate of cosmopolitan democracy to challenge the idea that the nation-state is democracy personified. Rengger (1997: 257) is critical of the idea that the nation-state is an indispensable setting for democracy in the contemporary world: "there is no reason to suppose that the nation-state is a particular friend of democracy, and considerable reasons for supposing the opposite." Nation-states, even western liberal democracies, regularly suppress dissent within their own boundaries. This is usually done in the name of democracy. The defence of democracy legitimates the need to suppress further democratization. In the words of Beck (1997: 83), "the internal democratization of a society can be held in check by enemy stereotypes without having to forgo consensus. Enemy stereotypes . . . make it possible to dismiss democracy with the blessing of democracy."

There is another important dimension to the relationship between democracy and the nation-state that should be borne in mind. The international order founded upon relations between sovereign nation-states has been one in which support for and commitment to democracy has been conditional upon other factors considered to be in the national interest. During the Cold War the West's perception of an external threat made it acceptable to forego a deepening of democracy at home. By the same token the incremental democratization of enemy states was much less of a priority than their military containment or neutralization. In the struggle to establish rival spheres of influence the democratic credentials of a "friendly" regime in Africa or Latin America were largely irrelevant. Cold war priorities permitted a great deal of democratic latitude to those who professed to be loyal to the West. To this day, Britain, the United States and other western countries have reputations for supporting foreign regimes which are far from democratic, while at the same time reminding the world of the extent to which they themselves embody the democratic ideal.

Of course, in many parts of Europe there are powerful tendencies towards polarization, and conflicts which revolve around the determination of belonging on the basis of ascribed identity. Also, in the absence of an external enemy to replace communism, the far right have discovered a new "enemy within" in immigrants (Mouffe 1993: 4). But the nationalist and ethnic struggles which continue in certain parts of Europe are no substitute for democratic contestation. Such ideas do not contribute to the formation of a European democracy, they are merely attempts to play out the identity politics of the nation-state on a wider stage. European democratic identity can never be a projection of nationalist xenophobia to the supranational level. The terms of the democracy debate are far broader and much more diverse. There are no simple distinctions between "us and them," self and other. European democratic identity (when distinguished from the democratic identity of European nation-states) is not fixed or settled, but emergent, hesitant and provisional, and is characterized by contending sets of ideas struggling to gain momentum and achieve dominance.

After reviewing the ways in which democracy and the EU are typically associated (transferred upwards and downwards between the nation-state, its constituent regions, and the supranational EU), and the debates on the democratic nature and potential of the EU *vis-à-vis* member states, this chapter gives consideration to two important contemporary approaches to democracy which seek to rethink democracy away from, and outside of, the nation-state paradigm. They also inform our understanding of the ways in which the EU relates to non-members and to its position within the changing international order. The first of these approaches is cosmopolitan democracy, which looks to the possibility of global democratic institutions beyond the nation-state working to democratize the international system. It also considers the EU to be a working example of cosmopolitan democracy: nation-states supplemented by new levels of democratic initiative.

The second approach is agonistic democracy, a radical theory of pluralism associated with the work of Mouffe and Laclau which places contestation at the very center of an understanding of democracy. This is democracy without any guarantees or predetermined outcomes, political identities and struggles are unstable, shifting, and open-ended. Democracy can never be final or complete, only provisional and inconclusive. Mouffe's work in particular, throws considerable light on the question of European democratic identity, especially the way in which this identity is often predicated on the need to demarcate a non-European "other" through which "we" Europeans might better know ourselves.

Democracy and the EU

The extent to which the EU is democratic is hotly contested. When Euro-democracy is placed under the spotlight it is invariably against the standards of the nation-state that the EU is measured. This gives rise to an understanding of democracy in the EU which emphasizes either that democratic gains at the European level are bestowed by member states,[3] or that the EU should work to develop a democratic structure in which democracy is parcelled out to the different levels on which it operates. Either way, the democratization process is assumed to be regulated by member states who form the building blocks of integration and who are the sole source of democratic imputs to the EU. That the EU could be democratized from elsewhere is rarely given serious consideration.

The work of Laffan (1999) contains a strong assumption that the democratization of the EU has come about because of the pervasive influence of member states within which democratic traditions are embedded. Thus, when these countries became members of the EU they set about increasing the democratic practices of the supranational organization of which they were now a part. The origins of the EU are profoundly democratic and stem from the desire to moderate inter-state relations in Europe, prevent nationalistic conflict, and achieve mutual peace and prosperity (Laffan 1999: 332). The values and traditions common to individual members states – liberty, democracy, respect for human rights, the rule of law – have been projected upwards onto the European level. In this sense, EU democracy "cannot be seen as distinct from democracy in the member states" (Laffan 1999: 340). Democracy comes from member states, and member states are the best means of ensuring the EU's democratic future. "If the Union is to transform itself from a system of democratic states into a democratic system of governance, it must first crucially remain a system of democratic states" (Laffan 1999: 340). This is a trenchant assertion of the primacy of the nation-state in the integration process and the necessity of the survival of the nation-state for the achievement of greater democracy. This is not an argument for a federalist, regionalist, or even internationalist solution to the democratic deficit. The EU is composed of nation-states, and, from the point of view of enhancing democracy, a union of nation-states is the best possible arrangement.

Moreover, the EU is not "suffering from a crisis of democracy or legitimacy" and for Laffan (1999: 347) the idea that the EU is undemocratic is "fallacious." The democratization of the EU continues in an incremental, piecemeal fashion ("democratizing the EU in bits and pieces"), and is accompanied by the institution of citizenship and by the symbols of European identity. Thus, a link between the processes leading to greater democracy and the need for European citizens to identify with the EU is emphasized. However, no European public space currently exists, save for an aggregate of national spheres which are still much more important. Although policymaking has become much more Europeanized, politics has remained much less so. The EU can never aspire to the status of a polity in the absence of a European public, with a European identity, operating in a genuinely European public space. For Laffan, with her preference for a national sovereignty basis for the EU's democratic development, this can only ever come about to a limited extent.

The idea that democracy in the EU is linked to both a European public space and the question of European identity is taken up by Giorgi, Crowley, and Ney (2001). They argue that a European polity will require a democratically viable public space. Crucially, such a space will likely adopt a much different form to that associated with the national level. In other words, a European public democratic space will not be simply an extension or aggregation of those found within the member states. Taking up more of the themes explored by Laffan they establish the following hypothesis: "the reduction of the European democratic 'deficit' – which implies the emergence of a 'public space' at the European level – depends on the restructuring of a genuinely European 'political field'" (Giorgi, Crowley and Ney 2001: 79). In other words, European political actors, participating and operating in a non-national political space must come into existence in order that the EU can become more genuinely democratic.

In contrast to the argument advanced in chapter 3, Giorgi, Crowley and Ney seek a single, unified European public space. For them the emergence of multiple, non-complimentary and autonomous public spaces which may or may not originate within the EU is not representative of the current situation, nor a sufficient precondition for ameliorating the democratic deficit. They hold that "a democratically viable Europe . . . requires a 'public space' or 'public sphere'" (Giorgi, Crowley, and Ney 2001: 74), and their notion of such a public space

– singular not plural – is much closer to the idea of civil society: "a sphere independent of both the market and the state." A European public space would allow for the discussion, evaluation, and contestation of European issues. Here too, the processes of democratization are linked to the building of European identity, but rather than seeing the latter as a prerequisite for the former they argue that greater democratization will lead to a growing identification with Europe, which in turn will promote further democratic tendencies; what they term a "virtuous cycle of truly European citizenship" (Giorgi, Crowley, and Ney 2001: 74).

The work of Giorgi and her co-authors makes an important contribution to the debate on the democratic deficit and the way in which thinking about democracy tends to be firmly embedded within national models. They emphasize that the emergence of a Euro-polity and a genuine EU public sphere is very much tied up with democratization. What is particularly useful about their work is the way that it draws attention to the importance of transnational democratic processes and a European dimension to political mobilization. In summary:

> The EU is not yet a polity and it lacks a public sphere. For this to emerge actions are needed that support trans-national mobilization and political contestation, the consolidation of a European party system, as well as the emergence of a cosmopolitan identity. (Giorgi, Crowley, and Ney 2001: 81)

Where their work is less successful is in assuming that a nascent European public space must be singular and must correspond to the space of European economic and political integration.

There exists a significant federalist tradition of thinking about the EU and democracy which assumes that the EU is naturally evolving a federal structure of governance. For example, the idea of a "Europe of the regions" is sometimes associated with a federalist vision of a division of authority between central and regional government. The EU is not a federal system and is unlikely to become one. Nevertheless, as Rosamond (2000: 22) indicates, the diversity among European states, and the desirability of an overarching unity, makes the attractions of European federalism obvious. Siedentop (2000) makes the case for a federal EU as a means of creating regional autonomy, dispersing power centers and promoting diversity. He recognises that existing democratic cultures are very much tied to the nation-state and that these can be deficient in that they tend to promote a passive form of citizenship and the national state over the regional and the local. Nevertheless, there is a danger that rapid political integration could damage democracy by diminishing national forms of democracy and promoting economic values over democratic ones: "sometimes it seems as if economic growth is the *only* criterion of public policy" (Siedentop 2000: 34–7). Federalism is a way of creating a regime in which regions, states and the federal level exist in harmony, and citizens are active within a civil society, which works to safeguard liberal democracy.

Siedentop (2000: 176) associates a "Europe of regions" with populism and non-civic democratic values. In distancing themselves from national authority, regions run the risk of losing civic cultures that incorporate democratic norms largely absent from regional political cultures. He writes:

> the kind of democracy unleashed by any project for a Europe made up of regions rather than nation-states would be ... a populist kind of democracy which is defined chiefly in terms of liberation from foreigners and which offers little guidance to the complex and hazardous business of self-government.

Citizenship is seen as the key to democracy. Our contemporary societies are too large and complex to allow for an active form of citizenship. As such we need a public sphere in which citizenship is fostered, the activities of the state are limited, and authority is devolved. Federalism encourages new spheres of public authority which can promote self-government, the devolution of power to regions, and the participation of the individual. Federalism "firmly anchors the individual in different layers of association" (Siedentop 2000: 63). The strength of Siedentop's analysis lies in his dismissal of an uncritical celebration of regionalism and the way he draws together questions of democracy and the nature of the European public sphere. He advances a strong argument for not relinquishing the beneficial influence of the nation-state on democratic culture.

A weakness in Siedentop's analysis, in addition to the optimistic assumption of a federal future, is the traditional notion of citizenship and civil society that he employs. Citizenship is conceived rigidly as a mode of civic participation "an active sense of public duty" nurtured by the nation-state, and he laments the substitution of the consumer for the citizen. Turning the citizen into the consumer "treats people simply as role-players, and can lead to a political outcome which ... takes [a] high toll of free-will and the human capacity for self-improvement" (Siedentop 2000: 128). In categorizing the status of citizen and consumer as antithetical, Siedentop declines to acknowledge the different forms of citizenship that are characteristic of modern society (Urry 1999), and the many origins of citizenship rights (Soysal 1994). According to contemporary social thought there is no strict opposition between citizen and consumer, indeed citizenship can be achieved via consumption. Another problem is that despite the emphasis on federalism as the government of diversity, its scope is strictly demarcated, and ultimately homogeneity within European civil society is valued more highly in the federalist scheme of things. "Cultural homogeneity, at least in the public sphere, is necessary if European federalism is to succeed one day" (Siedentop 2000: 147).

Another dominant theme in thinking about democracy and the EU is the emphasis placed on the need to distribute democracy more evenly throughout the various levels – subnational, national, supranational, global – on which the EU operates. This foresees the development of a European polity as a mixture of national, regional, and global governance (Moravcsik 1998). This is another way of saying that the future of the European Union is not as a more centralized "superstate" but as a balance between national and federal authority. Moravcsik's argument is not that the EU is in the processes of deepening its democracy, but that there is a limit to how democratic national publics and elites want the EU to become. In other words, he challenges the assumption that the EU will become progressively more democratic. He makes the pertinent point that a considerable proportion of national electorates oppose key elements of integration. Hence, in this sense "democratization is almost certain to undermine integration" (Moravcsik 1998: 50), and this he argues lies behind the reluctance to cede more power to the European Parliament.

One argument frequently used to demonstrate the inadequacy of EU democracy is that institutions of the EU favor the market, big business and trade liberalization, while working to block social policies and the development of Euro-welfare. Moravcsik sees the key issue in rather different terms. National leaders are able to "exploit constitutional foreign policy powers to conduct what would normally be domestic policies without parliamentary oversight" (Moravcsik 1998: 51). In other words, national leaders can circumvent

their own national democratic processes by skilfully utilizing opportunities at the European level. Therefore, in contrast to Laffan's belief
that the nation-state will succour and stimulate democracy throughout the EU, for Moravcsik it is the national elites and national public
opinion which act as fetters on the process of democratization.

What each of these perspectives share is the assumption that
democracy comes from within and that the democratization of the
EU is very much regulated by the member states. What these
accounts lack is a developed notion of extra-EU democratic resources
acting on and shaping the EU. In the rest of this chapter we will
consider two important theories which embrace the idea that the
democratization of the EU has an external, international or global,
dimension: cosmopolitan democracy and agonistic pluralism.

Cosmopolitan Democracy

One solution to the problem of how democracy can be extended both
beyond the nation-state and within it is identified by Held and others
who support the idea of cosmopolitan democracy. For Held, the
democratic process can no longer be assumed to occur only at the
national level. We must recognize the existence of a series of overlapping levels – regional, national, and global – which have their own
dynamics of democracy. Cosmopolitan democracy advocates the
redistribution of power between democratic agencies working within
and between these levels.

Cosmopolitan democracy, as a political theory, starts from the
observation that in the contemporary world the affairs of nation-
states are interrelated to an unprecedented degree. Many issues and
problems – pollution, the use of diminishing resources, the regulation
of global trade – cannot be acted on effectively by any single nation-
state. The transnational or global impact of the problems and the
forms of cooperation needed to regulate them point to both the
existence of "overlapping communities of fate" (Held 1998: 24) and
the difficulties of making transnational activities amenable to democratic control. One corollary of these developments is that new forms
of popular political participation exist in which citizens are concerned
with international affairs, in addition to the affairs of the nation-state
of which they are a member. Cosmopolitan democracy draws attention to "the creation of a democratic community which both involves
and cuts across democratic states" (Archibugi and Held 1995: 13).

What this means is that international affairs are now also the business of individual actors and their collective organizations: international relations are not the exclusive preserve of nation-states.

The emergence of new actors and new spaces within which they operate notwithstanding, the shifts mapped out by Archibugi and Held have the potential to bring about greater democracy in inter-state cooperation and within nation-states. Cosmopolitan democracy increases the likelihood that the democratic state will be the global norm, and also that democracy will be deepened in countries where it is newly established or insufficiently embedded. Hence, "[c]osmopolitan democracy aims at a parallel development of democracy both within states and among states" (Archibugi and Held 1995: 14). We are moving away from the situation that obtained during the Cold War when the spread of democracy was hampered by relations between states polarized according to ideological principle. Archibugi (1998: 204) makes the point that a world marked by international conflict is not a suitable setting for the maturation of democracy. As such, cosmopolitan democracy endorses two major developments in contemporary international relations which have emerged with the institution of a post-Westphalian world order: the regulation and control of international violence, and, more importantly, interference by the international community in the internal affairs of nation-states.

For the most part, cosmopolitan democracy aims to complement democratic institutions and practices which already exist at the level of the nation-state. It is a conception of democracy "based on the recognition of the continuing significance of nation-states, while arguing for a layer of governance to constitute a limitation on national sovereignty" (Held 1998: 24). In this sense it aims at the establishment of global institutions to monitor the international system of nation-states and thereby facilitate democracy. Some of these institutions are formed by governments working in cooperation, others are the product of citizens' initiatives. Cosmopolitan democracy envisages a new global institutional framework which overlaps with but does not threaten the existing system of inter-state and domestic relations: "cosmopolitan institutions must come to coexist with the established powers of states, overriding them only in certain, well-defined spheres of activity" (Archibugi and Held 1995: 14). Instances where cosmopolitan institutions might want to override the nation-state include cases where the actions of nation-states have transnational consequences (displacement of populations or weapons testing, for example), or where global initiatives are required for effective action (combating international crime or measures to counter the spread of epidemics). It also favors exerting pressure on national regimes to curb their use of repression and coercion and promotes the "direct interventions of democratic publics."

Archibugi and Held make the point that the rise of cosmopolitan democracy has been possible because of the ways in which citizens have been empowered by declarations and conventions sponsored by the UN, what we earlier referred to as the expansion of person-hood rights in the post-war period. Citizens have been given these new rights independently of their membership in a nation-state, although the latter is still the vehicle through which they are imple-mented and their legitimacy acknowledged. Whereas previously citizenship was a status bestowed by membership in a nation-state it is now available, to varying degrees, from an array of transnational and international sources. The relationship between citizens and their nation-state has been modified and the latter no longer represents the horizon of possibility for the former, who are increasingly able to identify with issues, communities and conflicts which have little or no basis in the nation-state in which they reside. As Goldblatt (1997: 145) points out, "international tribunals and declarations of human rights have posited and sustained the duties of individuals to a legal order beyond that of nation-states." Cosmopolitan democracy is an indicator of the non-correspondence of society and state: democratic communities exist without and beyond the nation-state.

Archibugi (1998: 216) states that the necessary global platform for cosmopolitan democracy is still lacking in two important respects. First, existing forms of "global governance" lack sufficient legal competence. Secondly, agencies of existing "global governance" are not necessarily guided by the principles of democracy. Cosmopolitan democracy aspires to both legitimate a range of transnational actors and to improve democratic practices throughout the globe. To achieve both of these aims a basis for intervention in the affairs of others is needed. An appropriate framework of international law is one mechanism, but by itself does not preclude the use of self-serving military force. In order to prove effective, cosmopolitan democracy must identify alternative means of interference, including "on the one hand, the creation of non-governmental authorities charged with pushing for democracy; and, on the other, the identification of new methods which minimize the use of violence" (Archibugi 1998: 210). New forms of intervention include the monitoring and approval of elections by international organizations, economic sanctions, conditions attached to aid and to membership in regional organizations (the EU, for example).

"Civil society" is identified as the main instrument of democratic interference with the aim of securing greater democratic participation. This idea is not without its problems. We have already critically assessed the coherence of the idea of global civil society (see chapter 4). One problem with the idea of global civil society as a tool of democratic interference is that while it suggests a collection of autonomous organizations with a transnational orientation, it also carries the implication that such organizations are linked to, working on behalf of, or subordinate to some kind of (international) state. Certainly, Archibugi's model places the nation-state at its center, both in the sense that it is still the "building block" of international cooperation and that cosmopolitan democracy is designed to exist alongside, rather than to replace, the existing international order very much founded on the sovereignty of the nation-state. For example, he states that cosmopolitan democracy can work to strengthen ties between states, thereby assisting in the development of intergovernmental institutions which can deal with global issues. The "international community" who desire the spread of democracy and need to find ways to legitimately interfere in the democratic development of certain countries and regions, is first and foremost a community of nation-states. The role of cosmopolitan democracy is to facilitate the forms of cooperation that exist between states, and to democratize their mutual relations, policy instruments, and internal processes.

Another problem for Archibugi's model of cosmopolitan democracy is the emphasis on the need for endogenous democratic development. "To be substantial and effective, the greatest part of the struggle for democracy should be based on endogenous, rather than exogenous, forces" (Archibugi 1998: 200). This means that although external interference in democratic affairs is sometimes necessary, lasting and stable democratic development will only be assured if there is a strong domestic democratic culture. In other words, democracy should have the support of the majority and should not be imposed from above but spring forth from below, when external conditions are right (when international conditions do not preclude a democratic awakening). If imposed by external forces democracy will only truly take hold when society is willing and able to embrace democratic principles. He cites the examples of Germany, Italy, Japan, and other countries after the Second World War. Democracy was able to develop only "because the reconstruction of the social fabric within these countries ensured the acceptance of such principles" (Archibugi 1998: 201). In this way, Archibugi establishes the central importance of endogenous democratic growth and outlines how it can be held in check by external factors, as was the case during the Cold War when both democratic deepening in the West and its export to non-democratic countries was circumscribed.

From the point of view of globalization we might want to question the appropriateness of the endogenous/exogenous model. Under conditions of globalization the borders of nation-states become increasingly porous to the point where internal and external, domestic and foreign become blurred. The flows, networks and spaces which constitute the landscape of globalization do not act upon nation-states in an orderly or systematic way, nor are they amenable to control by any one country or union of states. This has become evident through our investigation of the uneven, autonomizing, and de-totalizing impact of globalization upon the EU's regions and peripheries (chapters 6 and 7). Society, community, and locality no longer have the same referents as they did within the nation-state under conditions of modernity. If European society consists of disaggregated, plural, and non-territorial public spaces and "local" communities transcend national borders, there is little point maintaining the fiction of a system of nation-states with their corresponding domestic and international realms.

Archibugi, like Held, subscribes to a model of globalization which emphasizes not these facets of the "new world order," but the existence of multiple levels of international relations: the regional, the national, the international, and the global. Globalization heralds not the erosion of these categories but their increased interdependence, and their ordering along a continuum: the local and the global are separated by the intermediate levels of the national and the supranational. Cosmopolitan democracy is a theory of how new levels coexist and interact with the existing framework of relations between nation-states. Archibugi (1998: 212) states that the aims of cosmopolitan democracy "can be served only by institutional arrangements which would link across and within the existing states." Cosmopolitan democracy implies a union of states in a common purpose, and "the first international organization which begins to resemble the cosmopolitan model is the European Union" (Archibugi 1998: 219).

Cosmopolitan democracy simultaneously displaces the nation-state in favor of other agencies and levels of governance, and bolsters it by according it a privileged place in the new global order. One criticism that has been made of Held is that he underplays the continuing importance of nation-states (Nash 2000: 254). Nation-states cannot be subject to international laws since there is no global state capable of enforcing such laws.[4] Similarly, Nash observes that while no stringent controls over global capital exist, democratic rights will remain largely irrelevant for many people. While acknowledging these points, I would draw attention to the ways in which theorists of cosmopolitan democracy underplay the extent to which transnational processes are working to make untenable the idea of a global order consisting of the national, international and global levels. Rather than attempting to identify the mechanisms by which the "international community" can bring about the spread of democracy, or the means by which the international order of states can better cooperate, it would be more productive to map emerging forms of collective and community action, issue formation and claims-assertion, and mechanisms for governing conflict and dissonance resulting from the interaction of globalization and European integration. Moreover, such processes lead to a reordering of established social and geo-graphical hierarchies, one important outcome of which is a reassess-ment of the practices and institutions of democracy and the nature of representative politics. Cosmopolitan democracy holds to a rather undifferentiated and universalistic idea of democracy, comprising standardized forms of participation, representation, and institution-alization.

The idea of cosmopolitan democracy does have a particular rele-vance to a study of European integration and European democratic identity. Archibugi's claim that the EU is the first international organization which begins to resemble the cosmopolitan model is especially important, as is the idea that cosmopolitan democracy could form the basis for solving the democratic deficit in Europe. There would appear to be a great deal of correspondence between the idea of cosmopolitan democracy as the organization of relations between different democratic levels and the EU as a multi-level polity. European citizenship is a new form of democratic empower-ment which derives from a supranational rather than a national authority. Within the EU, the relationship between the citizens and nation-state has been reordered. The transnational movement of goods, services, people and capital is now commonplace, and broader European rather than narrowly national issues are an increasingly common feature of our political lives.

The features of cosmopolitan democracy which Archibugi found lacking at the global level – forms of transnational governance guided by democratic precepts – are certainly to be found in the EU. Similarly, the EU has adopted mechanisms of democratic interference in the workings of non-members which suggest complementarity with the principles of cosmopolitan democracy. Aided by the European Court of Human Rights, the EU – by means of the Copenhagen criteria – is able to interfere in the practices of other countries. The right to interfere is claimed on the basis that human rights are universal rights of which the EU is the bearer. In a recent speech (European Union 2000), Portugal's Minister for Foreign Affairs, speaking on behalf of the European Union, said, "No country should be free to invoke sovereignty or interference in internal affairs to prevent the people under its jurisdiction from fully enjoying their human rights." In other words, human rights are not a matter left to the discretion of the nation-state. An assertion of national sovereignty cannot form the legitimate basis for a refusal to conform. Non-compliance with global norms warrants EU interference.

There is another important way in which the idea of cosmopolitan democracy is associated with developments within the European Union. The problem of the "democratic deficit" mentioned in the introduction to this chapter has its root in the non-reproduction of participatory and representative institutions characteristic of national democracy at the European level. One way of addressing this problem would be to ensure the integration of different levels of democracy and citizenship. The European Union can clearly play an important role in the realization of this ambition. First, and foremost, overcoming the democratic deficit requires the acknowledgment and legitimacy of multiple European levels of allegiances and rights – subnational, national, supranational and global – combined with those applied by other relevant international bodies.

One question that suggests itself is this: why should the processes and practices associated with cosmopolitan democracy lead to the establishment and preservation of a multi-level system of states and international institutions, rather than its fragmentation and collapse? It would appear that there exists a major tension between the emergence of a multitude of global issues and new transnational forms of cooperation and conflict, and the extent to which these can be harnessed to and supportive of the international system of states. There is no good reason to suppose that having come into existence they will continue to work alongside the existing international order:

they are just as likely to subvert it or bypass it in order to achieve their increasingly self-generated objectives. Similarly, cosmopolitan democracy assumes that transnational actors and processes work for democracy. There is no reason to assume that this need be so. Globalization has no necessary direction and the presence of actors and processes oriented around an entirely different set of political concerns is a reality impossible to ignore.

Agonistic Democracy

The collapse of communism in eastern Europe in the late 1980s and early 1990s contributed in a major way to the to a crisis of democratic identity in western Europe. As Wallace (1994: 20) points out, the demise of communism was seriously disorientating for western Europe. "Once the certainties of the past 40 years had been swept away, it began to become evident that certain parts of the stabilizing framework of both EC integration and of some individual EC member states had also been weakened." The communist "other" was the reference point for democracy in the west. Identities were stabilized by this major antagonistic presence. In the international sphere the cold war divided the globe into three or four "worlds," and at the national level encouraged the institutionalization of class struggle, the expansion of citizenship rights and the subordination of economic, social, and cultural divisions to the need for national unity.

It is not only people in the former Soviet satellites who have engaged in a search for meaning through selfhood in the post-communist period. The fevered search for identity, what Picht (1993) suggests may be "the European disease," has gripped the continent following the demise of the stability and certainty held in place by the Cold War. It is not simply that populations freed from totalitarianism are discovering that nationalism, ethnicity, and religion can be very effective vehicles for collective self-expression and advancement. The very meaning of democracy has been transformed. Terms such as left and right, conservative and radical, east and west have all lost their former meanings. Cold War presuppositions are no longer valid in a world where the meaning of democracy is no longer given simply by its opposition to communism. According to Mouffe, the threat of communism was constitutive of western democracy. We are witnessing a "deep crisis of political identity that confronts liberal democracy following the loss of the traditional landmarks of politics. It is linked to the necessity of redrawing the political frontier between friend and enemy" (Mouffe 1993: 4).

Mouffe advocates a radical pluralism, a form of democracy which is guided by the principles of liberty and equality (Mouffe 1992: 2). She talks of "agonistic pluralism" which comprises a multiplicity of alternative and adversarial democratic positions each of which is legitimate and tolerated by the others. When pluralism is insufficiently developed other, non-democratic identifications based on ethnicity, nationalism or religion come to the fore. Such problems are caused by a lack of democratic political struggles with which to identify. In these cases, "the opponent cannot be perceived as an adversary to contend with, but as an enemy to be destroyed" (Mouffe: 1993:6), which is exactly what a pluralist democracy must avoid. A pluralist political community consists not simply of consensus and unanimity, but of contestation and rivalry, where each contestant acknowledges the "rules of the game" and shares a common political culture (Mouffe 1993: 4). In sum, pluralism requires a degree of commonality and consensus, but should not be taken to mean harmony or homogeneity. Contestation and struggle within clearly demarcated parameters is constitutive of democracy, not its enemy.

> The prime task of democratic politics is not to eliminate passions, not to relegate them to the private sphere in order to render national consensus possible, but to mobilize these passions in a way that promotes democratic designs. Far from jeopardising democracy, agonistic confrontation is in fact its very condition of existence. (Mouffe 1995b: 263)

For Mouffe, the aim of democratic politics is to transform an antagonism into an agonism. This requires some explanation. An antagonism separates friends from enemies and creates incommensurate political factions or communities which threaten and destabilize each other. An antagonism exists where commonality and consensus and a shared system of rules and mutual respect are absent. Antagonisms inhibit democracy, and must be overcome. Antagonisms can exist within societies as well as between them. For example, where class conflict exists or where there is a polarization between religious communities. More commonly, antagonisms exist between nation-states and where democratic countries define themselves by reference to a non-democratic "other" (communists and fundamentalists, for example).

An agonism implies another kind of "us and them" relationship, one in which the parties are not separated by a wide gulf, and where a degree of broad consensus already exists (as between Republican and Democrat, Conservative and Labour). Agonistic democracy does not eliminate internal conflict and struggle – it thrives upon it. Democratic (agonistic) opponents are not enemies to be destroyed but adversaries to be engaged. Adversarial positions are to be welcomed and lead to the mutual benefit of all parties. We accept an adversary as someone against whom we will struggle and at the same time legitimate the right of that person to occupy such a position. As we shall see, Mouffe points to the collapse of the left/ right distinction in western democratic systems and argues that this is harmful for democratic politics as it impedes the constitution of democratic identities and opens the way for exclusionary identities based on essentialist categories and non-negotiable moral values, ethnicity or religion.[5]

Mouffe projects these ideas onto post-1989 Europe, a political field transformed by the loss of its hitherto rigid democratic framework and where identity is once more unstable. The advent of deeper economic integration and the demise of social democratic certitudes has drawn attention to the need to create a common political identity to ensure that Europe is more than a common market. EU citizenship is therefore very important, but to be meaningful it cannot rest solely on legal status or a set of rights. EU citizenship must also identify with a set of political values and principles that are constitutive of modern democracy (Mouffe 1992: 8). Social democratic notions of citizenship with their debates limited to the issues of class, race and gender are no longer adequate, she argues. Social democratic citizenship postulates a homogenous public with differences relegated to the private sphere (Mouffe 1992: 9). The new European citizenship must be responsive to the political demands of new social movements and identity politics, in other words it must embrace difference: a plurality of alternative identities whose existence is constitutive of a radical, plural, democracy.

Mouffe's critique of the dynamics of pluralist democracy emerges from her earlier work in collaboration with Laclau, a self-styled project of post-Marxist "radical democracy" which involved displacing the working class as the central agent of socialist politics. In her recent work she has been much less concerned with a critique of

Marxism and much more concerned with pluralist democracy, and in their less collaborative work the positions of Laclau and Mouffe have begun to diverge. While Laclau emphasizes the impossibility of fixity and closure – "the impossibility of society" – Mouffe has furthered the idea of "agonistic democracy." The concepts of antagonism and agonism, as well as the idea that the erosion of the left/ right distinction has been bad for pluralist democracy, are underpinned by other key concepts in the work of Laclau and Mouffe. Before returning to a consideration of Mouffe's agonistic democracy we must examine the meaning and development of the key concepts of "difference" and "equivalence," as developed by Laclau and Mouffe in their earlier phase.

Difference can be thought of as the multiplicity of relations of subordination that exist in society. The idea of difference has to be understood in relation to the idea of equivalence: the two "logics of the social." The logic of equivalence is the separation of the social into two antagonistic factions, each of which seeks dominance. The logic of difference is the settling out of the social field into a relatively stable and peaceful system of relations of subordination, mutual acceptance, and toleration. If these relations of subordination and mutuality are not turned into antagonisms, the social will solidify and the potential for social disruption, particularly revolutionary change, will be foreclosed. In other words, an increasing number of relations of subordination leads to the complexity of society, a reinforcement of the status quo, and forms the basis for an inclusive and cohesive society, in which differential positions (relations of subordination) flourish.

Neither the logic of equivalence or the logic of difference is ever totally dominant, both tendencies are present in democratic societies. "The two logics limit each other such that neither one completely defines the social" (Smith 1998: 174). Antagonism is once again a central concept, firstly because it explains how difference can be disrupted, and also because it demonstrates that the social is not bounded, and that identities are dependent upon a constitutive outside. In fact these two points are closely related: antagonisms are not inherent to the relations of subordination (difference) but come from elsewhere. Laclau calls this elsewhere the constitutive outside. Moreover, as a post-Marxist, Laclau believes that antagonisms do not have to be economic, there are many potential sites for antagonisms: consumption as well as production, gender, identity, the state or bureaucracy, for example.

Let us examine Laclau's ideas further with the use of some concrete examples. The gendered division of labor, slavery, the exploitation of workers by capitalists are all examples of relations or subordination or difference. Throughout most of their existence these differential positions have been construed as relations of subordination. They have been seen as part of the natural order, the result of God's will, or the result of relations of power masked by ideology. People become habituated to living with these relations of subordination, they accept them, or at least do not actively rebel against them. Then, at a certain point in history, these relations become politicized, turned into antagonisms, and transformed into sites of oppression. When social groups see their subordination as oppression and begin to resist, the potential for political transformation is increased. In other words, the logic of equivalence comes into play, binding together social agents and political actors in a common cause. Equivalence makes it possible to see various forms of inequality as equivalent forms of oppression. Equivalence works to render the social into two antagonistic camps: "the logic of equivalence is a logic of the simpli-fication of political space, while the logic of difference is a logic of its expansion and increasing complexity" (Laclau and Mouffe, 1985: 130). The important point for Laclau, is that antagonism is not *inherent* to these relations, it comes from outside. In other words, the relations of subordination are not inherently antagonistic, they have to be politically constructed as antagonistic. Workers have to become polit-icized in order to resist their exploitation.

The logic of equivalence is the prerequisite for a revolutionary politics, the logic of difference underscores democratic pluralism. In their collaborative work Laclau and Mouffe's search for a post-Marxist socialist strategy placed greater emphasis on the former as the route to radical change. In Mouffe's more recent work the emphasis has been very much on the latter. She states that affirmation and mutual acceptance of difference leads to collective identifications, the creation of an "us" in contrast to a "them." When the mutual recognition engendered by difference breaks down, the us/them relationship can be transformed into a friend/enemy relationship; that is to say, into identities that threaten to destroy one another. In this sense, "us and them" is good as it leads to the constitution of stable, differential, and democratic subject positions.

According to Mouffe, until the collapse of communism, the most important political frontier of the friend/enemy type was that of democracy/totalitarianism. Now we are witnessing the redefinition of collective identity and the establishment of new political frontiers. Mouffe identifies two developments deriving from the fall of communism that are of particular importance. Firstly, "In the former Communist bloc, the unity created in the common struggle against Communism has vanished and the friend/enemy frontier is taking on a multiplicity of new forms linked to the resurgence of old antagonisms – ethnic, national, religious and others" (Mouffe 1993: 3). Mouffe does not differentiate between nationalism, ethnicity and religion, but assumes that they are antithetical to the development of democracy (in eastern European countries). The problem with these ethnic, national, and religious identities is that they make it difficult to create differential positions: the tendency is for the opponent to be seen as an enemy to be destroyed rather than an adversary whose existence is legitimate. There exists a lack of adversarial positions around which a pluralist politics could be constructed. For Mouffe, democracy is not possible where adversarial identities do not exist, and the growth of religious, nationalist or ethnic identities makes adversarial positions less likely. In other words, in situations where relations of the friend/enemy type dominate, it is not possible for relations of difference to exist.

The second development stemming from the fall of communism is that the identity of democracy is at stake in the West. This has two facets: first, the communist "other" was constitutive of democracy, but now communism is no more. Democracy requires a new frontier. Second, and most important for our discussion, the collapse of right/ left adversarial positions is a negative development, as it prevents the construction of distinct democratic identities. This is indicative of the shift undertaken by Mouffe since *Hegemony and Socialist Strategy*. Previously, Mouffe (in partnership with Laclau) was challenging the traditional class base of political identities, and identifying a whole range of non-economic antagonisms amenable to a socialist-led disruption of a social order founded upon relations of difference. Now Mouffe regrets the passing of the old left/right division of the political field as it was a positive element in cementing differential positions and consolidating the democratic order. "The blurring of political frontiers between right and left ... impedes the creation of democratic political identities and fuels disenchantment with political participation" (Mouffe 1995b: 263).

For Mouffe, pluralistic democracy requires difference; difference is constitutive of the social and prevents the agonistic "us and them" relation turning into an antagonistic friend/enemy relation. The complexity of the social is now a prescription for maintaining democracy. The aim is no longer to split the social into antagonistic camps through the creation of equivalence but to ensure the continuation of differential positions through encouraging political parties representing left/right positions. The purpose of politics is to "domesticate hostility" (Mouffe, quoted in Clarke 1999: 105). Those political identifications thought to represent the possibility of splitting the social – ethnic, nationalist or religious – are characterized as irredeemably anti-democratic and therefore undesirable.

Mouffe's agonistic pluralism is notable for the way in which it repositions democratic struggle within the twin logics of the social. Mouffe's trajectory mirrors other shifts within the core concerns of social science and the way societal change is studied. The nature of the social and the cleavages which define it have undergone profound changes in the period following the collapse of communism. Society has changed, and so too have the means by which it can be transformed: "Claims for social justice, economic democracy and struggles against inequalities are increasingly dismissed as relics of a foregone age dominated by the rhetoric of class struggle" (Mouffe 1995b: 295). This age was also characterized by the idea that society could split into two antagonistic camps. When searching for a politics which could bring about the logic of equivalence, Laclau and Mouffe were working with a model of the social which corresponded to the idea of a nationally sequestered society characterized by institutionalized class struggle. Their theory of a non-class socialist strategy, was based on their reading of Gramsci's notion of hegemony, which as we saw in chapter 3 was itself heavily invested with nationalist assumptions. It is not so much that socialism no longer has the potential to divide the social into antagonistic camps, but that the very nature of the social has changed. Nor is it simply the case that democracy must become more pluralistic: importantly, we must recognize that the social itself consists of plural, diverse, and disaggregated spaces. "The political community has to be viewed, then, as a diverse collection of communities, as a forum for creating unity without denying specificity" (Mouffe, quoted in Clarke 1999: 104).

Furthermore, the project of socialism has, out of necessity, undergone its own transformation. Socialist strategy must now embrace the goal of deepening pluralism and safeguarding liberty for all. Mouffe (1995b: 296) emphasizes that her project involves the complete reversal of the left's identity. Hitherto, it has been generally identified with a view of society that regards homogeneity, equality, and harmony as its central values. Pluralism, difference, and hetero-geneity were seen as ills of capitalist society that must be overcome because they were premised on inequality. The shift in emphasis from equivalence to difference is indicative of a broader realignment of political identities and objectives. The project of the socialist left is now conceived not in terms of the need to polarize the social through the creation of chains of equivalence which would fracture and divide, but in terms of the extension and deepening of pluralistic democracy which, in Laclau and Mouffe's terms implies the increas-ing complexity of the social through the multiplication of relations of subordination and difference.

What Mouffe provides us with is a way of thinking about European democratic identity which rejects the idea that it must be founded upon exclusion. Rather than a homogenous and primary identity Europe needs to think of itself in terms of accommodating otherness, hybridity, and openness to other influences.

> If we conceive of this European identity as a 'difference to oneself', as 'one's own culture as somebody else's culture', then we are in effect envisaging an identity that accommodates otherness, that demonstrates the porosity of frontiers, and opens up [our identity] to that 'exterior' which makes it possible. (Mouffe, quoted in Smith 1998: 140)

The prerequisites for agonistic pluralism – the ability to legitimate and struggle against contending positions – is a recognition that identities are multiple, contingent, and interdependent. Identity is never "pure" or primordial, always heterogeneous and multiple. Every identity needs the existence of an other, indeed always contains a recognition of that other: "without alterity and otherness, no identity could ever assert itself" (Mouffe 1995b: 265).

Thinking about democracy along these lines allows us to move beyond the idea that democracy is a European inheritance. The democracy advocated by Mouffe does not project itself backwards and claim a lineage with the city-states of ancient Greece. Mouffe's agonistic pluralism is of relatively recent origins, the antagonistic cleavages of modernity having given way to the differential logic of a plurality of contested public spaces. Another key feature is that agonistic pluralism is explicitly non-exclusionary: it is a form of democratic identification which accommodates otherness and breaks down boundaries between identities. Mouffe's work is not devoid of its exclusionary elements however, as in the case of those who do not recognize the rules of the democratic game. There is an "us and them" beyond the pluralist system and the possibility of an antagonistic friend/enemy relation developing between communities who differ on this principle. The category of the enemy can be displaced but never disappears completely.

Conclusion

The value of cosmopolitan and agonistic democracy for a study of democratic identity in contemporary Europe lies in the key features that they share, namely their ability to think democracy beyond the nation-state, and their projection of non-exclusive identities. Cosmopolitan democracy makes explicit its relation to developments within the EU: a multi-level polity which aims to extend its democratic practices both internally and towards the rest of the world through the stimulation of a variety of actors including citizen's movements, "civil society," and international organizations. The nation-state remains at the heart of this model. The EU offers the means through which to greater democratize member states and to ensure that the democratic nation-state is the global norm. Cosmopolitan democracy aims to develop an international order founded upon the democratic nation-state, and to this end identifies democratic practices which can supplement those existing at the national level.

Agonistic democracy is less in thrall to the nation-state model. Mouffe traces the passage from the antagonistic politics of the cold war to the pluralism characteristic of a Europe transformed by the collapse of communism and the expansion of the EU. Moreover, she charts changes in the nature of society, no longer coincident with the nation-state: diverse, autonomous, not easily bounded, increasingly self-constituted. As such, the idea of societal cohesion no longer applies nor constitutes one of the goals of democratic politics. Similarly, the "logic of equivalence," in which political positions form alliances in order to further their common aims, loses any meaning when societies are no longer unified. A plurality of social spaces lend themselves to the politics of pluralism. The social is constituted by a multiplicity of democratic contestations and conflictual differential positions. Difference and identity are the dominant features of the European political field, and identities are formed by democratic practice rather than inherited from the past and based on prescribed cultural and social hierarchies.

Cosmopolitan and agonistic democracy also works to challenge existing ideas regarding the necessary correspondence between a European public sphere, citizenship, identity, and democracy. The majority of approaches to the question of European democracy considered early in the chapter assume that all of these elements must exist in a functional unity. Moreover, Giorgi et al., Laffan, and Siedentop conceive the unifying principle to be civil society, whether it is named as such or not. It has been argued throughout this book, particular in chapter 4, that we must understand Europe without the reassuring notion of civil society. Furthermore, we must move away from the need to understand public spheres and political communities in terms of their integration or cohesiveness. Democracy which is pluralistic in nature demands a plurality of spaces within which it can operate. In the contemporary EU democracy, like social spheres, develops in and acts upon non-national contexts, and has no necessary correspondence with any traditional medium of political expression. Forms of democratic practice originating outside the national setting exercise an increasing hold on the imagination of Europeans.

9 EU Enlargement

The Problem of Enlargement

Enlargement is the biggest challenge facing the European Union at the present time and will remain so for the foreseeable future. The reason why the current round of enlargement constitutes such a challenge is not simply that it is far bigger in scope (as many as 13 countries currently engaged in or shortly to begin accession negotiations) than the enlargements that took place in the early 1970s (Britain, Ireland, and Denmark), the early and mid-1980s (Greece, Spain, and Portugal), or the mid-1990s (Austria, Sweden, and Finland), or even that the majority of these countries are poor by EU standards: "as a group, the ten CEEC applicants have a per capita GDP that is less than one-third the EU average, and less than half that of the EU's four poorest current members" (Baun 1999: 270–1).[1] The reason why the current round of enlargement constitutes such a challenge for the EU is that it is being conducted amidst a great degree of uncertainty. Put simply, no one knows exactly who the next member(s) of the EU will be, when they will join, and what conditions will be attached to their membership (opt-outs, transition periods). The EU is in the process of enlarging and possibly doubling its membership over the next few years, but as yet there is no firm timetable for the accession of even the leading candidates.[2]

Of growing importance is the fact that the enlargement process is not limited to the official candidate countries.[3] In addition to western European countries such as Norway and Switzerland who periodically reassess their decision to remain outside of the EU fold, there exists a growing number of countries with formal association status or who are otherwise loosely embraced by the EU, and who all have a prospect of membership at some unspecified time in the future. For example, the perspective of EU membership has been given to five south-eastern European countries (Albania, Bosnia-Herzegovina, Croatia, the Federal Republic of Yugoslavia, and Macedonia) as part of the Stability Pact for South Eastern Europe (Friis and Murphy 2001).

Another very significant feature of the enlargement process is that, in contrast with previous rounds, the burden of the adoption of the *acquis communautaire* falls very much on the applicant states. Financial assistance and support programmes to applicants prior to membership, even through official "cohesion" programmes, is limited and there is little prospect of generous benefits in terms of agricultural support and regional aid, at least not to anywhere near the same level enjoyed by Portugal, Spain, Ireland, and Greece – the EU's so called "poor four" – after graduation to full membership. It is easy to understand the EU's reluctance to extend existing levels of support to new members. Currently, approximately 80 percent of the EU's budget is devoted to regional aid and the common agricultural policy and "intended to subsidise poor people and farmers. As luck would have it, Central and Eastern Europe is full of poor people and farmers" (*The Economist*, May 25, 2001).

There is no precedent for the kind of wholesale enlargement that the EU is now contemplating and no blueprint or model for the EU to follow. Nor does the accession of other member states since the 1970s offer much in the way of guidance to the present crop of hopefuls. The experience of Portugal tells Poland very little, nor does the Spanish case assist Slovenia in preparing for full membership. To talk of EU enlargement as a linear process leading to a particular outcome is misleading. The process of accession is likely to lead to different outcomes for different countries and there is no fixed definition of full membership. New members will be obliged to accept seven-year transition periods before the free movement of citizens is possible (Czerwinska 2001) and participation in the EU's Common Agricultural Policy becomes a reality (Financial Times, May 20, 2001).[4] Hardly any are likely to participate in the single currency upon full membership or for some time afterwards.

Full membership is a subjective term. In the final analysis, the speed at which the leading candidates become members may well depend on how acceptable it is to agree to "less than full membership." For example, in the case of Poland a willingness to accept that agricultural support and the free movement of workers will not be possible without transition periods may well open the EU door, while a vigorous defence of the entitlement of all members to receive full rights and benefits may delay the process by several years. In other words, the EU "is likely to pursue trade-offs whereby the CEECs accept less favourable membership terms in return for earlier accession" (Fowler 2001). Applicant countries in this position will have to decide how much full membership their electorates are willing to forgo.

This chapter gives extended consideration to the politics of EU enlargement, Turkey's candidature, and prospects of accession. Turkey has only recently (December 1999) been accorded full candidate status despite having a formal association with the EU dating back to 1963. This makes Turkey's case an interesting one, not least because it allows for a consideration of a country moving from the outer orbits of the enlargement process to a closer level of pre-accession. Turkey is also interesting in the sense that it is one of the few candidate countries that actually attempts to resist some of the EU's moves to universalize its own model of democratic practice. Such resistance is often motivated by nationalistic and non-democratic motives, and Turkey is regularly and rightly criticized by the EU and international organizations for its poor record on human rights and democratization. The approach to enlargement adopted here is centered upon an examination of Turkey's relationship with the EU through a sociologically inspired globalization framework, rendering the subject compatible with the themes developed in the rest of the book. In addition to positioning enlargement within a globalization perspective this chapter also examines the Turkey–EU relationship from the perspectives of democracy developed in the previous chapter.

One of the most striking features about Turkey's relation with the EU is that Turkey still pursues integration according to norms which developed in the 1960s and '70s. On this understanding, the path to further integration will be trade-led and will center on the customs union agreement which came into force in 1996. The EU is first and foremost a common market and therefore integration is fundamentally an economic affair. Through incorporation in the EU's single market and by demonstrating that Turkey's economy is robust enough to withstand the rigors of EU competition, a place in the EU will be secured. Despite the widespread belief in Turkey that the economy is sufficiently integrated (periodic economic crises notwithstanding), Commission reports have regularly underlined deficiencies. The Copenhagen economic criteria state that membership of the Union requires both the existence of a functioning market economy and the capacity to cope with competitive pressure and market forces within the Union. A recent Commission report concluded that despite the fact that considerable parts of the Turkish economy are already able to sustain competitive pressure and market forces in a customs union with the EC, "the process of achieving a functioning market economy is not completed" (European Commission 2000b). While Turkey is reluctant to relinquish a trade-led vision of integration, the EU's expectations, rooted firmly in the Copenhagen criteria, are very much the result of contemporary concerns. The EU's frustrations with Turkey as both a candidate and a prospective member stem from Turkey's inability to grasp the nature and importance of EU-style human rights and respect for minorities.[5]

It is quite common for the CEECs to be treated as a group, or divided into two groups of first and second wave candidates. Turkey, it is fair to say, remains in a group of one. This is not only the case in terms of the longevity of the formal association (28 years) without full membership, or the way Turkey was pointedly excluded from the group of candidates launched at the Luxembourg Summit in December 1997, or even the way in which Turkey's European credentials are sometimes questioned by politicians and commentators. The most recent example of Turkey being in a group of one, and perhaps the most significant, was the decision at the Nice Summit to re-weight votes in the Council by taking into account the possibility of new members. Turkey held full candidate status but was not incorporated in the re-weighting process, and did not feature in the projections concerning the internal structure of an enlarged EU.

Turkey/EU Relations

European Commission reports typically conclude that "no substantial progress has been achieved as regards human rights and the democratic reform process in Turkey" (European Commission 1998b). The Commission report which paved the way for Turkey's promotion to candidate status at the Helsinki Council in December 1999 concluded that there were still "serious shortcomings" in terms of human rights and the protection of minorities (European Commission 1999c). When consideration is given to Turkey's candidature some of the biggest barriers to accession are thought to exist in the fields of democracy and human rights.[6]

The Luxembourg European Council of December 1997 denied Turkey full candidate status and, at the same time, offered enlargement negotiations to 11 other applicants. It was a watershed in Turkey's relations with the EU and appeared to constitute a major derailment of the process of integration which began in 1963 with the signing of the Ankara Agreement, a document which envisaged Turkey's eventual accession. Turkey's formal application for membership in 1987 was rejected. The Commission considered that Turkey was not yet capable of "bearing the constraints and disciplines" applying to member states, nor was the Community ready to cope with the problems that Turkey's integration would bring (European Commission 1989). This was a polite way of saying that Turkey was too big and too poor to be easily assimilated.

The Commission recommended that completion of the customs union foreseen by the Ankara Agreement would benefit Turkey through closer association with the single market. Turkey's customs union with the EU duly came into existence in January 1996, Greek approval being conditional on receiving guarantees that Cyprus would subsequently be granted candidate status (Onis 2001). The Commission also recognized the need for greater financial aid to Turkey and to this end prepared a Cooperation Program (the Matutes Package), although this was never brought into effect, a Greek veto preventing it being passed by the Council. It was clear that more than traditional Greek and Germany opposition was standing in the path of Turkey's accession. Concern was expressed at the burden Turkish membership would impose upon the Structural Funds, strongly suggesting the EU's poorer members viewed Turkey's candidature as a threat (European Commission 1989).

Many commentators view Turkey's continuing marginalization from the accession process as the product of perceived cultural differences (Williams 1994, Onis 1999). Christian Democrat politicians have propagated the idea that Turkey is not "of Europe." For example, just prior to the Luxembourg summit Wim van Welzen, President of the European Union of Christian Democrats, was quoted as saying that the EU had "cultural, humanitarian and Christian values different to Turkey's" (*Financial Times*, March 5, 1997). In a similar vein the Dutch Foreign Minister, Hans van Mierlo, said that Turkey's membership could be ruled out on the basis that Turkey was a Muslim country (Palmer 1997). In contrast, the European Parliament's long-standing reluctance to support Turkey's candidature has centered on the socialist-led objection to Turkey's human rights record, although this too is interpreted by some as evidence of prejudice against a Muslim society. There was more than a hint of cultural prejudice in the statements made by Luxembourg's Prime Minister Junker at the Luxembourg Council. He upset the Turkish government by claiming that Turkey was guilty of human rights abuses, and that torture happens every day. He also said that, "Turkey's leaders might bear a measure of direct responsibility" for the torture (Barchard 1998: 1). Such a country "could not sit down at the EU table" (*Electronic Telegraph*, December 12, 1997).

Turkey's marginal position in relation to enlargement is in no small part the product of self-exclusion. Turkey has never gone out of its way to shape itself according to EU wishes, and in many cases, particularly where national sovereignty in political matters is seen to be at stake, has wilfully resisted EU strictures. Onis (2001) raises the issues of why in the late 1970s Turkey did not apply for full membership at the same time as the Greeks, "considering that one of the motives for Turkey's application for associate membership back in 1959 was precisely to counteract the initial strategic move on the part of Greece." He gives three reasons. First, Turkey underestimated the problems that Greek membership would subsequently pose for Turkey. Second, the speed at which Greece could gain accession was not anticipated. Third, "the Turkish political elites . . . were reluctant to accelerate the pace of integration and expose Turkish industry to unnecessary and premature competition."

There have been other forms of self-exclusion. As has been already mentioned, Turkey's long association with the European Union has been characterized by the unshakeable belief that the route to greater integration is trade-led. In this regard Turkey has pursued a one-track strategy, which while perhaps appropriate through the 1960s and '70s became increasingly inappropriate during the 1980s and '90s. The customs union introduced in 1996 was the most tangible outcome of this approach, and it was genuinely believed for a while that the customs union would open the door to full membership.

Customs Union is no longer a narrow-scope exercise limited to abolishing customs duties and taxes having equivalent effect within the block and levying Common External Tariffs on third countries, but is perceived as a dynamic process also encompassing common rules of competition and trade. The negotiations for Customs Union with the Community have been approached from this standpoint. The aim has not been restricted to a classical customs union, but directed towards Turkey's full integration in the EU. (Duna 1996: 49)[7]

With hindsight it is not difficult to draw the conclusion that Turkey saw the customs union as something much more important than it really was in the context of eventual accession. It is also likely that the EU saw no reason to dissuade the Turks from this view. While Turkey was focusing very narrowly on trading arrangements the CEECs were busy maneuvering towards Europe and Partnership agreements which proved to be a more substantial base from which to launch a drive for full membership. This was certainly the EU's understanding of the situation at the Luxembourg summit where customs union did not count for much when Turkey's case was being considered.

Turkey's exclusion from the formal enlargement process at Luxembourg was tempered by the offer of a seat at the European Conference set for March 1998, and the inception of a "European Strategy for Turkey" designed to facilitate Turkey's subsequent candidature. The invitation to the European Conference was ignored by Turkey for whom the conditions attached were little more than a shopping list of Greek demands.[8] The purpose of the strategy document was to "prepare Turkey for accession by bringing it closer to the European Union in every field." Mention was made of a number of political issues on which progress should be made (including relations between Greece and Turkey and the Cyprus problem) and prominently "the alignment of human rights standards and practices with those in force in the European Union" and "respect for and protection of minorities" (in other words, the Copenhagen criteria).

Despite its avowed "commitment to developing a strategy to prepare Turkey for accession," the *European Strategy for Turkey* (European Commission 1998c) was not a great success. Turkey never welcomed it as a positive step towards full integration. The EU was unable to ensure that the initiatives outlined in the strategy received the appropriate financial backing. The strategy's one real weakness was not its dependence upon finance, although that was clearly a stumbling block, as the Commission subsequently confirmed (European Commission 1999c). Its real weakness was its preoccupation with reinforcing and extending the customs union arrangement above all else: a "customs union plus," as it was dubbed. Indeed, the advent of customs union further encouraged the idea that Turkey's integration would continue to be driven by greater trade flows and greater economic harmonization and that, in the context of possible accession, the customs union would cement Turkey's status of most economically integrated of the non-member countries. In short, that customs union was the closest form of economic integration with the EU short of full membership (Kramer 1996). More surprisingly, given the EU's earlier emphasis on human rights and democratization, the *European Strategy for Turkey* concentrated almost exclusively on trade, economic, and technical issues and the five-point strategy did not include human rights and democratization, nor did they feature in the work-plan for the first half of 1998 detailed in the strategy's conclusions.

In October 1999 the European Commission published a report in which it was recommended that Turkey be considered as a full candidate (European Commission 1999c). However, the report made it plain that Turkey did not meet the Copenhagen political criteria. "There are serious shortcomings in terms of human rights and protection of minorities. Torture is not systematic but is still widespread and freedom of expression is regularly restricted by the authorities." The Commission's report was the prelude to the decision reached at the Helsinki summit which formally granted Turkey the status of candidate country. The Presidency conclusions of the Helsinki summit had four main components as far as Turkey's membership aspirations were concerned. First, that Turkey was recognized as a candidate country on the basis as the same criteria as all the other candidates. Second, that Turkey would be the recipient of coordinated pre-accession assistance. Third, that the EU would seek enhanced political dialogue aimed at assisting Turkey in reaching the accession criteria, particularly in the area of human rights. The Helsinki Council made explicit the EU's position that compliance with the political criteria laid down at the Copenhagen European Council is a prerequisite for the opening of accession negotiations.[9] Fourth, that Turkey would be included in Community programs and agencies (European Commission 1999d).

While clearly representing a very positive step the Helsinki decision confronted Turkey with a new barrier in the form of the political elements of the Copenhagen criteria (the importance of which Turkey had chosen to downplay in the past). There were other stipulations which Turkey found a little unpalatable, particularly the reference to resolving border disputes within a reasonable time or refer them to the International Court of Justice (clearly a reference to disagreements with Greece over the Aegean coast and airspace). We might note in passing that a similar clause in the invitation to the European Conference proved totally indigestible. Similarly, the EU's statement that in the absence of a negotiated settlement the accession of Cyprus to the European Union would not necessarily be blocked would, under different circumstances, have been interpreted as an unacceptable concession to the Greeks.

There is much faith in the idea that the proximity of the European Union (and the possibility of future accession) will stimulate domestic political reform in Turkey (Keyder 1997), as it did in Spain, Portugal, and Greece (Gordon 2000).[10] In this respect, EU aid to Turkey is an important factor in the dual processes of political harmonization and domestic democratization. Overall, Community aid to Turkey since the inception of the Ankara Agreement has been relatively small (Euro 1, 561 billion – excluding loans),[11] and either disrupted (grants were frozen during 1980–7 following the military intervention) or blocked (the Fourth Financial Protocol worth Euro 600 million has been the subject of a Greek veto, or, in the Commission's language, "not allocated due to a lack of unanimity"). Since 1993 an average annual budget of Euro 500,000 has been made available for "actions aimed at defending and promoting human rights and civil society."

EU support for human rights initiatives in Turkey is still a contentious issue in some quarters. The Kemalists – the reforming elites of the patriarchal Turkish state (Bozdagan 1994) – draw a clear association between the promotion of human rights, support for the terrorist PKK (Kurdistan Worker's Party), and mobilization of anti-Turkish sentiment. Calls from the EU for greater human rights are frequently interpreted as little more than thinly veiled support for "enemies of the state." This is how we should understand Prime Minister Ecevit's request to EU countries "not to support terrorist groups either directly or indirectly under the pretext of human rights" (*Hurriyet*, March 23, 2000).[12] Danielle Miterrand's espousal of the Kurdish cause and the subsequent award, by the European Parliament, of the Sakharov Peace Prize to the imprisoned Kurdish activist Leyla Zana was interpreted by the Turkish political elite as blatant support for terrorism. The extent to which human rights and terrorism are often linked in the Kemalist mind is indicated by the comments attributed to then-Prime Minister Mesut Yilmaz on the occasion of the shooting of Akin Birdal, President of the Turkish Human Rights Association (HRA) in 1998. Yilmaz alleged that the HRA were connected to the PKK and that the shooting should be viewed as an "internal settling of accounts"(Human Rights Watch 2000).[13]

The Issue of Universalism

Within Turkey there is growing enthusiasm for instituting a "citizen-ship constituted foundationally around universally applicable civil rights" (Keyder 1997: 42). The proximity of the European Union has done much to stimulate domestic reform, indeed it could be argued that Turkey's hand has been forced by its desire for EU membership. During the 1990s the EU was less tolerant of excuses about the time not being right for reforms in the sphere of civil and political rights. "It became clear that refusal to institute the legal foundations of individual autonomy would be tantamount to giving up the geo-cultural claim of 'Europeanness'" (Keyder 1997: 47). EU pressure for change has had another important consequence, namely contributing to a domestic political environment in which the expectations of reform have been heightened. This has encouraged numerous groups to enter the political arena and engage in struggles for recognition, extensions of civil rights and freedoms, and access to media. How-ever, the assertiveness of minorities in Turkey, particularly the Kurds and Islamic groups, has been met, not with greater liberalization and extension of rights, but with resistance from the state. The dominant political discourse characterizes Islamic and Kurdish movements as a threat to Turkish democracy and the territorial integrity of the state. In this way it has been possible for leading Islamic and Kurdish political parties to be banned by the Turkish courts[14] (Gulalp 1999), a state of emergency to be maintained in several provinces in the southeast, elected mayors to be arrested on charges of aiding and abetting terrorists.[15]

One of the interesting features of the global field of democratization in which Turkey now has to operate is that it is constituted in part by competing claims to universalism. Minority groups claim human rights on the basis that they are universal rights. The European Union declares that its human rights values are universal values. The founding of the modern Republic in the 1920s provided Turkey with its own claims to represent the universal, stemming from the Kemal-ist elites' expressed equation of Westernization with civilization. "Turkish modernizers had readily identified modernization with Westernization – with taking its place in the civilization of Europe" (Keyder 1997: 37). The project of the "making" of modern Turkey (Ahmad 1993) was one in which perceptions of western nation-states figured large both as a template and as a goal, although as Gellner

(1994) points out it was a nineteenth-century vision of the modern nation-state that formed the working model. For Kemalists socio-economic development should be state led. Kemalism (named after Kemal Ataturk, founder and father-figure of the Republic) equates modernity with progress, where modernity, universality, and western values are synonymous. Kemalism "was premised on the equation of modernity with progress, that is, on the making of a modern nation through the introduction and the dissemination of Western reason and rationality into what was regarded as traditional and backward social relations" (Keyman 1995: 97).

Universalism is a key theme in contemporary sociology and social theory. In addition to the study of globalization where the relationship between the universal and the particular is a central issue, the nature of universalism is also a central component of debates on citizenship and identity (Soysal 1994 and 1997, Jary 1999), modernity and nationalism (Albrow 1996), and even the development of sociology itself (Turner 1990, Robertson 1992), to mention just a few examples. Given this general intellectual background it is not surprising that questions of Turkish identity, democratization, and political contestation are frequently posed in terms of the relationship between the universal and the particular. For example, Keyman (1995: 95) argues that, "Turkey exemplifies very clearly the tension between the universal and the particular, where at stake is the clash between the secular national identity as the bearer of cultural homogenization and the revitalization of the language of difference through the rise of Islam, the reemergence of Kurdish nationalism in organized form, and the feminist movement." Gole (1996: 17), writing about the rise of the Islamic movements, feminism, and ethnic movements in Turkey, holds that "identity politics, particularism, and localism against the uniformity of abstract universalism are common features of the postmodern condition." For Robins (1996) the emergence of these new social identities means that Turkey can no longer sustain a universal identity to the exclusion of the particular.

There are two main problems with such formulations. First, there is the assumption that the universal and the particular exist as polar opposites and must necessarily be counterposed. Against this it is argued that the relationship between the universal and the particular must be seen as relative, non-exclusive and interdependent. This is, broadly speaking, the position adopted by Beck, Laclau and Robertson, and discussed in full below. Although none of these writers have written about Turkey as such, it is argued that their ideas can be usefully employed to investigate the idea of universalism in the context of Turkish democratization. Second, in relation to Turkey the assumption that minorities represent the particular and the state the universal is challenged by the work of Beck, Laclau and Robertson who, in very different ways, problematize the relationship of minorities to the universal, allowing for the possibility that both the state and non-state actors can simultaneously claim to represent the universal.

Beck and "Contextual Universalism"

Beck's ideas on contextual universalism are advanced in the course of a general discussion concerning the impossibility of sustaining either a simple universalist or relativist perspective under conditions of globalization. Universalism means imposing one's truth on others, while relativism is an illusion of separate, incommensurate worlds. At first glance these positions appear to be polar opposites but Beck sees them more as "similarly *blind* to the truths of others. The one is blocked by the enemy image inherent in its own certainty, the other by the supposed impossibility of ever understanding another's standpoint" (Beck 2000: 83).

Beck's insight offers a useful way of approaching the issue of why, in contemporary Turkish politics, it is common for leading politicians to oscillate between two seemingly incompatible positions: a wholehearted embrace of EU norms on human rights and democratization, on the one hand, and a nationalistically inflected rejection of outside interference in domestic matters, on the other.[16] What appears to be an attempt to hold irreconcilable positions is in fact revealed as a consistent blocking out of the claims of others. In the first case, the particularity of Kemalist universalism is denied, and the fiction of a seamless incorporation into the West is maintained. In the second, there is refusal to acknowledge the legitimacy of the political claims of the Islamic or Kurdish minorities. We will further explore the idea of contextual universalism with reference to two areas of contestation central to Turkish politics: the dispute over Islamic identification in the "headscarf case," and the EU's claims to embody universal human rights.

Beck's idea of contextual universalism presupposes that intercultural interference and misunderstanding is the norm, "there is no escape from the unrest of mutual interference between exclusive certainties" (Beck 2000: 84). This provides the basis for his more inclusive approach: the integration of the contextual into the concept of the universal. Specifically, it allows for plural universalism, the idea that different groups can each claim to possess a version of universalism. In other words, universalism can be contested. The case of Merve Kavakci, a female MP whose attempt to wear a headscarf in the Turkish parliament caused a furore during the months of April and May 1999, is a good example of this contestation. The political conflict surrounding this event took the form of a public debate between the Kemalist political elite who were defending an idea of universalism couched in terms of progress and modernity, and Islamists who framed their claims within a discourse of globalized norms of human rights and individual freedom of expression.[17]

Merve Kavakci was elected to parliament as a representative of the (Islamic leaning) Virtue Party in the April 1999 general election. By entering parliament dressed in a headscarf she was accused of violating the principles of the secular Republic. Members of Prime Minister Bulent Ecevit's DSP (Democratic Left Party) initiated a parliamentary protest and Kavakci left the parliament building without taking her MP's oath of allegiance.[18] Kemalists see the headscarf as a symbol of a movement that seeks to replace the country's secular constitution with a strict Islamic code. Although Turkey is a Muslim country and the headscarf is widely worn in rural (and indeed, urban) areas, the secular elite regards it as a political symbol of Islamic fundamentalism and bans its use in universities and offices (although in practice the ban is far from uniformly applied). From the Islamists' perspective it was Kavakci's democratic right to wear the headscarf and covering the head is a matter of personal freedom and religious duty. The Islamists regularly invoke a language of democracy and human rights when explaining their actions. In a similar vein, the Turkish Human Rights Association holds that the right to wear a headscarf (in the universities, for example) is a matter of belief and freedom of thought (*Turkey Update*, October 13, 1998).

Both sides in the dispute ground their claims in the legitimacy bestowed by universalism. On the one hand, the demands for freedom of expression on behalf of the Islamic minority are expressed through universalistic not particularistic arguments. The universal status of personhood has become the conduit through which rights and privileges of citizenship are claimed and realized, and in global fora identities have been redefined as rights. As Soysal (1997: 513) points out, "the universal right to 'one's own culture' has gained political legitimacy, and collective identity has been redefined as a category of human rights." On the other hand, the secular establishment also talks in terms of democratic and human rights, but for them the Republic is the guarantor of human rights in Turkey. As such, demonstrating in favor of wearing a headscarf is a demonstration against the Republic. According to one commentator, "the challenge is directed against the very soul of the Turkish Republic, without which there can be no democracy and human rights" (Turkmen 1999). For the secularists progress, modernization and civilization are of a piece and the threat represented by the headscarf requires political mobilization: "It is time to defend this civilization" (Turkmen 1999). There is yet another dimension to the Kemalist reaction to the wearing of the headscarf, and this involves the status of women as citizens in the Kemalist ideology. According to Gole (1996: 143–4), for Kemalists "secularism, republicanism and gender equality" are the key indices of Turkish modernity. That the construction of women as public citizens is the "backbone of Kemalist reforms" explains why "the violation of women's rights and secularism hurts the feelings of the elite more than does the violation of human rights and democracy."

The usefulness of Beck's idea of contextual universalism as a means through which to study Turkish politics can also be demonstrated by applying his critique of the universalist claims of human rights to Turkey's failure to fulfil EU expectations on guaranteeing rights and protecting minorities. While Turkey falls short of meeting the Copenhagen criteria the EU projects its version of human rights as the embodiment of universal values. Beck's notion of contextual universalism seeks to relativize these positions. For Beck, human rights are not universal, in the sense that "they do not have to apply everywhere on earth in the form in which they were *invented* in the West" (Beck 2000: 85). He points out that even in Europe different versions of human rights exist. "In the Scandinavian countries, for example, economic rights are counted among basic rights, whereas in the postcommunist countries of Central and Eastern Europe civil and political rights are often highly valued by the population but not by the government" (Beck 2000: 85). Beck's analysis of the universality of human rights norms raises several important issues. Not least of these is the fact that for the EU, human rights are universal values applicable to all peoples in all places. One aspect of this universality, that no country should be free to invoke sovereignty or interference in internal affairs to prevent the people under its jurisdiction from fully enjoying their human rights, causes particular friction with Turkey (European Union 2000). For the Kemalist elite the Turkish Republic's modern, secular, western orientation and its indivisible territorial unity is the embodiment of freedom and democracy, and, as such, represents the very possibility of human rights.

Beck's position is critical of the claims of both the EU and Turkey. The universal pretensions of the EU are undermined, while Turkey's reluctance to bow to international pressure is rejected. Embracing the principle of contextual universalism does not mean that one has to accept human rights violations in other countries, nor does it sanction invasion on the pretext of preventing persecution. Rather, contextual universalism implies that one must accept that it is extremely presumptuous to expect that values will automatically be agreed and accepted by others. Each group must attempt to see how others, even in countries where human rights appear to be violated, conceive of human rights. In other words, contextual universalism demands both a self-scrutiny of claims to universalism and a dialogue between value systems. It also means that each party must create a value system that is reflexive and responsive to others' perceptions of what are projected as universal standards.

Beck's analysis would suggest that the EU's universal notion of rights needs to be relativized and Turkey's own human rights perspective be given more credence if genuine progress can be made. It is certainly the case that the EU stance on human rights does not take into account that its own universal values have been shaped, and continue to be shaped, by the global human rights discourse, and by contestations surrounding the appropriateness and universal applicability of those rights. Nevertheless, there are many commentators who take the line that "Human Rights organizations and campaigns cannot afford to compromise on universalism" (Zubaida 1994: 10–11). Furthermore, the idea that European notions of human rights are culturally specific to the west is countered by pointing out that far from being inherent, rights are the outcome of political contestation, and that in many European countries the establishment of liberal rights is a recent phenomena. Zubaida (1994: 11) emphasizes that "human rights in Europe were only won after protracted political struggles against entrenched political and religious interests."

Beck's position would appear to legitimate Turkish intransigence in the face of globalized human rights norms of which the EU is a bearer. His rather liberal approach may even work to undermine what he wishes to achieve: a greater pluralism of approaches to human rights. In the Turkish context, the Islamists draw upon the legitimacy of the EU's rights discourse to defend and strengthen their own minority freedoms. Global conceptions of personhood rights and the proximity of the EU as a rights-bearing institution exist as a valuable political resource for suppressed and marginalized groups. If EU human rights values are seen as but one value system among many the struggle of minorities for recognition may well become more difficult.

Laclau: The Interdependance of the Universal and the Particular

Laclau's work on the categories of the universal and the particular provides a valuable framework for reinterpreting Turkey's relationship to the universal. Laclau says that under conditions of modernity universality meant transforming society in such a way as to overcome all particularism and "bring about a society reconciled with itself" (Laclau 1996: 51). This was very much the Kemalist project. Laclau argues that the period of modernity is now over and we no longer believe in the claims of universalism. Indeed, universalism may now be viewed with suspicion and dismissed as an "old-fashioned totalitarian dream" (Laclau 1996: 26). In the contemporary context political struggles involve a "strong assertion of their particularity, the conviction that none of them is capable, on its own, of bringing about the fullness of the community" (Laclau 1996: 51). However, this does not mean that we can simply celebrate the new particularisms. Laclau states, "an appeal to pure particularism is no solution to the problems we are facing in contemporary societies" (Laclau 1996: 26). Particularism is not enough. If particularism is the only valid principle we have to accept the right to self-determination, not only of ethnic and sexual minorities for example, but all kinds of reactionary and unwelcome groups: ethnic nationalism and other forms of exclusionary politics.

For Laclau, the right of an ethnic group to cultural autonomy "can only be justified on universal grounds. The assertion of one's own particularity requires the appeal of something transcending it" (Laclau 1996: 48). Particularism only gains purchase when grounded in the universal. In other words: "The more particular a group is, the less it will be able to control the global communitarian terrain within which it operates, and the more universally grounded will have to be the justification of its claims" (Laclau 1996: 46). This is an important formulation as it encapsulates the essence of the relationship between the universal and the particular for Laclau: the particular having no meaning outside of a universalistic context. The universal and the particular are not exclusive categories: the universal and the particular exist in a relation of mutual and reciprocal dependence.

From this it follows that the demands of minority groups within society cannot be made in terms of particularism, but in terms of some universal principles that the minority shares with the rest of the community. He gives an example; "The right of everybody to have access to good schools, or live a decent life, or participate in the public space of citizenship, and so on" (Laclau 1996: 28). In this way the universal is part of the identity of the minority group. Laclau argues that particularism requires universality, not that it must supplant it. The establishment of common ground between different discourses and identities is made possibly by the non-exclusive relationship between the universal and the particular.

> For the very emergence of highly particularistic identities means that the particular groups will have to coexist with other groups in larger communities, and this coexistence will be impossible without the assertion of values that transcend the identities of all of them. The defence, for instance, of the right of national minorities to self-determination involves the assertion of a universal principle grounded in universal values. These are not the values of a 'universal' group, as was the case with the universalism of the past but, rather, of a universality that is the very result of particularism. (Laclau 1994: 5)

But as Beck has demonstrated, different particularisms will have different conceptions of the universal, and as such a consensus may not be possible. The "headscarf" case outlined in the previous section demonstrates that universalism is not simply opposed to particularism: universalism is perspectival and contested. What is less clear is the degree to which coexistence between contending universal claims will be possible. The same problem is identified by Bozdogan and Kasaba (1997) who take the line that Turkish modernization must adapt if is to continue to be a progressive force. They acknowledge that the Kemalist project may have failed inasmuch as it has been responsible for the increasingly apparent division and fragmentation of Turkish society. What is required, they argue, is "a new consensus that makes communication across social, political, and theoretical divides possible while upholding the universal principles of truth and justice" (Bozdogan and Kasaba 1997: 6). This raises several important issues. On the one hand it gravitates towards the idea of the non-exclusive nature of the universal and the particular as advanced by Laclau. On the other hand it demonstrates the problems inherent in laying claim to universalism. Whose "universal principles of truth and justice" are to be upheld? Different particularisms have different conceptions of the universal and as such the consensus desired by Bozdogan and Kasaba (and assumed by Laclau) may not be forthcoming. In this sense, Beck's idea that contending universalisms would in practice tend to relativize each other appears to be the superior formulation. It does, however, leave unresolved the question of the differential power relations that are likely to exist between contending visions of the universal.

There are two other issues connected with Laclau's formulation of the universal and the particular which deserve our attention. In the first place, although there is no rigid separation of the universal and the particular it is assumed that ethnic minorities, for example, represent the particular. He suggests that particularistic groups "fill out their incomplete identities by invoking the common principles of the broader community," and that ethnic groups should invoke universal principles shared in a broader social space (Smith 1998: 187). Laclau suggests that the struggle of a subordinate group to assert its identity can result in either ghettoization, or a struggle with dominant institutions which may result in loss of identity. Dominant groups can marginalize smaller groups and their cultural values "can be easily retrieved as 'folklore' by the establishment" (Laclau 1996: 49). Appadurai (1990: 304) makes a similar point about difference becoming "museumized" and appropriated via "heritage politics." Alternatively, in the struggle for recognition the subordinate groups may be rendered harmless through division and/or incorporation. This leads Laclau to advance a variation on the thesis that the universal and the particular are counterposed and antagonistic, albeit one which allows for their complex interpenetration: in situations of struggle, particular groups can attempt to "undermine the hegemonic discourse's universalistic dimensions by drawing attention to its particularistic dimension" (Smith 1998: 189).

The second problem concerns the nature of the "broader community" referred to above. From Laclau's formula that "minorities equal particularisms" it is reasonable to infer that the broader community normally refers to the nationally contained state, although this is never made explicit. However, Smith (1998: 187) draws attention to the ways in which Laclau works with a "multiplicity of universal spaces": different groups invoke different universalities – nations, language groups, economic trade communities, global rights communities. Clearly this is an important consideration. In contestations over political rights in Turkey the "imagined communities" to which the rights apply vary considerably depending upon who is doing the imagining. For example, the community to whom citizenship rights are extended and the "community" of Islam are not coeval. Laclau rightly points out the transnational and transcultural dimensions of the "broader community." A subordinate group can utilize the resources of global discourses and the norms and practices of transnational institutions to further its cause. The political struggles for Kurdish autonomy or Islamic politics in Turkey are not circumscribed by domestic politics, nor do the conflicts necessarily take place within Turkish territory as such. They are also played out across European space, as with the controversy over MedTV for example, and within European institutions: 3,880 cases against Turkey are currently lodged with the European Court of Human Rights (*Turkish Daily News*, December 30, 1999).

Robertson: A "Globewide Cultural Nexus"

For Robertson the universal and the particular are mutually implicated, and one key aspect of globalization is the way it brings about the institutionalization of the universalization of particularism and the particularization of universalism (Robertson 1991: 80). One consequence of this is that is impossible to identify particularism with the local or minority culture, and universalism with global, dominant or "official" culture. "Rather than simply viewing the theme of universalism as having to do with principles which can and should be applied to all and that of particularism as referring to that which can and should be applied only 'locally', I suggest that the two have become tied together as a globewide cultural nexus" (Robertson 1991: 76).

The idea that the universal and the particular exist in a "globewide cultural nexus" is a crucial step towards seeing universalism in terms other than those imposed by thinking about nationally contained societies, and, as such, is of great relevance for an understanding of Turkey where universalism has been claimed by the Kemalists as the rightful property of the state. The Kemalists' dependence upon the politics of modernization and their tendency to monopolize ideas of Turkishness and nationhood, and to define and deploy ideas such as democracy, rights, and freedom in a way that renders them absolute and non-negotiable has led to the construction of the interests of the Islamists and Kurds as antithetical to those of the Republic.

Increasingly these groups face each other not simply as actors within a nationally bounded society, but also via interaction within the global frame of reference. Globalization means that nation-states are "increasingly subject to the internal, as well as external, constraints of multiculturality or, which is not quite the same thing, polyethnicity" (Robertson 1992: 98). In other words, the Kemalist project of producing a culturally homogenous population of modern, national citizens is undermined by the degree to which minority and ethnic groups are increasingly mobilized not just from within but also from afar. As Robertson (1995) notes, "much of what is called local is in large degree constructed on a trans- or super-local basis." Equally important is the fact that these groups claim rights and entitlements which are bestowed not by the national state but by international organizations such as the UN and the EU (even if it is nation-states who are held responsible for the implementation of human rights).

An interpretative framework which posits the political field as being delineated by the borders of national societies is not a suitable platform from which to investigate the political rights of Islamists and their claims to universalism. The discourses of universalism within which such political groups situate themselves are only intelligible within a global perspective. It is precisely their ability not to be contained with the national frame, and their ability to resist ghettoization as mere particularisms that creates the conflict with the dominant elites in Turkey. In the terms employed earlier by Laclau we can say that the Kurds, Islamists, feminists, and others prevent the reconciliation of society with itself. This resistance is made possible not because minority or subordinate groups are engaged in conflicts over the exercise of state power, but precisely because their conflicts are animated and their causes legitimated through their insertion into global discourses of rights and freedoms, and sustained by transnational religious, feminist, or ethnic support networks.

The Kurdish struggle, to take one example, is not something that can be nationally regulated and contained. It is a transnational conflict played out across Europe, the Middle East, and elsewhere.

Turkish troops regularly pursue the PKK into Iraq and Syria. Abdullah Ocelan, leader of the PKK, was captured by a group of Turkish commandoes operating covertly in Kenya. Pro-Kurdish demonstrators set fire to themselves on the streets of London. Belgium refuses to extradite a suspected terrorist on the grounds that the death penalty remains on Turkey's statutes. The Kurdish parliament in exile meets in various European cities. The European Parliament and the Council of Europe criticize Turkey for arresting three mayors elected from the pro-Kurdish HADEP party, and so on.

Robertson's ideas can be usefully applied to an interpretation of the "headscarf" case. The Islamists' defence of rights is couched in terms of global norms which they want applied to themselves in order that they may better promote their identity and, closely linked to this, pursue their political agenda. They are not seeking recognition as a national minority denied civil equality, but on the basis of global and universal rights to which they assert their entitlement. Their claim to universalism is constitutive of their particularism. As Soysal (1994: 160) comments, "[c]laims to particularistic identities, cultural distinctiveness, and self-determination are legitimated by reference to the essential, indisputable rights of persons, and, thus, are recast as world-level, postnational rights." This is what precisely what Robertson has in mind when he speaks of the universalization of particularism and the particularization of universalism, or in slightly different terms, the global production and reproduction of locality.

Viewed from Robertson's perspective, the apparent resistance of the Turkish state to the globality of human rights and democracy as manifested by their insistence upon continuing to forge a homogeneous national community and actively denying difference is opposition, "not merely to the world as one, homogenised system but also ... to the conception of the world as a series of culturally equal, relativised, entities or ways of life" (Robertson 1991: 77). Turkey's reluctance to make headway towards the EU's Copenhagen criteria or to embrace global human rights norms by, for example, abolishing the death penalty or signing Protocols 4, 6 and 7 of the European Charter for Human Rights, is a form of "global rejection" which is self-defeating. It is self-defeating because in its failure to conceptualize the world in terms of cultural equivalence it is unable to grasp that it is quite simply impossible to escape globalization, and, more importantly, to see that globality offers Turkey a legitimate means of safeguarding the values which are perceived as being so fundamentally threatened by the "energy and unruliness" of the globalizing trends which "ensnarl the country" (Bozdogan and Kasaba 1997: 5). By internalizing the EU's Copenhagen criteria Turkey could occupy a place in a world order in which international organizations, transnational movements, and global actors are working to secure a common ground upon which cultural expression is guaranteed and all ways of life protected. Rather than threaten the Kemalist project these developments make it easier to guard against threats to democracy and strengthen the principles which Kemalism has worked so hard to guarantee, while at the same time underpinning minority and democratic rights.

Turkey's encounters with globalization are not new. Indeed, from its inception in the 1920s the Turkish Republic sought to take its place within the emerging global order of nation-states. Moreover, it is evident that Ataturk himself had a nuanced understanding of the global order. When asked to justify Turkey's borrowing from the West, Ataturk is reported to have replied that "the national principle itself had become internationally accepted" (quoted in Matossian 1994: 220), thereby anticipating a key element of Robertson's globalization thesis – that the idea of nationalism develops only in tandem with internationalism – by 70 years (Robertson 1992: 103). Rather than seeing Turkey's national development as being subordinated to that of the West or being unable to bridge the gap between its own particularism and the universalism of the West (Robins 1996), Robertson allows for a different interpretation of Turkey's place in the world order. Turkey's particularism as a nation-state is a product of its insertion into a globalizing system of nation-states, the universality of which permitted Turkey's particularism. In other words, the "nationally sequestered society" as the internationally recognized norm provided the ground upon which the constitution of a particular *Turkish* state became possible. The universal and particular are not polar extremes separated by an unbridgeable gap: they exist in a "globewide nexus."

Democratization in Turkey within the Global Frame

EU candidature requires Turkey to harmonize with global political and human rights practices, and disputes between individuals and the state, or organized groups and the state, can no longer remain an "internal" matter. When Islamists in Turkey feel constrained by the nationalist secular Republic fostered by the Kemalists they seek legitimacy for their political agenda via global discourses on minority and human rights. Their claims are "embedded in universalistic principles and dominant discourses of equality, emancipation, and individual rights" (Soysal 1997: 518). Working through institutions of representative democracy at the national level is no longer the political *sine qua non* of the oppressed or marginalized.

Turkey has chosen to integrate with the EU, and, as such, must work to realign its domestic political practices with pan-European norms. We can identify two general types of solution advanced to solve the problem of reconciling the need for state control over domestic political activity with the demand voiced from both within and without Turkey for greater freedoms and plurality. The first is to call for an extension or a completion of the Kemalist project for the modernization of Turkey (Keyder 1997). This is based on the idea that the top-down transformation of Turkish society is incomplete and needs to be revitalized in order to guarantee full, western-style citizenship rights and civil liberties. While there is a growing realization that the authoritarian, paternalistic form of national development favored by the Kemalists is an inappropriate model from which to derive greater democracy and individual freedom, there is a great reluctance to abandon the project entirely (Bozdagan and Kasaba 1997). Modernization can still serve Turkey but must be extended and taken to its logical conclusion if Turkey is to emerge with a robust and fully functioning democracy.

The second type of solution is to argue that the emergence of a number of groups and minorities on the political scene over the past 20 years should be seen as the development of civil society, the consolidation of which will work to ensure the stability and inclusiveness of Turkish democracy (Robins 1996, Gole 1997). It is the liberal democratic version of the idea of civil society that has been taken up, much as it was in eastern Europe: civil society as the realm of possibility for political change. On this model there is a strong association of civil society with the idea of democratic progress in the face of state intransigence: the realm of political and economic freedoms, expression of opposition to an existing regime, and democratization. Of course, this is not civil society conceived as a realm in which democratic rule is exercised, or which sees that government also works through the agencies and manageable spaces of civil society. As Navaro-Yashin (1998: 4) points out, such an optimistic reading of developments in Turkey confuses "a changing discourse or technique of state power with an autonomous rise of civil society."

The idea that the Kemalist project of modernization as the bearer of democracy, rights, justice, and truth can provide the vehicle for democratization is called into question by the way in which it positions minorities and rights-asserting groups as particularisms subordinate to its own universalism. Beck, Laclau, and Robertson all emphasize the problems inherent in constituting universal-particular relations in this way. Similarly, civil society is posited as the realm where conflict between particularisms and the state can be resolved, diffused, accommodated. Equally importantly, both of these models work within a nationally constituted society view of political change. Both the modernization and the civil society route to democratization both assume that this is an endogenous, national project which can be generated by, and of benefit to, nationally constituted actors working within a domestically constituted (and state regulated) political field. Such assumptions are also called into question by the ideas of universalism and globality advanced by Beck, Laclau, and Robertson (even if Laclau is not a globalization theorist as such). From a globalization perspective the solutions to the problem of democratization outlined above are severely limited by their exclusive concern with the form that political contestation assumes in Turkey (who the protagonists are, what they stand for, and the extent to which they have access to the political process). In doing so they reproduce the modernist logic that political struggles are naturally contained within national societies.

Turkey's political elites are increasingly aware that international treaties and conventions, as well as European integration, work to limit national sovereignty. Nevertheless Turkey actively resists the logic of globalization in certain respects. Foremost among these is the insistence on equating Kemalism with universalism, a strategy which strives to preserve the "naturalness" of the national social space as the primary arena of political contestation. In doing so the Turkish political elites deny the reality that particularism is now very much part of the "universal core of humanness and selfhood" (Soysal 1997: 513). Despite this fetter, political actors within Turkey are animated by the possibilities that changing conceptions of universalism can bring and seek to further their cause by drawing on transnational resources and positioning themselves according to global criteria. By contesting their democratic rights in international fora and moving onto a global terrain of struggle they are forcing the state to confront some rather rigid notions about Turkey's place in the world order.

Pre-conditions for Democracy in Turkey

In a speech given at the Norwegian Nobel Institute, the Turkish Prime Minister, Bulent Ecevit, outlined the ways in which the Turkish state, business, and education are increasingly operating transnationally. Turkish state television broadcasts to central Asia, Europe and Australia, Turkish military contingents contribute to UN and NATO operations, thousands of Turkish firms trade and invest in the former Soviet Central Asian Republics, Turkish schools are established all over the world (Ecevit 2000).[19] He was much less enthusiastic about another consequence of transnationalism: support given to Kurdish groups, especially the PKK, by neighbouring countries and political groups in Europe. While globalization offers Turkey opportunities in terms of expanding markets and spheres of influence, it also introduces new challenges to national sovereignty and the regulation of domestic political actors.

This helps to explain why, from Turkey's point of view, the progress that can be achieved in the field of human rights is limited by perceived threats to the democratic system. The Justice Minister expressed this very clearly (Turk 1999):

> There are two reasons why Turkey has not been able to reach a more advanced level in the fields of democratisation and human rights. Firstly, Turkey has had to fight a separatist terrorist movement for 15 years. Secondly, fundamentalist attacks against secularism, which is the primary value of the Republic of Turkey and ensures social harmony among beliefs, religions and sects. These two sensitive issues have brought with them certain limitations in the field of human rights. We are making efforts to overcome these limitations, particularly on the freedom of conscience, but to do so completely requires the elimination of the aforementioned dangers.

Viewed from a different perspective, it can be argued that the rise of political Islam and the issue of minority rights represent "two basic challenges which Turkey has not been able to handle adequately" (Onis 1999: 131). Greater democratization has been viewed with suspicion by certain sections of the political elites. "For years it was believed and accepted to some degree that full provision of freedom of thought and human rights would increase terrorist acts, spread fundamentalism, and further divide the country" (Birand

2000). These challenges continue to delineate and limit the process of democratization. For example, there is a widespread consensus that political Islam is incompatible with the process of democratic consolidation. Similarly, the Kemalist elite continues to insist that minority rights for the Kurds conflict with the interests of the state and as such "any discussion of cultural rights or cultural autonomy is out of the question" (Onis 1999: 133). The political field is restricted by the (state induced) need to propagate an "authentic" form of democracy that guarantees (secular) freedoms and (nationalist) civil liberties while at the same time countering those groups perceived as enemies of the Republic.

What is conveniently ignored in Kemalist accounts of the threat posed by political Islam and the Kurds is that the political parties representing these groups have frequently held power in Turkey at a variety of levels over the past decade or so. The Refah Party was the leading member of the coalition government in 1996 with the Islamist Erbakan as Prime Minister (Onis 1997, Gulalp 1999). Since the mid-'90s Islamic-leaning political parties have run the municipalities of Istanbul and Ankara and the scare-stories that proceeded their election (prohibition of the public consumption of alcohol in areas under their jurisdiction, for example) have proved groundless (Navaro-Yasin 1999). At the present time many municipalities are run by either the Islamic Virtue Party (Fazilet) or the Kurdish HADEP.[20]

To draw attention to the nascent pluralism in Turkish democracy is not the same as saying that Turkey has a fully functioning democratic system in which all parties stand a fair chance of election and hence there is no reason for the EU and international agencies to be concerned. Rather, the point that needs to be made is that the dominant political discourse, in choosing to characterize Islamic and Kurdish politics *only* as a national threat is denying the reality that both Fazilet and HADEP are functioning within the system and are continuing to be relatively successful in elections. That there may be elements within these parties who wish to establish Islamic law or create an independent state for the Kurds does not divest their parties of democratic credentials, nor does it diminish their ability to administer municipalities and to get re-elected. This suggests that they are already adapted to and conversant with the democratic system, and that they do not simply use their elected offices as a power base from which to plot the break-up of the Turkish state.

It is clear that Turkey must embrace both a greater degree of pluralism and greater respect for minority rights if EU membership is ever to become a reality. This will begin to happen only when political Islam and the Kurdish problem begin to be seen in terms other than a threat to national security. A discursive space is needed in which Islamic and Kurdish tendencies in Turkish politics can begin to be seen as an assertion of citizenship rights in accordance with globalized norms. On this basis, political Islam would cease to be seen only as the threat of an alternative political order and become recognized as a legitimate political actor. Rather than a simplistic and monolithic portrayal of Islamic politics as fundamentalist, what is needed is the recognition that within Islamic politics a multiplicity of positions exist ranging from the fundamental to the liberal democratic. Both Kurdish and Islamic political tendencies need to be recognized as both a straightforward demand for cultural and political space on behalf of a minority, and a legitimate element of a pluralist social order. The idea that the EU's democratic expectations and human rights principles could in any way make it easier to guard against threats to democracy and strengthen the principles which Kemalism has worked so hard to guarantee, while at the same time underpinning minority and democratic rights, seems to not have entered the political calculations of the Kemalists. In other words, it is possible to have Kurdish cultural autonomy *and* territorial integrity, and pluralistic political representation *and* secularism.

Conclusion: Applicants or Supplicants?

Consideration of the enlargement process is usually framed within a discussion of the process of harmonization and adoption of the *acquis communautaire*, the impact on the economies of candidate and member state countries, and the economic and political problems and prospects created by an enlarged bloc. Clearly, there are many outstanding issues surrounding the enlargement process, including fundamental ones such as who will be included, when it will start to happen, and whether new members will be offered full membership, as traditionally understood. Despite an initial enthusiasm for enlargement existing member states have been extremely reluctant to make the process a straightforward or smooth one.

What is surprising about this state of affairs is not that the EU has been rather indecisive about who it wants to admit and how it wants to conduct the enlargement process, or unenthusiastic about setting a timetable for its completion and making firm commitments as to the funding that will be on offer to new members. What is surprising is that the candidate countries, on the whole, remain uncomplaining about this state of affairs. Shifting goalposts, lack of a timetable, and uncertainty over costs and benefits have not deterred EU candidate countries from central and eastern Europe and the Mediterranean from staying true to their vocation. Europe appears to possess a "magnetic attraction" (Rachman 2001) for the candidate countries, for whom the price and the wait are worthwhile. But by occluding the accession timetable, creating a queue for membership, and by imposing strict norms and values on its neighbours the EU has created supplicants, rather than applicants.

There is another, much more important, aspect to the acquiescence of the candidate states. The norms, values, principles and priorities of the EU towards applicants, as codified in the Copenhagen criteria, and the way in which the EU projects these values and expectations as universal, remain largely unchallenged within the accession processes. In much the same way as theorists of cosmopolitism democracy see the need for peaceful means of interference in the domestic democratic practices of recalcitrant states, the EU reserves the right to interfere peacefully in the democratic development of former communist countries and other non-members.[21] For instance, in the context of promoting human rights the EU believes it must take a pro-active stance. In Commissioner Patten's words, the "moral case for action is unquestionable" (European Commission 2001a).

Adoption of the *acquis communautaire* is expected to be completed before membership is possible (and in Turkey's case before accession negotiations can begin). The EU is now very active in imposing its expectations and standards upon aspiring members. Assistance, such as it is, political dialogue and trade relations are conditioned by the ways in which candidates or potential candidates embrace the Copenhagen criteria. In contrast with the practices of the 1970s and '80s this process now begins at a much earlier stage. There are non-candidate countries within the wider orbit of the EU whose internal democratic development is now influenced by the proximity of the EU as a rights-bearing organization. Democracy now means very much more than the rule of law and a functioning parliamentary system. Satellites of the EU now have to take into account the EU's preference for "good governance," the abolition of the death penalty, and non-discriminatory treatment of minorities. By adopting a cosmopolitan democracy-style approach to interference in the democratic practices of others, and occupying the moral high ground in respect of the universality of its own position, the EU extends its sphere of influence beyond that of its pan-European networks, its single market, and its Europe agreements. "By framing its relations with outsiders in terms of the perspective of membership, by establishing structures and stepping stones towards accession, the EU can more effectively govern beyond its territory" (Friis and Murphy 2001).

The addition of Turkey to the enlargement equation throws up some very interesting questions to do with the way in which the EU develops relations with non-members and the extent to which its norms are non-negotiable. Turkey positions herself as an applicant, not a supplicant. In asserting a marked difference from the EU (and other candidates) Turkey becomes yet more marginalized from the accession processes. More than any cultural and "civilizational" differences Turkey's Otherness stems from an adherence to a model of democracy, universalization, and progress and development which is no longer widely endorsed.

Nevertheless, Turkey's model remains a major irritant for the EU. According to the ECHR, Turkey did not violate human rights when it banned the Welfare Party, a decision that has confounded most commentators' instincts regarding Turkey's rather casual approach to upholding democratic standards. The criticisms levelled at Turkey when the decision to ban the Welfare Party (and later the Virtue Party) was announced were that the ban would widen the gap between EU expectations and democratic practices in Turkey (Dorsey 1998), and concern was raised regarding the ability of Turkey to uphold democratic standards of pluralism and freedom of expression. However, rather than positioning Turkey outside the European democratic fold, the judgment of the ECHR has in fact confirmed that Turkey's democracy is aligned with European and global norms, and in doing so has bolstered the legitimacy of the Turkish state. Put simply, the ECHR has acknowledged that it is legitimate to ban political parties who constitute a threat to democracy. The decision of the ECHR confirms the Kemalist position that the Welfare Party was anti-democratic, not a view shared by many outside of Turkey at the time the ban was imposed. In terms of the EU's Copenhagen political criteria, the "stable institutions guaranteeing democracy" have received a ringing endorsement.

This is not to say that Turkey is right to limit cultural autonomy to the Kurds or is not guilty of the democratic and human rights shortcoming frequently highlighted by any number of international organizations. Turkey has a considerable way to go before being able to claim parity with other western countries in these matters. Nevertheless, Turkey is not wrong to expect that there should be greater openness on the part of the EU to engage in a productive debate about different forms of democracy, where its own norms and practices came from, and how they only emerged in their present form in the relatively recent past.

10 Conclusion

If we were to construct a history of European integration from the perspective of the sociological framework developed in this book we would not begin with the nation-state and the changes that it has undergone, or sacrifices that it has had to make, in order to bring about European integration. Rather than viewing the development of the EU as inhering in the unfolding of an intergovernmental bargain or the rise of a supranational authority, we should view it as a strategy for the management of emerging transnational spaces occasioned by the acceleration of globalization. In other words, the EU should not be viewed as the agglomeration of nation-state space but as an example of transnational space. This is the point at which the benefits of a sociological interpretation of European integration become most obvious. As the study of the EU comes to terms with global rather than nation-state dynamics, a globalization-inspired sociology stands well placed to make an important contribution.[1]

On this interpretation, the integrative structuring of (western) Europe in the post-war period has been one consequence of Europe's incorporation into the international and transnational frameworks which have themselves become increasingly dominant features of the second half of the twentieth century. The EU was born into a rapidly transnationalizing world ushered in by the global institutions of the post-war capitalist economic system: the UN, the IMF, the World Bank, and GATT. For example, we have seen how the European Union's Common Agricultural Policy, to many a symbol of EU member states at their most parochial and introspective – and an expression of a distinct "European model of agriculture" – was occasioned and sustained by the external pressures coming from global export regimes.

Within a globalization-inspired political sociology frame integration is revealed to be more than the building of supranational structures of governance or the conservation of individual nation-states, and just one of a range of important processes at work in Europe. Integration can be best thought of as an attempt to manage a multiplicity of (sometimes) contradictory dynamics. We saw in chapter 6 how the European region is animated from afar and by forces working outside the influence of the EU in such a way as to confound the project of European integration. Similarly, the terms "Europe" and "integration" can be decoupled, and the idea of Europe freed from being synonymous with the EU. The term "Europe" is not exhausted by EU attempts to monopolize it. In order to complete our sociological study of European integration we must turn our attention to the issue of to what extent the terms "Europe" and "integration" are indivisible and inseparable, implying and reinforcing each other, or whether they can be conceived independently. In other words, how are we to best understand the idea of integration? And does Europe exist distinct from and without the EU?

This book constitutes a sustained attempt to problematize the idea of integration, and one of its central arguments has been that an appreciation of globalization is the key to understanding the dynamics of the contemporary EU. On the one hand, globalization allows us to see how actors and agencies within the EU (NGOs and regions, sectors, and citizens) can be (partially) mobilized from afar: the EU is not the horizon of opportunity for Europeans. This is particularly true in the case of citizenship – which has multiple origins, only some of which can be attributed to member states or the EU. On the other hand, globalization fragments as well as integrates: globalization should not be seen purely as an external threat requiring "ever closer union." For example, sub-national regions do not neatly aggregate into a cohesive whole at the EU level. Under conditions of globalization regions are experiencing autonomization as well as integration and are freed of any necessary dependence upon a centre, whether the national capital or Brussels. Indeed, the many territorial assumptions upon which conventional accounts of integration are based can be rejected in favor of a model of networks and flows, which in turn erodes the idea of a fixed and bounded European space.

But we cannot do away completely with territorialist assumptions, no more than we can dispense with existing notions of integration, society, or the nation-state. The old and the new coexist: the nation-state and the transnational; territorial space and networks; national, supranational, and postnational citizenship. The fact that they continue to operate and have an effectivity within the same space creates the tensions and disjunctures which are responsible for the most interesting phenomena of the present day, namely the EU's attempts to domesticate the global through its policies and programs: attempting integration through subnational regions; maintaining the economic dependency of "peripheral regions"; the contradiction between high unemployment and the need to recruit large numbers of immigrant workers; the mismatch between nationally derived models of democracy and the democratic potential of transnational spaces.

Perhaps the best example of the tension produced by imposing old categories on new phenomena is the way the EU views European society. In an attempt to address the democratic deficit, the need for a European social space or society has been identified by the European Commission as a necessity if European integration is to become meaningful to its citizens. This European society is conceived very much along the lines of a national civil society, a cohesive and harmonized space in which a range of state and non-state actors can formulate policy and solve social and economic problems according to the model of "good governance." What this vision neglects is the fragmented and partial nature of European social space(s). Contemporary European society is characterized by division without overall unity. It is constituted by the forces of transnational fragmentation acting on its nation-state underpinnings, and by the transformatory impact of non-consensual social fissures which recognize no national limits. Society is unruly and fragmented, no longer obeying the commands of a nation-state from which it is increasingly divorced.

From the perspective of how to best to approach the study of the EU our political sociology approach can identify two developments of note. First, the EU is changing, not merely in the obvious ways – enlargement, monetary union, acquiring a defence capability – but in unpredictable and extremely challenging ways. Under the impact of globalization, as understood in this book, the EU is finding it difficult to control its various components – citizens, regions, enterprises, NGOs – and render them amenable to integration. Second, EU studies is wrestling with the problem of how best to understand the EU in flux. It has become untenable to view the EU as a collection of nation-states or an emerging supranational authority, and a direct outcome of the need to apprehend, understand, and manage this change has been the rise to prominence of the idea of multi-level governance.

The appeal of multi-level governance is that it both strives to capture the transformed capacity of the EU as a state – working at multiple levels through governance – and gives expression to its aspirations for greater democracy, social inclusion, and participatory citizenship. In short, multi-level governance theory attempts to embrace the dynamism of the contemporary EU at the same time as domesticating it and rendering it amenable to investigation within a familiar political science framework. Multi-level governance works to accommodate the contradictory logics correctly identified by Axford and Huggins (1999). On the one hand it embraces the inclusive "social" model of the EU as a nation-state "writ-large," while at the same time accepting that the EU is responsible for giving rise to and managing a transnational European space. In sum, multi-level governance attempts to reconcile the idea of a fluid and differentiated Europe of the network with that of a more traditional notion of integration.

The conclusions on how to study European integration reached in this book, emphasizing the broadness of the field and the need to contextualize the role of the European Union within the array of integrative (and disintegrative) processes characterizing contemporary Europe, invite a reconsideration of Etzioni's pioneering sociological study of European unification mentioned in the Introduction. Two main features of Etzioni's 1960s study were highlighted: his scepticism regarding the degree of integration resulting from EEC initiatives, and the ability of the EEC to mythologize its origins and attributes. Both are also very real issues in the contemporary context. For Etzioni, integration was something for the future, not an actually existing reality, and depended upon the functioning of a true political community. As we have seen, in the contemporary setting there exists a consensus that there is still no real basis for a political community and that this is a flaw in the EU project, contributing in no small measure to the "democratic deficit." The more sceptical among us may believe that the sort of political community sought by many will never come about, not simply because it is undesirable or beyond the capabilities of the EU, but because a political community in the singular, an integrated and cohesive entity created by a unified public space and a common citizenry, with shared values, principles and aspirations and embracing and representing diverse and disparate Europeans, is a vision consistent with the politics of modernity, taking the nation-state as its template. One conclusion to be drawn from the present survey is that Europe isn't like that, and attempts to make it conform to such a model will do incalculable harm to the diversity of individuals, groups and communities which occupy

European spaces, and who may have divergent, contradictory – even incompatible – wants and needs.

Secondly, Etzioni saw that from the very beginning the EEC was very good at narrating its own history as one of success in overcoming difficult obstacles, and was not slow to take the credit for economic growth which may have happened anyway. The EU has never shied away from a strategy of self-aggrandizement. What Etzioni's work points to is that we should not assume that the EU exhausts the meaning of the term "Europe," that the EU is the only body involved in integrating Europe, and most importantly that not all processes acting upon and shaping Europe emanate from or can be controlled by the EU. What was true in the 1960s is also true today: Europe is much more than can ever be represented by European Union integration.

Is it possible to speak of Europe having an existence distinct from the EU? Or is the EU discourse of integration so dominant that the term Europe dovetails with the idea of integration so as to invoke the unity and oneness of a natural entity? To speak of Europe as an integrated entity is of course a relatively recent phenomenon, as until the dissolution of Soviet-dominated communist regimes Europe was generally prefixed by either western or eastern, a division which many held to have a genuine and historical "natural" basis.[2] Since 1989 the EU has increasingly been the focus of attempts to create a "New Europe" – the desire of the former communist satellites to "return to Europe," and their perception of the important role of the EU in this process consolidating the EU's hegemonic status yet further. But there exist many European spaces, many Europes, which are not, and cannot, be easily contained by the EU.

It is much more appropriate to our task to speak of "Europes" in the plural. The reading of integration and the role of the EU in shaping current events preferred in this book suggests that not only is the EU but one player shaping the politics, economy and society of contemporary Europe, but that what is emerging is a multiplicity of Europes – both in relation to EU membership (full members, official candidates, associates countries, non-members), and in relation to other pan-European bodies (the Council of Europe, for example), but also in terms of the plethora of social and political spaces which actors are able to construct, inhabit, and move within and between. European communities are proliferating, not tied to or limited by national spaces or EU initiatives, but transnational and global, connecting Europeans to each other and the wider world in myriad ways, and which may or may not have a relation to the EU. If "Europes" were to be recognized as spaces of political freedoms, democratic contestation, cultural and economic pluralism and social diversity, the idea of Europe would be invested with the sort of meaning and identity that the EU has only been partially successful in capturing.

One area in which this is particularly true is that of human rights. During the military campaign against the Taliban in Afghanistan following the events in New York and Washington on September 11, 2001 and at a time when the US was applauding the solidarity shown by Britain in the "fight against terrorism," Britain was said to have angered the US by indicating that it would not extradite suspects accused of involvement in the events of September 11 unless the US waived its right to impose the death penalty (*Electronic Telegraph*, October 7, 2001).[3] Britain, in common with other EU member states, is bound by the European Convention of Human Rights which prohibits extraditions in cases where capital punishment can result. The European Convention of Human Rights does not derive from the EU, nor has the EU signed the convention (although all of its member states have). The Convention originates with the Council of Europe, and was adopted in 1950, thereby predating the EEC. The human rights identity of the EU, increasingly an integral part of its dealings with non-members via the Copenhagen criteria, is both a recent development and owes a considerable debt to the groundbreaking activities of other regional and international bodies. The "integration" of EU member states around a common set of "European" human rights values is, in this instance at least, the work not of the EU, but of another important European body. As such, it is possible to assert that there are very good reasons for wanting to resist attempts by the EU to colonize the meaning of Europe, and every advantage in ensuring that "Europes" proliferate.

Notes

1 Introduction: A New Approach to Studying European Integration

1 The 12 members were Belgium, Denmark, France, Germany, Greece, Ireland, Italy, Luxembourg, the Netherlands, Portugal, Spain, and the UK. According to the Treaty, the EU comprises the European Communities – the European Coal and Steel Community (ECSC), European Atomic Energy Community (EURATOM), and the European Economic Community (EEC) – plus two intergovernmental "pillars": Common Foreign and Security Policy (CFSP) and Cooperation on Judicial and Home Affairs.

2 The 12 listed in note 1, plus Austria, Finland, and Sweden who joined in 1995.

3 The ECSC began operation in 1952. The six nations that formed the European Coal and Steel Community – West Germany, France, Italy, and the Benelux countries – were later to become the founding members of the EEC. The ECSC formally merged with the EEC in 1967.

4 The use of the term social theory and its relation to sociology requires clarification. Social theory is a broader category than sociology, although the two are closely related. Social theory is interdisciplinary in character and concerned with a theoretical understanding of the organization and transformation of social life. It probes social science assumptions concerning the forces shaping social relations, and focuses particularly on issues such as the nature of identity, agency and subjectivity, political and social power, modernity and postmodernity. There are two reasons why social theory provides an important resource for a political sociology of the EU. First, sociology as a discipline has become aware of its rootedness in the study of national societies and needs to draw upon a body of work which can stimulate a "sociology beyond societies." Second, sociology, like many other disciplines, does not always find it easy to embrace or engage with new ideas and theories. As a consequence such ideas and theories remain outside or marginal to the field

of sociology (at least for a period). Examples include the way in which the emerging discipline of cultural studies was seen as a threat to sociology, prompting some sociologists to react by policing their discipline's boundaries. More recently, theories of postmodernism and globalization have not been enthusiastically received by the discipline and are still seen as marginal to a subject whose core consists of studies of class and inequality, gender, race and ethnicity, and economic life. In the same way as there is no clear cut distinction between sociology and political sociology, the boundary between sociology and social theory is a porous one.

2 The European Union and Globalization

1 The phrase is Robertson's and designates a sociologically grounded but necessarily trans-disciplinary approach to understanding globalization and one which avoids its reduction to a simple causality.

2 On this charge I must plead guilty. My *European Cohesion? Contradictions in EU Integration* (2000a) analyzes the contradictions apparent in the EU's regional and cohesion policies without incorporating the ideas of globalization under consideration here. In my defence I would point out that the conclusions reached in that study are consistent with a globalization perspective.

3 Consider the following comments made by Robert Reich, Secretary of State for Labor in the Clinton administration: "During the Cold War, we used the Soviet threat to get the public to accept certain changes and to build certain institutions, from the national highway system to the space programme. They were all justified in national security terms. Today, with the Soviet threat gone, governments now use the global markets in the same way. We have to adopt this economic policy, initiate this training program for our workforce, because if we don't we won't be able to attract global capital and raise our standard of living," quoted in Bruton (1996: 35).

4 *The Rise of the Network Society: Volume 1* (second edition) (Castells 2000a), *The Power of Identity: Volume 2* (Castells 1996), *End of Millennium: Volume 3* (second edition) (Castells 2000b).

5 Castell's ideas on the network society are also explored in some detail in chapter 6 *Rethinking Core–Periphery Relations.*

6 The assertion that "capital is global, labour local" is examined in more detail later in the chapter.

7 We need to be clear about what we mean by the terms the Modern Age, modernity, and so on. We can say that the term modernity stands for a cultural experience – the Enlightenment, rationality, scientific method, notions of domination and progress, western values. It is also associated

with a certain type of politics – democracy, citizenship, the nation-state. Modernity is the ideas, experiences, and values characteristic of the modern epoch. Modernization, on the other hand, refers to the set of socioeconomic processes that constitute the dynamics of modernity; capitalism, industrialization, technological innovation, mass social movements associated with political ideologies (Berman 1983). Neither modernity nor modernization complete the configuration of the Modern Age, which includes the rural, the poor, the old world religions. "Traditional cultures were not bypassed by modernity. They were ever present features of the Modern Age, without being modern" (Albrow 1996: 55). The Modern Age is a broad category which embraces the tension between the modern and the non-modern.

8   We should bear in mind that Albrow prefers the term globality to globalization as it carries less connotations of historical direction (teleology) (Albrow 1996: 121).

9   And notable for the way it tends to read all Islamic politics as fundamentalist.

10 It should be noted that Albrow's treatment of the EU in his book *The Global Age* is perfunctory. His thoughts on the subject are developed more fully in Albrow 1998a.

11 This is not to suggest that Albrow wishes to detach "our time" from any general historical narrative. He writes of the need to "grasp our own time in its unique configuration and therefore in contrast to other times and places, but at the same time to uphold the essential requirement for effective analysis we seek to identify truths which cross times, places and cultures" (Albrow 1998a).

12 For a sociological account which cuts the other way and locates globalization within the wider processes of postmodernity, see Rattansi (1994).

13 Robertson (1995) holds that the tendency to think of the global/local as polar opposites is a product of the type of thinking consistent with modernity. Thus, we find accord between Robertson and Albrow on the point that it is impossible to fully understand globalization within the paradigm of modernity.

14 See the article entitled "Planet Mac" in *The Guardian*, April 7, 2001.

15 The truth of this is born out by the fortunes of the high-street retailer C&A. In June 2000 the closure of the entire British operation and 4,800 redundancies were announced. Critics pointed to C&A's policy of centralizing fashion buying in Dusseldorf and Brussels, and attempting to sell the same styles in all of its European stores without taking into account local tastes. The "selective, style-aware British shopper did not want her wardrobe to be a homogenous, style equivalent of the euro [and] did not see herself as a Frau Smith in a T-shirt with shoulder-pads" (*Electronic Telegraph*, June 16, 2000).

16 However global capital has the potential to be, in reality a significant

proportion of it does tend to stick to tried and trusted routes. Britain continues to attract the highest level of inward investment in the G7 group of countries. In 1999 investment accounted for 27 percent of GDP (*Electronic Telegraph*, February 13, 2001).

17   The Delors White Paper *Growth, Competitiveness and Employment* (European Commission 1993) emphasized the need to reduce non-wage labor costs and to increase labor flexibility. As Amin and Tomaney (1995: 28) point out, this is an example of the subordination of EU social policy to needs of industry rather than defending the rights of employees.

18   There have been many reports concerning the ways in which state aids to the UK motor industry have been used to offset production costs thereby attracting investment that would otherwise have gone elsewhere (see Rumford 2000a: 150–3).

19   The EU's *Draft Charter of Fundamental Rights* is notable for the rights it confers on non-EU nationals. For example, the right to working conditions equivalent to those of citizens of the EU (Article 15), the right to social security benefits (Article 34), right of access to EU documents (Article 42), right to petition the European Parliament (Article 44), freedom of movement (Article 45).

3   The Question of the European State

1   The multi-level governance approach was developed in the field of regional policy studies but has developed into a general model of EU decision-making (Hix 1999: 200). The issue is covered here in some detail in chapter 6.

2   I prefer the term harmonization to Albrow's standardization. This is because harmonization better encapsulates the way the EU is attempting to reconstitute Europe as an economic, social and political space, and also better captures the nature of the policy process. Harmonization implies not rigid established standards but a "settling out" process around pragmatic norms. Standardization also implies a uniformity of response, while harmonization allows for a differential adoption of EU norms. Harmonization does not proceed with equal intensity across all sectors and countries. There are sectors, for example R&D, which have actively resisted attempts by the EU to harmonize them (Peterson 1996). Nor does harmonization always emanate from the EU: it may be sector or member state led. It is also important to bear in mind that harmonization is not the only regulatory approach available to the EU. Majone (1996: 268–9) points out that where harmonization is seen to be over-regulatory or inflexible "mutual recognition" of national standards is sometimes the preferred option.

3 ASEAN (Association of South East Asian Nations); NAFTA (North American Free Trade Agreement).

4 According to Scholte (2000: 137), under conditions of globalization, the classical (Westphalian) model of sovereignty can no longer be sustained. No country can maintain supreme, comprehensive, unqualified, and exclusive rule over its territorial jurisdiction. National borders are no longer impermeable to external processes and "transworld relations influence circumstances in a country without ever directly touching its soil."

5 Although such ideas are frequently encountered in the media and in the political debate about European integration, particularly in Britain where former Conservative leader William Hague said of the European Rapid Reaction Force – the so-called "Euro-army": "This has nothing to do with the defence of our country and everything to do with going with the flow in Europe and building a European superstate" (*Electronic Telegraph*, November 23, 2000).

6 Or in Kaldor's (1995: 74–5) formulation the nation-state is too large to prevent "the elimination of lesser cultures" (from the cultural homogeneity involved in nation-building), and "too large for efficient democratic decision making." At the same time it is "too small to regulate . . . a global economy [and] to prevent wars."

7 It should be borne in mind that Stone Sweet and Sandholtz are contributing to a theoretical debate dominated by neo-functionalism and intergovernmentalism. Within the terms of this dichotomous division they align themselves with neo-functionalism, with certain reservations.

8 "Eurosclerosis" refers to the stagnation and lack of progress on European integration characteristic of the period following the 1973 Oil Crisis when member states chose to pursue individual solutions to economic problems. This period lasted until the early 1980s.

9 Audit is elsewhere described by Rose as "the control of control" (1999: 154).

10 Barry (1993 and 2001) is an exception. It is worth noting that although the governmentality theorists have applied themselves to the issue of "Governing Australia" (Dean and Hindess 1998) no comparable work has been carried out on "governing Europe."

11 The Commission has made plain that the CAP tends to favor the larger, more profitable farms of northern Europe rather than the smaller ones of the south. Also, one of the "poor four," Portugal, continues to be a net loser from the CAP (European Commission 1996a and 2001c).

12 According to Grant (2001) historically speaking the drivers of reform have been budgetary pressures, external trade negotiations (the Uruguay Round), and eastern enlargement. Recently, the issue of food quality and safety has also spurred reform.

13   It should be noted that the "second pillar" of the CAP currently receives only about 10 percent of available funds.

4   European Society

1   Dean (1999) and Urry (1999) contain interesting discussions of Thatcher's speech.
2   Urry (1999: 5–12) summarizes how different sociological traditions work with the concept of society.
3   We need to clarify the use of the terms "society" and "the social." "The social" is generally used by sociological thinkers and social theorists in one of two ways. In the first case, "the social" may be employed where attention is being drawn to the incomplete or partial nature of society. This is the case in the work of Laclau and Mouffe (1985) for whom the idea of society as a bordered totality is an impossibility. Alternatively, "the social" is used to express the idea that society comprises different social forces and elements which exist independently of whether or not they happen to be bound together to form a society. This perspective holds that the forces and collectivities termed "the social" are the "building blocks" of society, the raw material out of which society can be constructed. In the second case, "the social" is the preferred term for those writers emphasizing the postnational nature of societies under conditions of globalization, thereby implying that the term "society" is best reserved for discussions of the nation-state society of modernity. This is also how the term is used in the work of the governmentality theorists, who characterize the dynamics of social change rather differently.
4   Hay, Watson, and Wincott (1999) "unpack" the European social model to reveal four distinct conceptions. First, a generic European model that has emerged in the post-war period based on social protection and institutionalized social cleavages. Second, within this overall context a variety of national models. Third, "the development of a distinctive trans-national social model," with the EU replacing some of the functions previously carried out at the national level. Fourth, new social models emerging from within former state socialist regimes.
5   Delors was President of the European Commission from 1985 to 1995. The influence of the idea of the "European model of society" endured well into the period of the Santer Commission (1995–9).
6   Indeed, a "Euro-welfare state" has never developed as members states have chosen to retain a pretty tight grip on social policy. The welfare state remains primarily national in scope (Pierson 1998: 143).
7   The European Commission (2000c) defines NGOs as no-profit, voluntary, accountable, independent organizations active in the public arena.
8   On this point, see also Barry (1993) and Axford and Huggins (1999).

9   The idea of good governance has been carried through into the Prodi Commission (1999–present).

10 Similarly, whereas welfare provision was once justified by its direct contribution to social inclusion, increasingly it is subordinated to "perceived economic imperatives", that is to say, competitiveness (Hay, Watson, and Wincott 1999).

11 Mann (1998: 184) uses the term "Euro" to designate "that unit defined by the boundaries of a succession of acronyms, the ECSC, the EEC, the EC and now the EU." Mann's work on the network society will be discussed at greater length in chapter 6.

12 He does not appear to take into account the non-national potential and global scope of the Internet.

13 See for example Hosking (1991), especially chapter 3. The idea of the growth of civil society as the "return of the repressed" has been employed in a similar way in commentaries on Turkey. See, for example, the work of Robins (1996) and Kramer (2000).

14 The use of the term "political society" in this context should not be confused with Gramsci's equation of political society with the state itself. For an example of a distinction between civil and political society similar to that employed by Cohen and Arato, see Pelczynski (1988).

15 Although the extent to which totalitarian societies actually eliminated all forms of opposition and dissent is the subject of some debate. See for example Tismaneanu (1990a and 1990b).

16 However, belief in the possibility of "top-down" reform was reignited by Gorbachev's policies in the Soviet Union. *Glasnost* and *perestroika* were the catalysts of change in eastern and central Europe (Tismaneanu 1990c: 183).

17 Compare Giddens' (2000: 51) assertion that a "democratic order, as well as an effective market economy, depends upon a flourishing civil society. Civil society, in turn, needs to be limited by the other two."

18 These private interests do not include economic interests. For Gramsci, following Hegel, civil society is separate from both the state and the economy.

19 "Having redefined what it means to be left wing, Tony Blair plans to do the same for Britishness" ("A new brand for Britain," *The Economist*, August 23, 1997).

20 By asserting this "enlarged conception of the state" (Mouffe 1979) he confirms that civil society does not enjoy the freedom and protection from the state that the more liberal theories of civil society proclaim.

21 Dean (1999: 210) defines liberalism as "a critique of excessive government." "Liberalism is an art of government not only because it recognizes that there are limits to the role of the state but because what it determines as falling outside the political sphere is itself necessary to the ends of government" (Dean 1999: 51).

22   Urry proposes replacing "society" with networks, flows, and mobilities as the central focus of sociology: "a 'sociology of mobilities' disrupts a 'sociology of the social as society'" (Urry 1999: 4). However, the position developed in this book is that it is not necessary to counterpose societies to mobilities. As outlined in this chapter and chapter 7 it is quite possible to retain both concepts in an analysis of contemporary Europe.

23   Appadurai is not suggesting that passive consumption of the media is empowering in this way. He is thinking of a much more active form of consumption in which "images of the media are quickly moved into local repertoires of irony, anger, humor, and resistance" (Appadurai 1996: 7).

24   The use of civil society in this context should not be taken to mean that Soysal endorses the civil society thesis that was criticized earlier in this chapter. As used here the term refers to a nationally constituted model of social order and to the idea that this order is necessarily based on a rationally derived consensus. Her preference for the phrase "European public spheres" rather than "European civil society" in the title of her paper suggests a deliberate distancing from the problematic notion of civil society.

5   Unemployment, Social Exclusion, and Citizenship

1   The December 2000 figure was an improvement on the 8.9 percent registered 12 months earlier. National rates continue to vary enormously across the EU: from 2.1 percent in Luxembourg to 13.7 percent in Spain (European Commission 2001b).

2   Thereby opposing the view that reducing working hours could contribute to a reduction in unemployment. UNICE cites the case of Germany where the working week is the shortest in Europe but where unemployment in still high.

3   "While there is widespread agreement that labour-market flexibility (variously measured) is increasing, no such consensus exists over either its causes or its consequences" (Peck 1995: 158).

4   In support of this Michie (1995: 86) notes that in the UK productivity growth has been translated into falling employment rather than output growth. Hudson (1999: 34) writes that, "Labour productivity consistently grew more rapidly than output so that much of western Europe experienced 'jobless' or even 'job shedding' growth as companies strove to respond to global competitive challenges and depressed national economies in Europe."

5   But not the same sort of unskilled jobs characteristic of industrial society, or as Beck terms it "first modernity." The new unskilled jobs are in the service industries, "MacJobs" as they are sometimes referred to.

6 Giddens (2000: 76) states that "In almost all industrial countries there are more jobs now than a quarter of a century ago." However, the rate of growth in new jobs is lower in Europe than in North America or Japan.

7 Preuss also believes that the experience of citizenship will have a greater European dimension for non-nationals of another EU state than for nationals. He is thinking in particular of the way in which the Maastricht Treaty instituted the right to move and reside freely within the territory of the EU, and the right of Union citizens resident in other member states to vote and stand as candidates in municipal elections and elections to the European Parliament.

8 It should be noted that the work of the governmentality theorists on the government of unemployment is concerned mainly with the situation in the UK, Australia and the United States of America, rather than Europe as such.

6 Cohesion Policy and Regional Autonomy

1 When the EU talks of economic and social disparities it is not referring to class or gender inequalities for example, but to disparities in the level of development and economic well-being between regions or member states.

2 Structural Funds grew from ECU 18 billion in 1992 to ECU 31 billion in 1999 (at 1992 prices). This approximates to one third of the total EU budget. In addition, approximately ECU 14.5 billion was spent on the Cohesion Fund between 1994 and 1999 (Dinan 2000).

3 Variations are quite pronounced. Judged by Purchasing Power Standards (PPS) the poorest region is Ipeiros in Greece, with a GDP per person standing at 43 percent of the EU15 average. The richest is Inner London, at 222 percent. There are 50 regions below 75 percent of the EU15 average, while at the other end of the scale 10 regions have a GDP per person around 1½ times the EU15 average. In nine member states GDP per person in the richest region is approximately double the lowest. Regional differences in Germany and the UK are much more pronounced. In the UK, there are regions with a third of Inner London's 222 percent. There is an even greater disparity between Hamburg and some of the former GDR regions of Germany (European Commission, 1999a).

4 Of this group Ireland's growth has been the most impressive, GDP increasing from 64 percent of the Community average in 1983 to 80 percent in 1993, and 90 percent in 1995. However, Mathews (1994: 5–6) reminds us that GDP growth is not necessarily the most accurate indicator of economic performance. He argues that GNP per head is a more reliable indicator, in terms of which Ireland improved only slightly

between 1973 (Ireland's date of EU accession) and 1990 (from 59 percent of the EU12 average to 62 percent). The difference between GDP and GNP growth is due to the way increased production is generated: government spending financed by foreign borrowing and by foreign investment. Both sources have lead to outflows of interest on foreign debt and profit repatriation.

5 There is a wealth of information on disparities between individual member states, and between their regions. Interestingly, the EU has very little to say about disparities *within* regions, arguably a problem of even greater importance (Allen et al. 1998), and it has been argued that the method of indicating economic inequality through per capita GDP figures and levels of unemployment works to mask intra-regional disparities (Amin and Tomaney 1995: 13).

6 The Structural Funds comprise the European Regional Development Fund (ERDF), the European Social Fund (ESF), the guidance section of the European Agricultural Guidance and Guarantee Fund (EAGGF), and the Fisheries Guidance Instrument (FGI).

7 We have already encountered the idea of multi-level governance in the context of the European Union as a form of state (chapter 3).

8 Reflexive modernization, it should be noted, is preferred by both Beck and Giddens to the term postmodernism. According to Giddens (1990: 51) "We have not moved beyond modernity but are living precisely through a phase of its radicalisation." Reflexive modernization does not designate counter-modernity or that the Enlightenment project has come to an end, rather that simple modernization has been extended and taken to a higher level.

9 One consequence of this is that the direct impact of cohesion policies on disparities is extremely difficult to disentangle from the effects of other factors (European Commission 1996a: 94).

10 Member states have much larger budgets at their disposal than the EU, and their economic priorities do not always coincide with EU cohesion strategy. Member states allocate between 40 percent and 60 percent of national GDP to public spending, while the EU budget is about 1.2 percent of EU GDP (European Commission 1996a: 6).

7   Rethinking Core–Periphery Relations

1 When considering the impact on cohesion of extending the single market to the transport or telecommunications sectors the Commission concluded that, "In general, such policies seem not to be to the *absolute* disadvantage of less favoured regions or social groups, but they tend to benefit them less *relatively* to *central regions or more favoured groups*" (European Commission 1996a: 86–7).

2   The Commission (1999a: 79–93) identifies four factors that explain variations in GDP per head between regions (regional disparities). First, the structure of economic activity: richer regions have more people employed in manufacturing and services. Second, innovative activity, the presence of which is correlated to economic success. Third, accessibility: the less peripheral a region the higher its GDP tends to be. Fourth, the existence of a highly qualified work force. Whilst being aware of the limitation of these factors in explaining the pattern of regional disparities, the report claims that they account for two-thirds of GDP variation. As such, the cause of disparities is held to be an absence of the factors which contribute to the success of the richer regions: competitiveness. The less well-off regions should aim to emulate their better-off neighbours, aided by EU policy. This is an attempt to explain disparities in terms of the remedial measures that are available to tackle them. At no point is it suggested that differential growth is a contributing factor to differing levels of regional GDP (although it is acknowledged that increases in GDP may lead to changes in the structure of economic activity), or that regional success is non-generalizable.

3   The Commission makes the claim that if transaction costs can be reduced "peripheral regions could well benefit more than the more central ones" (European Commission 1996a: 75). Elsewhere it is acknowledged that "transport costs do not generally account for a significant element of business costs" (European Commission 1996a: 76).

4   An example of both the productivist and "northern" bias underlying cohesion programmes is provided by the EU's explanation for regional variations in GDP per head (see note 1 above). What poorer regions lack is precisely what the richer, northern, "core" regions are thought to possess. Each of the four factors – economic structure, innovative activity, accessibility (to markets), and educated workforce – is central to production.

5   Nodes comprise networks, but what a node actually is, "depends on the kind of concrete networks of which we speak" (Castells 2000a: 501). They can be stock exchange markets, European Commissioners, mobile telephones etc. Their importance comes from their place within a network.

6   Somewhat confusingly Castells sometimes talks of the network state – exemplified by the EU – and at other times of the network society, without adequately differentiating between them. On this point see Axford and Huggins (1999: 196).

7   Castells shows scant interest in the sociological theories of globalization, nor does he acknowledge the pioneering work of Robertson and Albrow in developing globalization as a sociological field.

8   Although he does quote Touraine approvingly for criticizing the tendency to reduce societies to economies, economies to markets, and markets to financial flows (Castells 2000b: 356).

9   In a short summary it is not possible to do justice to the impressive theoretical foundations upon which Mann's work is constructed. His seminal work on the origins of social power is underpinned by a non-reductionist view which identifies four main power networks: ideological/cultural, economic, military, and political (see Mann 1986). His analysis of the EU is conducted in terms of the spatial networking of his power networks.

10   The international network is the one most closely associated with the EU or "Euro" as Mann terms it. The transnational is equated with "Northern networks" indicating that "Euro" is incorporated within an important "transnational slice" of the world which stretches beyond Europe (Mann 1998: 187).

11   See also Axford and Huggins (1999).

12   The term culture is not defined by Appadurai but can be understood in its broad sense: including both artefacts and institutions as well as ideas and practices which give meaning to the world. He wishes to move us away from the idea that globalization is about capital flows and markets, and is keen to demonstrate that his ideas are as relevant to international clothing styles as international capital (Appadurai 1990: 297). Hence the term global cultural economy.

13   He does, however, claim to reside in the Marxist camp and at certain points in his thesis relies upon a variation of the base–superstructure model.

14   But in saying that ideoscapes are directly related to the struggle over state power he is ignoring a whole range of struggles which ethnic and other movements are engaged in.

15   While focusing on the global flows made possible by the disjunctures between the various scapes Appadurai says very little about the ways in which nation-states and other political units are subjected to transformation. Nation-states and networks remain rather static in contrast to the "world in motion" represented by global flows.

16   But today's EU peripheries will become tomorrow's internal borders as the EU expands eastwards and southwards.

17   The economies of peripheral regions are less robust and more prone to succumb to adverse developments. At the same time central regions are more "naturally resilient" (European Commission 1994: 105).

8   Europe and Democracy

1   The EU summit in Copenhagen in 1993 established conditions that should apply to prospective EU states. The "Copenhagen criteria" require applicant countries to fulfil certain basic conditions if they wish to join the EU. Politically, the country must have stable institutions

guaranteeing democracy, the rule of law, human rights, and the protection of minorities. In economic terms, the country must have a functioning market economy and the capacity to handle competitive pressure on
the Union's internal market. Administratively, the country must have
public authorities capable of implementing and enforcing EU law.

2   "Fortress Europe" has a broad repertoire of applications. In addition to
being a metaphor for European barriers to immigration, it is frequently
used to indicate the measures taken to ensure competitiveness *vis-à-vis*
the US and Japan (see Hix 1999) during the 1980s. It is also used in
relation to the way the EU has attempted to insulate itself from the
democratic agenda stimulated by the political transformations of the
former Soviet bloc (see Rich 2000: 207).

3   Critics of EU democracy sometimes claim that gains at the European
level are at the expense of those enjoyed at the national level.

4   A criticism founded on a rather Hobbesian view of law giving and law
enforcement.

5   Essentialism is the tendency to conceive identity as being an expression
of an inner nature, or essence. In other words, identities have an
unchanging core nature which defines them, and of which their aspirations and behaviour patterns are an expression. To the essentialist,
identity is primordial: "it predates history and culture. It is part of our
fixed, essential being, persisting from time immemorial without significant change or alteration. . . . If identity is indeed fixed, primordial and
immutable, then politics is irrelevant in the face of the deeper, more
fundamental forces – biological or cultural inheritance, kinship, home-
land – which really, in this view, regulate human conflict" (Gilroy 1997:
310). Essentialism holds that identity can be grounded in a set of fixed
categories and guaranteed by nature or the economy, for example.
Essentialism denies that identity is a politically and culturally constructed category. When Laclau talks of essentialism in relation to
Marxism, he means that all identities are class identities, and are given
as a datum of social existence, economically determined by reference to
the means of production. Marxism assumes the non-political, that is to
say economic, constitution of classes, and social relations, rather than
being constructed, are "given" by class positions.

9   EU Enlargement

1   CEEC – a standard abbreviation for the central and eastern Europe
countries.

2   At one point Jacques Chirac and Helmut Kohl, "promised that Poland
would be in the EU by 2000. The applicant countries joke grimly that
they have been promised membership of the EU within five years –

every year since 1990" (Rachman 2001). When formal negotiation began in 1998 no one in the EU dared to suggest that accession for the "fast track" candidates would not be possible within a few years. Indeed, in 1997 the candidate countries were upset when a Commission document was leaked in which it was predicted that enlargement could not begin until 2002. Nowadays no one expects the first new member before 2004 and every day that sort of target looks more and more unrealistic.

3   The current candidate countries are Bulgaria, Cyprus, the Czech Republic, Estonia, Hungary, Latvia, Lithuania, Malta, Poland, Romania, Slovakia, Slovenia, and Turkey.

4   The situation regarding transition periods prior to participation in the CAP is made more complicated by the insistence of Poland that a transition period of 18 years is introduced to prevent EU citizens (meaning Germans) from buying land in Poland. For similar reasons the Czech Republic and Hungary want a 10-year delay (Financial Times, May 20, 2001). Candidate countries are also asking for long transition periods for the sale of meat and dairy products not conforming with EU quality and hygiene standards (*Frankfurter Allgemeine Zeitung*, May 25, 2001).

5   For example, Turkey's "National Programme for the Adoption of the Acquis" deals with the political criteria only in a cursory manner.

6   Turkey recently (August 2000) signed the International Covenant on Civil and Political Rights (ICCPR) and the International Covenant on Economic, Social and Cultural Rights (ICESCR).

7   Duna was one of the chief architects of the customs union agreement on the Turkish side.

8   For example, "commitment to peace, security and good neighbourliness, respect for other countries' sovereignty, the integrity and inviolability of external borders and the principles of international law and a commitment to the settlement of territorial disputes by peaceful means, in particular through the jurisdiction of the International Court of Justice in the Hague."

9   This would appear to contradict point one, that Turkey is a candidate on the same basis as all other candidates. None of the other 12 has been told that the Copenhagen criteria have to be fulfilled *prior to the start* of accession talks.

10   For example, the signing of two international treaties in August 2000 (see note 6) can be seen both as harmonization with the EU, and an EU-inspired step towards greater democratization.

11   All figures in this section taken from the website of the Representation of the European Commission to Turkey www.eurptr.org.tr/english/e-mali-overview.html accessed on September 12, 2000.

12   In March 1995 there was a heated exchange between Turkey's President Demirel and French Foreign Minister Alain Juppe. Juppe said that in

European countries there were people who believed that the PKK terrorists were struggling for the social and political rights of the Kurds. "The President argued that European demands for a 'political solution' were in reality calls for the granting of autonomy for the Kurds which he insisted would lead the country into a state of anarchy" (Kirisci and Winrow 1997: 174).

13 Members of the ultranationalist Turkish Revenge Brigade were subsequently arrested and face trial for the offence.

14 In July 2001 the European Court of Human Rights (ECHR), an institution of the Council of Europe not the European Union, upheld Turkey's Constitutional Court ruling against the Welfare Party on the grounds that it was undermining secular principles. The ECHR ruling stressed the threat to democracy posed by welfare: "the sanctions imposed . . . could reasonably be considered to meet a pressing need for the protection of democratic society" (ECHR 2001).

15 On February 21, 2000 three elected mayors representing HADEP (Peoples' Democracy Party) were arrested and charged with having links with, and providing funding to, the outlawed PKK (Kurdistan Workers' Party). "Aiding the PKK" is a catch-all legal charge often invoked in Turkey against leading figures who challenge the establishment position on the Kurdish conflict that the group's members are terrorists who must be dealt with by military means alone (*Reuters*, December 23, 1999) (see also Rumford 2001a).

16 In the wake of the Helsinki decision Prime Minister Bulent Ecevit pledged rapid human rights and democratic reform in line with EU entry expectations. Following the arrest of the HADEP mayors (see note 15) leading Turkish politicians defended the state's actions on the basis that this was a domestic matter about which the EU should not be concerned. Prime Minister Ecevit said, "This is Turkey's local issue and comes under the jurisdiction of the Turkish legal system" (*Cumhuriyet*, February 22, 2000). President Demirel took much the same line and argued that "each and every state has the right to implement its own laws and regulations and Europe has no right to pressure Turkey not to apply its laws" (*Turkish Daily News*, February 24, 2000).

17 Although there is considerable debate regarding the extent to which the Islamists actually believe in rights-based democracy or whether they are merely utilizing the discourse of rights for political advantage. The democratic claims of the Islamists are viewed with great suspicion by the Kemalists, for whom Islamic politics can only mean fundamentalism. Gulalp (1999: 36) takes the line that, "if Refah [Welfare Party] had come to power with enough of a majority to implement its program freely, there were strong indications that it might actually have pursued totalitarian policies." Not everyone shares this view. Ozbudun (1996: 133) takes the position that "it is unclear whether Refah seriously intends

to establish an 'Islamic state' based on the *shari'a* (sacred law) or would be satisfied by certain, mostly symbolic, acts of Islamization in some areas of social life."

18   Shortly afterwards events took an unexpected turn. President Demirel approved a governmental decree to withdraw Kavakci's citizenship (and her status as a Deputy) on the grounds that she had failed to declare her newly acquired US citizenship when registering as a candidate for the General Election.

19   Although ironically many of the schools are Islamic ones.

20   In the 1999 local elections HADEP won 37 municipalities (including 3 urban centers) and Fazilet (FP) 488 (including 17 urban centers).

21   As it did in the case of Austria, one of its own members. During 2000, 14 EU member states applied sanctions against Austria on the basis that they were unhappy with the coalition between the Austrian People's Party (OVP) and the (far right) Freedom Party (FPO). The 14 imposed these sanctions before any violation of EU treaties and in doing so ignored the EU's own procedures for dealing with such matters. One interpretation of these events was that in acting against one of its own members in this way the EU was sending a warning message to candidate countries. However, the overwhelming impression was that the EU's policy of interference in the affairs of nation-states now extends to questioning the right of an electorate to democratically elect the candidates of their choice.

10   Conclusion

1   In a very different context (that of transmigration between the US and Mexico), Pries' account of the emergence of transnational social spaces emphasizes that social space is uncoupled from national belonging and "different social spaces with no relationship to each other in geographic terms can become *stacked* within one and the same geographic space . . . in addition . . . a social space can also expand over several and distinct geographical spaces" (Pries 2001: 57).

2   Derived from the divide between Latin and Orthodox Christianity. The cold war division of Europe held a strong grasp over the academic imagination, many scholarly works dealing with either one or the other, or when dealing with both, treating the two halves as distinct, even when the period in question predated the ideological division of Europe (for example, Anderson 1979). The point is that for a long period the duality of Europe was treated as "natural."

3   The US is increasingly out of step with global norms in this area of human rights. When, in May 2001 the US was voted off the UN Human Rights Commission after serving on the body since its inception in 1947,

US criticism of the human rights record of other nations was cited as the most likely explanation. Another interpretation is that less than whole-hearted commitment to core human rights values was a contributory factor.

References

Ahmad, F. 1993: *The Making of Modern Turkey*. London: Routledge.

Albrow, M. 1996: *The Global Age: State and Society Beyond Modernity*. Cambridge: Polity Press.

Albrow, M. 1998a: "Europe in the Global Age," Amalfi Prize Lecture, Amalfi, Italy, May 30.

Albrow, M. 1998b: "Frames and Transformations in Transnational Studies," Transnational Communities Working Paper 98–02, Institute of Social and Cultural Anthropology, Oxford University.

Albrow, M. 1999: *Sociology: The Basics*. London: Routledge.

Albrow, M. 2001: "Society as social diversity: the challenge for governance in the global age," in *Governance in the 21st Century*. Paris: OECD.

Allen, D. 1996: "Competition policy," in H. Wallace and W. Wallace (eds.), *Policy-making in the European Union*. Oxford: Oxford University Press.

Allen, J., Massey, D., and Cochrane, A. 1998: *Rethinking the Region*. London: Routledge.

Amin, A. and Tomaney, J. 1995: "The challenge of cohesion," in A. Amin and J. Tomaney (eds.), *Behind the Myth of European Union: Prospects for Cohesion*. London: Routledge.

Anderson, B. 1983: *Imagined Communities: Reflections on the Origins and Spread of Nationalism*. London: Verso.

Anderson, J. 1996: "The shifting stage of politics: new medieval and postmodern territorialities?" *Environment and Planning D: Society and Space*, 14.

Anderson, P. 1979: *Lineages of the Absolutist State*. London: Verso.

Anderson, P. 1997: "Under the sign of the interim," in P. Gowan and P. Anderson (eds.), *The Question of Europe*. London: Verso.

Appadurai, A. 1990: "Disjuncture and difference in the global cultural economy," in M. Featherstone (ed.), *Global Culture: Nationalism, Globalization and Modernity*. London: Sage.

Appadurai, A. 1996: *Modernity at Large: Cultural Dimensions of Globalization*. Minneapolis: University of Minnesota Press.

Archibugi, D. 1998: "Principles of cosmopolitan democracy," in D. Archibugi, D. Held, and M. Kohler (eds.), *Re-imagining Political Community: Studies in Cosmopolitan Democracy*. Cambridge: Polity Press.

Archibugi, D. and Held, D. 1995: "Editors' introduction," in D. Archibugi and D. Held (eds.), *Cosmopolitan Democracy: An Agenda for a New World Order*. Cambridge: Polity Press.

Axford, B. and Huggins, R. 1999: "Towards a post-national polity: the emergence of the Network Society in Europe," in D. Smith and S. Wright (eds.), *Whose Europe?: The Turn Towards Democracy*. Oxford: Blackwell.

Barchard, D. 1998: *Turkey and the European Union*. London: CER.

Barrett, M. 1991: *The Politics of Truth: From Marx to Foucault*. Cambridge: Polity Press.

Barry, A. 1993: "The European Community and European government: harmonization, mobility and space." *Economy and Society*, 22 (3).

Barry, A. 1996: "The European Network." *New Formations*, 26 (Autumn).

Barry, A. 2001: *Political Machines: Governing a Technological Society*. London: Athlone Press.

Baun, M. 1999: "Enlargement," in L. Cram, D. Dinan, and N. Nugent (eds.), *Developments in the European Union*. Basingstoke: Palgrave.

Beck, U. 1992: *The Risk Society: Towards a New Modernity*. London: Sage.

Beck, U. 1994: "The reinvention of politics: towards a theory of reflexive modernization," in U. Beck, A. Giddens, and S. Lash, *Reflexive Modernization: Politics, Tradition and Aesthetics in Modern Social Order*. Cambridge: Polity Press.

Beck, U. 1997: *The Reinvention of Politics: Rethinking Modernity in the Global Social Order*. Cambridge: Polity Press.

Beck, U. 2000: *What is Globalization?* Cambridge: Polity Press.

Beck, U., Giddens, A., and Lash, S. 1994. *Reflexive Modernization: Politics, Tradition and Aesthetics in the Modern Social Order*. Stanford, CA: Stanford University Press.

Berman, M. 1983: *All That is Solid Melts into Air: The Experience of Modernity*. London: Verso.

Birand, M. A. 2000: "Will Turkey be able to meet the Copenhagen criteria?" *Challenge Europe Online Journal*, June 8. http://www.theepc.be/Challenge_Europe/top.asp

Bottomore, T. 1993: *Political Sociology* (second edition). London: Pluto.

Bozdagan, S. 1994: "Architecture, modernism and nation-building in Kemalist Turkey." *New Perspectives on Turkey*, 10 (Spring).

Bozdogan, S. and Kasaba, R. 1997: "Introduction," in S. Bozdogan and R. Kasaba (eds.), *Rethinking Modernity and National Identity in Turkey*. Seattle: University of Washington Press.

Branch, A. P. and Ohrgaard, J. C. 1999: "Trapped in the supranational-intergovernmental dichotomy: a response to Stone Sweet and Sandholtz." *Journal of European Public Policy*, 6 (1).

Bruton, A. 1996: *A Revolution in Progress: Western Europe Since 1989*. London: Little, Brown.

Burchell, G. 1993: "Liberal government and the techniques of the self." *Economy and Society*, 22 (3).

Burchell, G., Gordon, C., and Miller, P. (eds.) 1991: *The Foucault Effect: Studies in Governmentality*. London: Harvester.

Byrne, D. 1999: *Social Exclusion*. Buckingham: Open University Press.

Caporaso, J. 1998: "Regional integration theory: Understanding our past and anticipating our future," in W. Sandholtz and A. Stone Sweet (eds.), *European Integration and Supranational Governance*. Oxford: Oxford University Press.

Castells, M. 1996: *The Rise of the Network Society: The Information Age: Economy, Society and Culture: Volume 1*. Oxford: Blackwell.

Castells, M. 1997: *The Power of Identity: The Information Age: Economy, Society and Culture: Volume 2*. Oxford: Blackwell.

Castells, M. 1998: *End of Millennium: The Information Age: Economy, Society and Culture: Volume 3*. Oxford: Blackwell.

Castells, M. 2000a: *The Rise of the Network Society: The Information Age: Economy, Society and Culture: Volume 1* (second edition). Oxford: Blackwell.

Castells, M. 2000b: *End of Millennium: The Information Age: Economy, Society and Culture: Volume 3* (second edition). Oxford: Blackwell.

Castells, M. 2000c: "Materials for an exploratory theory of the network society." *British Journal of Sociology*, 51 (1).

Clarke, T. 1999: "Feyerabend, Rorty, Mouffe and Keane: On realising democracy." *Critical Review of International Social and Political Philosophy*, 2 (3).

Coates, K. 1998: "Unemployed Europe and the struggle for alternatives." *New Left Review*, 227.

Cohen, J. 1995: "Interpreting the notion of civil society," in M. Walzer (ed.), *Towards a Global Civil Society*. Providence: Berghahan Books.

Cohen, J. and Arato, A. 1992: *Civil Society and Political Theory*. Cambridge, MA: MIT Press.

Cooke, P., Christiansen, T., and Schienstock, G. 1997: "Regional economic policy and a Europe of the regions," in M. Rhodes, P. Heywood and V. Wright (eds.), *Developments in West European Politics*. Basingstoke: Palgrave.

Crompton, R. and Brown, P. 1994: "Introduction," in P. Brown and R. Crompton (eds.), *Economic Restructuring and Social Exclusion*. London: UCL Press.

Czerwinska, I. A. 2001: "Who's afraid of Poland's workforce?" *The Warsaw Voice*, 19 (655), May 13. www.warsawvoice.pl

Dean, M. 1999: *Governmentality: Power and Rule in Modern Society*. London: Sage.

Dean, M. and Hindess, B. 1998: "Introduction: government, liberalism, society," in M. Dean and B. Hindess (eds.), *Governing Australia: Studies in*

Contemporary Rationalities of Government. Cambridge: Cambridge University Press.

Dehousse, R. 1997: "European integration and the nation-state," in M. Rhodes, P. Heywood and V. Wright (eds.), *Developments in West European Politics*. Basingstoke: Palgrave.

Delanty, G. 1995: *Inventing Europe: Idea, Identity, Reality*. Basingstoke: Palgrave.

Delanty, G. 1998: "Social theory and European transformation: Is there a European society?" *Sociological Research Online*, 3 (1). http://www.socresonline.org.uk/

Delanty, G. 2000: "The resurgence of the city in Europe? The spaces of European citizenship," in E. F. Isin (ed.), *Democracy, Citizenship and the Global City*. London: Routledge.

Delors, J. 1999: "Introductory address," First Convention on Civil Society Organised at European Level, Brussels October 15–16, 1999.

Diamantopoulou, A. 2000a: "The European social model: past its sell-by-date?" Speech at the Institute for European Affairs, Dublin, July 20. http://europa.eu.int/comm/dgs/employment_social/speeches/2000_en.htm

Diamantopoulou, A. 2000b: "The European social model and enlargement." Speech at Seminar on the Harmonization of Turkey's Social Policy and Legislation with EU Standards, Istanbul, June 23. http://europa.eu.int/comm/dgs/employment_social/speeches/2000_en.htm

Dinan, D. 1994: *Ever Closer Union? An Introduction to the European Community*. Basingstoke: Palgrave.

Dinan, D. 2000: "Cohesion policy," in D. Dinan (ed.), *Encyclopedia of the European Union* (Updated Edition). Basingstoke: Palgrave.

Dorsey, J.M. 1998: "Turkish court ban on Islamic Welfare Party boomerangs, widening gulf with EU." *Washington Report on Middle East Affairs*, March. www.washington-report.org

Drake, G. 1994: *Issues in the New Europe*. London: Hodder and Stoughton.

Du Gay, P. 1997 "Organizing identity: making up people at work," in P. du Gay (ed.), *Production of Cultures/Cultures of Production*. London: Sage.

Duna, C. 1996: "On the verge of customs union with the EU," in *Turkey Almanac 1996*. Istanbul: Intermedia.

Ecevit, B. 2000: "Turkey on the threshold of the 21st century," Speech given at the Nobel Institute, Oslo, June 6.

Economic and Social Committee (ESC) 2000a: "Opinion of the Economic and Social Committee on the Role and Contribution of Civil Society Organisations in the Building of Europe," in *The Civil Society Organized at European Level: Proceedings of the First Convention, Brussels, 15 and 16 October 1999*. Brussels: European Economic and Social Committee.

Economic and Social Committee (ESC) 2000b: *The Civil Society Organized at*

European Level: Proceedings of the First Convention, Brussels, 15 and 16 October 1999. Brussels: European Economic and Social Committee.

Economic and Social Committee (ESC) 2001: *Opinion of the Economic and Social Committee on Organised Civil Society and European Governance: the Committee's Contribution to the Drafting of the White Paper.* Brussels: European Economic and Social Committee.

Esping-Anderson, G. 1990: *The Three Worlds of Welfare Capitalism.* Cambridge: Polity Press.

Esping-Anderson, G. 1999: *Social Foundations of Postnational Economies.* Oxford: Oxford University Press.

Etzioni, A. 1965: *Political Unification: A Comparative Study of Leaders and Forces.* New York: Holt, Rinehart and Winston.

European Commission 1989: *Commission opinion on Turkey's request for accession to the Community – 20 December 1989.* www.mfa.gov.tr/grupa/ad/adab/opinion.htm

European Commission 1993: *Growth, Competitiveness and Employment.* Luxembourg: Office for Official Publications of the European Communities.

European Commission 1994: *Competitiveness and Cohesion: Trends in the Regions: Fifth Periodic Report on the Social and Economic Situation and Development of the Regions in the Community.* Luxembourg: Office for Official Publications of the European Communities.

European Commission 1995: *White Paper on Education and Training: Teaching and Learning; Towards the Learning Society COM(95) 590 Final.* Luxembourg: Office for Official Publications of the European Communities.

European Commission 1996a: *First Cohesion Report.* Luxembourg: Office for Official Publications of the European Communities.

European Commission 1996b: *Report from the Commission on Developments in Relations with Turkey Since the Entry into Force of the Customs Union COM (96) 491 final.* Luxembourg: Office for Official Publications of the European Communities.

European Commission 1997: *Grants and Loans from the European Union: A Guide to Community Funding.* Luxembourg: Office for Official Publications of the European Communities.

European Commission 1998a: *Economic and Social Cohesion in the European Union: The Impact of Member States' Own Policies.* Luxembourg: Office for Official Publications of the European Communities.

European Commission 1998b: *Report from the Commission on Developments in Relations with Turkey Since the Entry into Force of the Customs Union COM (98) 147 final.* Luxembourg: Office for Official Publications of the European Communities.

European Commission 1998c: *European Strategy for Turkey: the Commission's Initial Operating Proposals, COM (98) 124 final.* Luxembourg: Office for Official Publications of the European Communities.

European Commission 1999a: "Eurostat Press Release, N° 1199," February 9.

European Commission 1999b: *Sixth Periodic Report on the Social and Economic Situation and Development of the Regions of the European Union.* Luxembourg: Office for Official Publications of the European Communities.

European Commission 1999c: *Regular Report from the Commission on Progress Towards Accession: Composite: 13 October 1999.*
http://europa.eu.int/comm/enlargement

European Commission 1999d: *Euromed Report,* 3 (16) December.

European Commission 1999e: *The CAP Reform: A Policy for the Future.*
http://europa.eu.int/comm/agriculture/publi/fact/policy/en.pdf

European Commission 1999f: *CAP Reform: Rural development.*
http://europa.eu.int/comm/agriculture/publi/fact/rurdev/en.pdf

European Commission 2000a: *White Paper on European Governance: Enhancing Democracy in the European Union, SEC (2000) 1547/7 final.* Brussels: European Commission.

European Commission 2000b: *Turkey 2000: Regular Report from the Commission on Turkey's Progress Towards Accession.*
http://europa.eu.int/comm/enlargement/dwn/report_11_00/pdf/en/tu.pdf

European Commission 2000c: *Commission Discussion Paper: The Commission and Non-governmental organizations: Building a Stronger Partnership COM (2000) 11 final.* Brussels: European Commission.
http://europa.eu.int/comm/secretariat_general/sgc/ong/en/index.htm

European Commission 2001a: "Commission proposes a fresh strategy for promoting Human Rights and democratisation," Press Release IP/01/666.

European Commission 2001b: "Euro-zone unemployment unchanged at 8.7%," Eurostat Press Release 16/2001, January 31.

European Commission 2001c: *Unity, Solidarity, Diversity for Europe, its People and its Territory: Second Report on Economic and Social Cohesion.*
http://www.inforegio.cec.eu.int/wbdoc/docoffic/official/report2/contentpdf_en.htm

European Court of Human Rights (ECHR) 2001: "Judgement in the case of Refah Partesi (The Welfare Party) Erbakan, Kazan and Tekdal v. Turkey," Press Release 566, July 31. www.echr.coe.int

European Union (EU) 2000: "Statement by Mr Jaime Gama Minister for Foreign Affairs of Portugal on behalf of the European Union at the 56th session of the Commission on Human Rights," EU Press Release, Geneva, March 21.
http://ue.eu.int/newsroom/

Falk, R. 2000: "The decline of citizenship in an era of globalization." *Citizenship Studies,* 4 (1).

Featherstone, M. and Lash, S. 1995: "Globalization, modernity and the spatialization of social theory: an introduction," in M. Featherstone, S. Lash, and R. Robertson (eds.), *Global Modernities.* London: Sage.

Fowler, B. 2001: "Enlargement of the European Union: Impacts on the EU, the candidates and the 'next neighbors.'" *ECSA Review*, 14 (1).

Franceschet, A. 1998: "Cosmopolitanism, sovereignty and the theory of European integration: a Kantian contribution." *Journal of European Integration*, 21 (2).

Friedmann, J. 2000: "Reading Castells: Zeidaignose and social theory." *Environment and Planning D: Society and Space*, 18 (1).

Friis, L. and Murphy, A. 2001: "Enlargement of the European Union: Impacts on the EU, the candidates and the 'next neighbors.'" *ECSA Review*, 14 (1).

Garton Ash, T. 1989: *The Uses of Adversity*. Cambridge: Granta Books.

Gellner, E. 1994: *Encounters with Nationalism*. Oxford: Blackwell.

Giddens, A 1990: *The Consequences of Modernity*. Cambridge: Polity Press.

Giddens, A 1991: *Modernity and Self-identity: Self and Society in the Late Modern Age*. Cambridge: Polity Press.

Giddens, A. 2000: *The Third Way and its Critics*. Cambridge: Polity Press.

Gilroy, P. 1997: "Diaspora and the detours of identity," in K. Woodward (ed.), *Identity and Difference*. London: Sage.

Giorgi, L., Crowley, J., and Ney, S. 2001: "Surveying the European Public Space – a political and research agenda." *Innovation: The European Journal of Social Sciences*, 13 (2).

Gledhill, J. 1999: "The challenge of globalisation: reconstruction of identities, transnational forms of life and the social sciences." *Journal of European Area Studies*, 7 (1).

Glos, M. 2001: "Is Turkey ready for Europe?" *Internationale Politik: Transatlantic Edition*, 2 (2). http://www.dgap.org/english/tip.htm

Goldblatt, D. 1997: "At the limits of political possibiliy: the cosmopolitan democratic project." *New Left Review*, 225.

Gole, N. 1996: *The Forbidden Modern: Civilization and Veiling*. Ann Arbor: The University of Michigan Press.

Gole, N. 1997: "The quest for the Islamic self within the context of modernity," in S. Bozdogan and R. Kasaba (eds.), *Rethinking Modernity and National Identity in Turkey*. Seattle: University of Washington Press.

Gordon, C. 1991: "Government rationality: An introduction," in G. Burchell, C. Gordon, and P. Miller (eds.), *The Foucault Effect: Studies in Governmentality*. Chicago: University of Chicago Press.

Gordon, P. 1989: *Fortress Europe: The Meaning of 1992*. London: The Runnymede Trust.

Gordon, P. 2000: "Turkey and the European Union after Helsinki," *The Changing Environment of Turkish Foreign Policy* conference organized by the Institutute of Turkish Studies, February.

Gowan, P. 1997: "British Euro-solipsism," in P. Gowan and P. Anderson (eds.), *The Question of Europe*. London: Verso.

Gramsci, A. 1971: *Selections from Prison Notebooks*. London: Lawrence and Wishart.

Grant, W. 2001: "Is real reform now possible?" accessed from webpage http://members.tripod.com/'WynGrant/Overview.html on October 4, 2001.

Grundmann, R. 1999: "The European public sphere and the deficit of democracy," in D. Smith and S. Wright (eds.), *Whose Europe?: The Turn Towards Democracy*. Oxford: Blackwell.

Gulalp, H. 1999: "The poverty of democracy in Turkey: the Refah Party episode." *New Perspectives on Turkey*, 21 (Fall).

Habermas, J. 1992: "Citizenship and national identity: some reflections on the future of Europe." *Praxis International*, 12 (1).

Hadjimichalis, C. 1994: "The fringes of Europe and EU integration." *European Urban and Regional Studies*, 1 (1).

Hall, S. 1991: "Europe's other self." *Marxism Today*, August.

Harvie, C. 1994: *The Rise of Regional Europe*. London: Routledge.

Hay, C., Watson, M., and Wincott, D. 1999: *Globalization, European Integration and the Persistence of European Social Models*. Working Paper 3/99 POLSIS, University of Birmingham.

Hebdige, D. 1979: *Subculture: The Meaning of Style*. London: Methuen.

Held, D. 1989: *Political Theory and the Modern State*. Cambridge: Polity Press.

Held, D. 1998: "Democracy and globalization," in D. Archibugi, D. Held, and M. Kohler (eds.), *Re-imagining Political Community: Studies in Cosmopolitan Democracy*. Cambridge: Polity Press.

Held, D., McGrew, A., Goldblatt, D., and Perraton, J. 1999: *Global Transformations: Politics, Economics and Culture*. Cambridge: Polity Press.

Hetherington, K. and Law, J. 2000: "After networks." *Environment and Planning D: Society and Space*, 18 (2).

Hirst, P. and Thompson, G. 1996: *Globalization in Question: The International Economy and the Possibilities of Governance*. Cambridge: Polity Press.

Hix, S. 1999: *The Political System of the European Union*. Basingstoke: Palgrave.

Hooghe, L. 1996a: "Reconciling EU-wide policy and national diversity," in L. Hooghe (ed.), *Cohesion Policy and European Integration: Building Multi-level Governance*. Oxford: Oxford University Press.

Hooghe, L. 1996b: "Building a Europe with the regions: the changing role of the European Commission," in L. Hooghe (ed.), *Cohesion Policy and European Integration: Building Multi-level Governance*. Oxford: Oxford University Press.

Hooghe, L. 1998: "EU cohesion policy and competing models of European capitalism." *Journal of Common Market Studies*, 36 (4).

Hosking, G. 1991: *The Awakening of the Soviet Union*. London: Mandarin.

Hudson, R. 1999: "The new economy of the new Europe: eradicating divisions or creating new forms of uneven development?" in R. Hudson and A. M. Williams (eds.), *Divided Europe: Society and Territory*. London: Sage.

Hudson, R. and Williams, A.M. 1999: "Re-shaping Europe: the challenge of new divisions within a homogenized political-economic space," in R. Hudson and A. M. Williams (eds.), *Divided Europe: Society and Territory*. London: Sage.

Human Rights Watch 2000: *Turkey, Human Rights and the European Union Accession Partnership*, 12 (10 D).
www.hrw.org/reports/2000/turkey2/

Huntington, S. 1993: "The clash of civilizations?" *Foreign Affairs*, Summer.

Huntington, S. 1996: *The Clash of Civilizations and the Remaking of World Order*. New York: Simon and Schuster.

Jary, D. 1999: "Citizenship and human rights – particular and universal worlds and the prospects for European citizenship," in D. Smith and S. Wright (eds.), *Whose Europe? The Turn Towards Democracy*. Oxford: Blackwell.

Jeffery, C. 1997: "Conclusions: sub-national authorities and 'European domestic policy,'" in C. Jeffery (ed.), *The Regional Dimension of the European Union: Towards a Third Level in Europe?* London: Frank Cass.

Kaldor, M. 1995: "European institutions, nation-states and nationalism," in D. Archibugi and D. Held (eds.), *Cosmopolitan Democracy: An Agenda for a New World Order*. Cambridge: Polity Press.

Kasaba, R. 1997: "Kemalist certainties and modern ambiguities," in S. Bozdogan and R. Kasaba (eds.), *Rethinking Modernity and National Identity in Turkey*. Seattle: University of Washington Press.

Keane, J. 1988a: *Democracy and Civil Society*. London: Verso.

Keane, J. 1988b: "Despotism and democracy," in J. Keane (ed.) *Civil Society and the State*. London: Verso.

Keyder, C. 1997: "Whither the project of modernity? Turkey in the 1990s," in S. Bozdogan and R. Kasaba (eds.), *Rethinking Modernity and National Identity in Turkey*. Seattle: University of Washington Press.

Keyman, F. 1995: "On the relation between global modernity and nationalism: The crisis of hegemony and the rise of (Islamic) identity in Turkey." *New Perspectives on Turkey*, 13 (Fall).

Kirisci, K. and Winrow, G. 1997: *The Kurdish Question and Turkey: An Example of a Trans-state Ethnic Conflict*. London: Frank Cass.

Konrad, G. 1984: *Antipolitics*. London: Quartet Books.

Kramer, H. 1996: "The Turkey/EU customs union: economic integration amid political turmoil." *Mediterranean Politics*, 1 (1).

Kramer, H. 2000: *A Changing Turkey: The Challenge to Europe and the United States*. Washington: Brookings Institution Press.

Kumar, K. 1994: "Civil society," in W. Outhwaite and T. Bottomore et al. (eds.), *The Blackwell Dictionary of Twentieth-Century Social Thought*. Oxford: Blackwell.

Laclau, E. 1994: *The Making of Political Identities*. London: Verso.

Laclau, E. 1996: *Emancipation(s)*. London: Verso.

Laclau, E. and Mouffe, C. 1985: *Hegemony and Socialist Strategy: Towards a Radical Democratic Politics*. London: Verso.

Laffan, B. 1999: "Democracy and the European Union," in L. Cram, D. Dinan, and N. Nugent (eds.), *Developments in the European Union*. Basingstoke: Palgrave.

Lash, S. 1994: "Reflexivity, modernity and aesthetics," in U. Beck, A. Giddens, and S. Lash, *Reflexive Modernization: Politics, Tradition and Aesthetics in Modern Social Order*. Cambridge: Polity Press.

Lash, S. and Urry, J. 1994: *Economies of Signs and Space*. London: Sage.

Leontidou, L. and Afouxenides, A. 1999: "Boundaries of social exclusion," in R. Hudson and A. M. Williams (eds.), *Divided Europe: Society and Territory*. London: Sage.

McCormick, J. 1999: *Understanding the European Union: A Concise Introduction*. Basingstoke: Palgrave.

Machiavelli, R. 2000: "Forward," in *The Civil Society Organized at European Level: Proceedings of the First Convention, Brussels, 15 and 16 October 1999*. Brussels: European Economic and Social Committee.

Majone, G. 1996: *Regulating Europe*. London: Routledge.

Mann, M. 1986: *The Sources of Social Power: Volume 1: A History of Power From the Beginning to* A.D. *1760*. Cambridge: Cambridge University Press.

Mann, M. 1998: "Is there a society called Euro?" in R. Axtman (ed.), *Globalization and Europe: Theoretical and Empirical Investigations*. London: Pinter.

Markoff, J. 1999: "Our 'common European home' – but who owns the house?" in D. Smith and S. Wright (eds.), *Whose Europe?: The Turn Towards Democracy*. Oxford: Blackwell.

Marks, G. and McAdam, D. 1996: "Social movements and the changing structure of political opportunity in the European Union," in G. Marks, F. W. Scharpf, P. C. Schmitter, and W. Streek, *Governance in the European Union*. London: Sage.

Marks, G., Nielsen, F., Ray, L., and Salk, J. 1996: "Competencies, cracks and conflicts: regional mobilization in the European Union," in G. Marks, F. W. Scharpf, P. C. Schmitter, and W. Streek, *Governance in the European Union*. London: Sage.

Mathews, A. 1994: *Managing the EU Structural Funds in Ireland*. Cork: Cork University Press.

Matossian, M. 1994: "Ideologies of delayed development," in J. Hutchinson and A. D. Smith (eds.), *Nationalism*. Oxford: Oxford University Press.

Mayes, D. 1995: "Introduction: conflict and cohesion in the single European market: a reflection," in A. Amin and J. Tomaney (eds.), *Behind the Myth of European Union: Prospects for Cohesion*. London: Routledge.

Melucci, A. 1988: "Social movements and the democratization of everyday life," in J. Keane (ed.), *Civil Society and the State*. London: Verso.

Miall, H. 1993: *Shaping the New Europe*. London: RIIA/Pinter.

Michie, J. 1995: "Unemployment in Europe," in A. Amin and J. Tomaney (eds.), *Behind the Myth of European Union: Prospects for Cohesion*. London: Routledge.

Micklethwait, J. and Wooldridge, A. 2000: "The market shall make you free." *The Spectator*, June 24.

Miller, P. and Rose, N. 1990: "Governing economic life." *Economy and Society*, 19 (1).

Milward, A. 1992: *The European Rescue of the Nation-state*. London: Routledge.

Milward, A. 1997: "The Springs of Integration," in P. Gowan and P. Anderson (eds.), *The Question of Europe*. London: Verso.

Milward, A., Lynch, F., Romero, F., Ranieri, R., and Sorensen, V. 1993: *The Frontier of National Sovereignty: History and Theory 1945–1992*. London: Routledge.

Mitchell, J. and McAleavey, P. 1999: "Promoting solidarity and cohesion," in L.Cram, D. Dinan, and N. Nugent (eds.), *Developments in the European Union*. Basingstoke: Palgrave.

Moravcsik, A. 1998: "Europe's integration at century's end," in A. Moravcsik (ed.), *Centralization or Fragmentation? Europe Facing the Challenge of Deepening, Diversity and Democracy*. New York: Council on Foreign Relations Press.

Mouffe, C. 1979: "Hegemony and ideology in Gramsci," in C. Mouffe (ed.), *Gramsci and Marxist Theory*. London: Routledge.

Mouffe, C. 1992: "Democratic politics today," in C. Mouffe (ed.) *Dimensions of Radical Democracy: Pluralism, Citizenship, Community*. London: Verso.

Mouffe, C. 1993: "Introduction: For an agonistic pluralism," in *The Return of the Political*. London: Verso.

Mouffe, C. 1995a: "Pluralism and the left identity," in M. Walzer (ed.), *Towards a Global Civil Society*. Providence: Berghahan Books.

Mouffe, C. 1995b: "Post-Marxism: democracy and identity." *Environment and Planning D: Society and Space*, 13.

Murray, P. 2000: "European integration studies: the search for synthesis." *Contemporary Politics*, 6 (1).

Nash, K. 2000: Contemporary Political Sociology: Globalization, Politics and Power. Oxford: Blackwell.

Nash, K. 2001: "The 'cultural turn' in social theory: towards a theory of cultural politics." *Sociology*, 35 (1).

Navaro-Yashin, Y. 1998: "Uses and abuses of 'state and civil society' in contemporary Turkey." *New Perspectives on Turkey*, 18 (Spring).

Navaro-Yasin, Y. 1999: "The historical construction of local culture: gender and identity in the politics of secularism versus Islam," in C. Keyder (ed.), *Istanbul: Between the Global and the Local*. Lanham, Maryland: Rowman and Littlefield.

Onis, Z. 1997: "The political economy of Islamic resurgence in Turkey: the rise of the Welfare Party in perspective." *Third World Quarterly*, (18) 4.

Onis, Z. 1999: "Turkey, Europe, and paradoxes of identity: perspectives on the international context of democratization." *Mediterranean Quarterly* (Summer).

Onis, Z. 2001: "An awkward partnership: Turkey's relations with the European Union in comparative-historical perspective." *Journal of European Integration History*, 7(1).

Ozbudun, E. 1996: "Turkey: how far from consolidation?" *Journal of Democracy*, 7 (3).

Palmer, J. 1997: "Dutch diplomat turns Turkey," *The Bulletin*, February 20.

Peck, J. 1995: "Regulating labour: the social regulation and reproduction of local labour-markets," in A. Amin and N. Thrift (eds.), *Globalization, Institutions, and Regional Development in Europe*. Oxford: Oxford University Press.

Pelczynski, Z. A. 1988: "Solidarity and 'the rebirth of civil society,'" in J. Keane (ed.), *Civil Society and the State*. London: Verso.

Peterson, J. 1996: "Research and development policy," in H. Kassim and A. Menon (eds.), *The European Union and National Industrial Policy*. London: Routledge.

Phillips, A. 1999: *Which Equalities Matter?* Cambridge: Polity Press.

Picht, R. 1993: "Disturbed identities: social and cultural mutations in contemporary Europe," in S. Garcia (ed.), *European Identity and the Search for Legitimacy*. London: Pinter.

Pierson, P. 1998: "Social policy and European integration," in A. Moravcsik (ed.), *Centralization or Fragmentation? Europe Facing the Challenge of Deepening, Diversity and Democracy*. New York: Council on Foreign Relations Press.

Preuss, U. K. 1998: "Citizenship in the European Union: a paradigm for transnational democracy?" in D. Archibugi, D. Held, and M. Kohler (eds.), *Re-imagining Political Community: Studies in Cosmopolitan Democracy*. Cambridge: Polity Press.

Pries, L. 2001: "The disruption of social and geographic space: Mexican–US migration and the emergence of transnational social spaces." *International Sociology*, 16 (1).

Procacci, G. 1996: "A New Social Contract? Against Exclusion: the Poor and the Social Sciences," European University Institute Working Paper, RSC No. 96/41.

Prodi, R. 2000a: "2000–2005 : Shaping the New Europe," Speech to the European Parliament, Strasbourg, February 15.

Prodi, R. 2000b: "Towards a European civil society," speech at the Second European Social Week, Bad Honnef, April 6.

Rachman, G. 2001: "Europe's magnetic attraction." *The Economist*, May 17.

Rattansi, A. 1994: "Western' racisms, ethnicities and identities in a 'postmodern' frame," in A. Rattansi and S. Westwood (eds.), *Racism, Modernity and Identity on the Western Front*. Cambridge: Polity Press.

Rengger, N. 1997: "Beyond liberal politics? European modernity and the nation-state," in M. Rhodes, P. Heywood, and V. Wright (eds.), *Developments in West European Politics*. Basingstoke: Palgrave.

Rex, J. 1999: "Prologue," in D. Smith and S. Wright (eds.), *Whose Europe?: The Turn Towards Democracy*. Oxford: Blackwell.

Rhodes, M., Heywood, P., and Wright, V. 1997: "Towards a new Europe?" in M. Rhodes, P. Heywood, and V. Wright (eds.), *Developments in West European Politics*. Basingstoke: Palgrave.

Rich, P. 2000: "Identity and democratisation in Europe," in B. Axford, D. Berghahn, and N. Hewlett (eds.), *Unity and Diversity in the New Europe*. Bern: Peter Lang.

Rieger, E. 1996: "The Common Agricultural Policy: External and internal dimensions," in H. Wallace and W. Wallace (eds.), *Policy-making in the European Union*. Oxford: Oxford University Press.

Robertson, R. 1990: "Mapping the global condition," in M. Featherstone (ed.), *Global Culture: Nationalism, Globalization and Modernity*. London: Sage.

Robertson, R. 1991: "Social theory, cultural relativity and the problem of globality," in A. D. King (ed.), *Culture, Globalization and the World-System*. Basingstoke: Palgrave.

Robertson, R. 1992: *Globalization: Social Theory and Global Culture*. London: Sage.

Robertson, R. 1995 "Glocalization: time-space and homogeneity-heterogeneity," in M. Featherstone, S. Lash, and R. Robertson (eds.), *Global Modernities*. London: Sage.

Robertson, R. 2001: "Globalization theory 2000+: Major problematics," in G. Ritzer and B. Smart (eds.), *Handbook of Social Theory*. London: Sage.

Robins, K. 1996: "Interrupting identities: Turkey/Europe," in S. Hall and P. Du Gay (eds.), *Questions of Cultural Identity*. London: Sage.

Robins, K. 1997: "What in the world's going on?" in P. Du Gay (ed.), *Production of Culture/Cultures of Production*. London: Sage.

Rosamond, B. 2000: *Theories of European Integration*. Basingstoke: Palgrave.

Rose, N. 1998: "Death of the social? Refiguring the territory of government." *Economy and Society*, 25 (3).

Rose, N. 1999: *Powers of Freedom: Reframing Political Thought*. Cambridge: Cambridge University Press.

Ross, G. 1995: *Jacques Delors and European Integration*. Cambridge: Polity Press.

Ross, G. 1998: "European integration and globalization," in R. Axtman (ed.), *Globalization and Europe: Theoretical and Empirical Investigations*. London: Pinter.

Rumford, C. 2000a: *European Cohesion? Contradictions in EU Integration.* Basingstoke: Palgrave.

Rumford, C. 2000b: "From Luxembourg to Helsinki: Turkey, the politics of EU enlargement and prospects for accession." *Contemporary Politics,* 6 (4).

Rumford, C. 2000c: "European cohesion? Globalization, autonomization, and the dynamics of EU integration." *Innovation: the European Journal of Social Science Research,* 13 (2).

Rumford, C. 2001a: "Human rights and democratization in Turkey in the context of EU candidature." *Journal of European Area Studies,* 9 (1).

Rumford, C. 2001b: "Social spaces beyond civil society: European integration, globalization and the sociology of European society." *Innovation: the European Journal of Social Science Research,* 14 (3).

Stone Sweet, A. and Sandholtz, W. 1998: "Integration, supranational governance, and the institutionalization of the European polity," in W. Sandholtz and A. Stone Sweet (eds.), *European Integration and Supranational Governance.* Oxford: Oxford University Press.

Schlesinger, P. 1994: "Europeanness: a new cultural battlefield?" in J. Hutchinson and A. D. Smith (eds.), *Nationalism.* Oxford: Oxford University Press.

Scholte, J. A. 2000: *Globalization: A Critical Introduction.* Basingstoke: Palgrave

Scholte, J. A. 2001: "Civil Society and Democracy in Global Governance." CSGR Working Paper No. 65/01, Department of Politics and International Studies, University of Warwick.

Siedentop, L. 2000: *Democracy in Europe.* Harmondsworth: Penguin.

Simon, R. 1982: *Gramsci's Political Thought: An Introduction.* London: Lawrence and Wishart.

Smith, D. 1999: "Making Europe – processes of Europe-formation since 1945," in D. Smith and S. Wright (eds.), *Whose Europe?: The Turn Towards Democracy.* Oxford: Blackwell.

Smith, D. and S. Wright (eds.) 1999: *Whose Europe?: The Turn Towards Democracy.* Oxford: Blackwell.

Smith, A. M. 1998: *Laclau and Mouffe: The Radical Democratic Imaginary.* London: Routledge.

Soysal, Y. 1994: *Limits of Citizenship: Migrants and Postnational Membership in Europe.* Chicago: University of Chicago Press.

Soysal, Y. 1997: "Changing parameters of citizenship and claims-making: Organized Islam in European public spheres." *Theory and Society,* 26 (4).

Soysal, Y. 2000: "Changing citizenship in Europe: Postnational membership and the national state," in G.G. Ozdogan and G. Tokay (eds.), *Redefining the Nation, State and Citizen.* Istanbul: Eren.

Standing, G. 1997: "The new insecurities," in P. Gowan and P. Anderson (eds.), *The Question of Europe.* London: Verso.

Starie, P. 1999: "Globalisation, the state and European economic integration." *Journal of European Area Studies*, 7 (1).

Swann, D. 1995: *The Economics of the Common Market: Integration in the European Union* (eighth edition). Harmondsworth: Penguin.

Tismaneanu, V. 1990a: "Unofficial peace activism in the Soviet Union and East-Central Europe," in V. Tismaneanu (ed.), *In Search of Civil Society: Independent Peace Movements in the Soviet Bloc*. London: Routledge.

Tismaneanu, V. 1990b: "Against socialist militarism: the independent peace movement in the German Democratic Republic," in V. Tismaneanu (ed.), *In Search of Civil Society: Independent Peace Movements in the Soviet Bloc*. London: Routledge.

Tismaneanu, V. 1990c: "Epilogue," in V. Tismaneanu (ed.), *In Search of Civil Society: Independent Peace Movements in the Soviet Bloc*. London: Routledge.

Turk, H. S. 1999: "Human rights in Turkey." *Perceptions: Journal of International Affairs*, 3 (4).

Turkmen, F. 1999: "All about Merve." *The Guide: Istanbul*, 47 (July/August).

Turner, B. 1990: "The two faces of sociology: global or national?" in M. Featherstone (ed.), *Global Culture: Nationalism, Globalization and Modernity*. London: Sage.

Turner, B. 1992: "Outline of a theory of citizenship," in C. Mouffe (ed.), *Dimensions of Radical Democracy: Pluralism, Citizenship, Community*. London: Verso.

Urry, J. 1999: *Sociology Beyond Societies: Mobilities for the Twenty-first Century*. London: Routledge.

Waever, O. 1995: "Europe since 1945: crisis to renewal," in K. Wilson and J. van der Dussen (eds.), *The History of the Idea of Europe*. London: The Open University/Routledge.

Wallace, H. 1994: "The EC and Western Europe after Maastricht," in H. Miall (ed.), *Redefining Europe*. London: Pinter.

Wallace, W. 1996: "Government without statehood: the unstable equilibrium," in H.

Wallace and W. Wallace (eds.), *Policy-making in the European Union* (third edition). Oxford: Oxford University Press.

Walzer, M. 1995a: "Introduction," in M. Walzer (ed.), *Towards a Global Civil Society*. Providence: Berghahan Books.

Walzer, M. 1995b: "The concept of civil society," in M. Walzer (ed.), *Towards a Global Civil Society*. Providence: Berghahan Books.

Weiss, L. 1997: "Globalization and the myth of the powerless state." *New Left Review*, 225.

Wieviorka, M. 1994: "Racism in Europe: unity and diversity," in A. Rattansi and S. Westwood (eds.), *Racism, Modernity and Identity on the Western Front*. Cambridge: Polity Press.

Williams, A. M. 1994: *The European Community* (second edition). Oxford: Blackwell.

Wishlade, F. 1996: "EU cohesion policy: facts, figures, and issues," in L. Hooghe (ed.), *Cohesion Policy and European Integration: Building Multi-level Governance*. Oxford: Oxford University Press.

Zubaida, S. 1994: "Human rights and cultural difference: Middle Eastern perspectives." *New Perspectives on Turkey*, 10 (Spring).

Index